Praise for *Billionaire Democracy*

"The economic inequalities of our era are bad enough in themselves. Far worse is their distorting effect on America's political processes. Everyone knows about these problems. George Tyler offers clear, original, and inventive solutions."

—**James Fallows**, *The Atlantic*

"George Tyler's *Billionaire Democracy* is a profound, clearly and provocatively written indictment of the American political system by an insider who has seen up close how it works. This book is a must-read for all sentient American citizens."

—**Clyde Prestowitz, author of *The Betrayal of American Prosperity* and president of the Economic Strategy Institute**

"A powerful critique of America's dysfunctional democracy. Tyler vividly illustrates how government policy is bent to serve the needs of the wealthy few and shows that only fundamental political reforms can make America truly democratic."

—**Martin Gilens, author of *Affluence & Influence: Economic Inequality and Political Power in America***

BILLIONAIRE DEMOCRACY

THE HIJACKING OF THE AMERICAN POLITICAL SYSTEM

GEORGE R. TYLER

BenBella Books, Inc.
Dallas, TX

BenBella Books, Inc.
10440 N. Central Expressway, Suite 800
Dallas, TX 75231
www.benbellabooks.com
Send feedback to feedback@benbellabooks.com

Printed in the United States of America
10 9 8 7 6 5 4 3 2 1

Library of Congress Cataloging-in-Publication Data is available upon request.
ISBN 978-1-942952-92-3 (paperback)
ISBN 978-1-944648-93-0 (electronic)

Editing by Eric Wechter
Copyediting by J.P. Connolly
Proofreading by Lisa Story and Cape Cod Compositors, Inc.
Indexing by George R. Tyler
Text design by Publishers' Design and Production Services, Inc.
Text composition by PerfecType, Nashville, TN
Front cover by Bradford Foltz
Full cover by Sarah Avinger
Cover illustration by Ralph Voltz
Printed by Lake Book Manufacturing

Distributed to the trade by Two Rivers Distribution, an Ingram brand
www.tworiversdistribution.com

Special discounts for bulk sales (minimum of 25 copies) are available. Please contact Aida Herrera at aida@benbellabooks.com.

Toward a Better Democracy
for Alexia, Tibber, and Tippi

☆ CONTENTS ☆

INTRODUCTION   Removing the Dead Hand of Pay-to-Play   1

Section 1   America Is a Low-Quality Democracy   13

CHAPTER 1   Faux Democracy: America's Decline to History's Dismal Default Setting   15

CHAPTER 2   Documenting Low-Quality American Democracy: The Income Bias and International Evidence   35

CHAPTER 3   The *Buckley* Era: Constitutionally Shielding Vote Buying   53

CHAPTER 4   The Donor Class Buys Itself a Political Party   67

Section 2   Reducing the Role of Money to Improve the Quality of American Democracy   81

CHAPTER 5   The Roberts Republicans: A Partisan Court of Sumner Darwinians   83

CHAPTER 6   Rejection of Political Equality by the Constitution   93

CHAPTER 7   Political Bribery Decriminalized: Vote Buying as "Free Speech"   99

CHAPTER 8   The *Buckley* Era: Cynicism and Diminished Faith in Democracy   113

CHAPTER 9   International Dismay with the Variant
                 of Capitalism Produced by Low-Quality
                 American Democracy   125

Section 3   Achieving Political Equality   135

CHAPTER 10   Other Wealthy Democracies Corral Oligarchs   137
CHAPTER 11   Recriminalizing Vote Buying   147
CHAPTER 12   Rehabilitating America's Flawed Democracy:
                 A Framework for Ending Vote Buying   161

Section 4   Original Intent to Prevent Fake News   187

CHAPTER 13   Original Intent: A Fact-Based Media   189
CHAPTER 14   Fake News Exacerbates Political Polarization,
                 Tribalism, and the Income Bias   199
CHAPTER 15   Closing the "Hate Factories": Avoiding the
                 Farce Feared by Madison   215
CHAPTER 16   Epilogue   229

                 Notes   239

                 Acknowledgments   284

                 Index   285

Removing the Dead Hand of Pay-to-Play

Fifty-seven percent of surveyed Albuquerque voters think that federal elections are overly influenced by special interest money. In contrast, only 23 percent think that Albuquerque elections are overly influenced by special interest money . . . Seventy-one percent believe that [campaign] spending limits improve the fairness of elections by ensuring that ordinary citizens, not just the very wealthy, can run for office in Albuquerque without having to raise so much money from special interest groups.[1]

—US District Court, D. New Mexico, September 2001

Well, I checked the Citizens' Clean Election commission website this morning and it says that this act was passed to "level the playing field" when it comes to running for office. Why isn't that clear evidence that it's unconstitutional?[2]

—Chief Justice John Roberts, *Arizona Free Enterprise Club's Freedom Club PAC v. Bennett*, 2011

In Germany, giving money in politics is always seen as trying to buy access.[3]

—Andrea Römmele, Hertie School of Government (Berlin)

F OUR IN FIVE AMERICANS support higher minimum wages, mandated paid sick leave, and filling gaps in Social Security coverage by raising taxes on the wealthy. These and a host of similar popular policies are commonplace in wealthy democracies like Australia and Germany, but not in America. This country's failure to reflect supermajority preferences in its public policies marks it as a low-quality democracy.

The search for ways to improve the quality of America's democracy begins with an examination of a system as old as mankind: the exchange of goods for value. Inherent in this system, at the intersection of politics and economics, is a default setting that occurs in virtually all societies, including capitalist ones: A handful of powerful individuals inevitably come to dominate both economic and political life. Democracy was devised to neutralize this default setting, and the quality of a democracy is measured by how effectively it disrupts that default—by how well its political process succeeds in dispersing the gains from economic activity. Aristotle argued over two millennia ago that the quality of democracy can best be measured by the extent of influence enjoyed by the landless.[4]

Aristotle also observed that oligarchs are naturally displeased by democracy. Democracy's evolution in Europe over the last millennium—especially after voting for representatives began in Britain in 1430—has been a struggle marked by revolution, regicide, and debate as kings and elites resisted being corralled. Democracy, let alone high-quality democracy, has historically been a tenuous condition—it is under continuous threat from plutocrats and authoritarians and is thus hard won and hard to sustain. Today's America provides real-time evidence of that historic fact, and *Billionaire Democracy* explains why.

America's founding fathers* and constitutional framers made two significant contributions to democracy's global evolution—the Bill of Rights and an unprecedented expansion of the franchise. Other republics of their day restricted the franchise to elites and the educated. But our founding fathers adopted low property thresholds, enabling 60 to 70 percent of white males to vote. By the nineteenth and twentieth centuries, other nations had adopted this broad American-style franchise and crafted democracies that flourish today, the superior ones characterized by political equality where

---

*As used herein, the founding fathers refer to those involved with the Declaration of Independence and the Articles of Confederation, not the later constitutional framers.

voters are sovereign. But American democracy has floundered because it never followed suit. In 1787, only a handful of years after expanding the vote, America adopted a constitution that explicitly rejected the seminal principle of political equality.

At the root of this rejection is a protest known as Shays' Rebellion. In 1786, farmers in western Massachusetts protested high taxes and limited credit. In response, the Massachusetts legislature in early 1787 rushed through laws imposing progressive taxes, providing debt relief, and facilitating the printing of (easy) money. Their reaction revealed for the first time in the new nation the power of a vastly expanded electorate to sway lawmakers.

Bankers, wealthy colonials, and merchants were stunned, and quickly developed misgivings about the consequences of a grandly expanded electorate. To address their concerns about an electorate that had proven ill-informed and too easily misled, these elites gathered later that year in Philadelphia to replace the too-democratic Articles of Confederation crafted by the founding fathers. The design and architecture of the resulting Constitution was driven by a compelling fear, expressed by Alexander Hamilton in what proved to be his last letter, capitalization included, sent one day before his calamitous duel: "Our real disease . . . is DEMOCRACY."[5]

Three Imperatives of the Constitution

The framers not only had misgivings about the outsize influence voters could wield on policy decisions when given full equality and sovereignty, but they also wanted to ensure that lawmakers themselves could not be unduly influenced. The Constitution addressed their concerns about legislative decision making in three ways.

First, the framers stripped power from voters, placing policy decisions in the hands of senators, federal judges, and a president selected by elites. Hamilton expressed the intent that "All men of respectability . . . must [ensure] that the power of government is entrusted to proper hands."[6] James Madison, the primary author of the Constitution and the smartest man in the room, explained in *Federalist 10* that the Constitution was designed for lawmakers to naturally second-guess voters, their duty being to "refine and enlarge the public views, by passing them through the medium of a chosen body of citizens, whose wisdom may best discern the true interest of their country . . ."[7]

The framers' retreat from a government featuring voter sovereignty was quickly criticized by advocates of democracy. Within days
of the Constitution's unveiling, the *Federal Farmer,* on October 12, 1787,
lamented ordinary voters' lack of power as well as the hurdles placed by
the framers to prevent reformers from unwinding the new, undemocratic
constitution with amendments: "Every man of reflection must see, that
the change now proposed, is a transfer of power from the many to the few,
and the probability is, the artful and ever active aristocracy, will prevent
all peaceable measures for changes . . ."[8]

As historian Michael Klarman accurately summarized, "The
Constitution was designed to reverse the democratic trajectory of
American politics."[9]

Second, the framers sought to enhance the independence and integrity
of the representatives by banning bribery of public officials. Indeed, they
viewed the buying of lawmaker votes a seminal threat to the new nation.
In his *Federalist 52* essay, for example, the meticulously prepared Madison
insisted that members of Congress must resist entreaties by donors and
favor seekers.[10] Their fear was existential: The framers believed the success
of the new nation hinged on preventing bribery in any guise.

The third way the framers sought to elevate decision making in the
new nation was to strengthen the electorate itself. One option was to mimic
Britain, where the limited franchise was buttressed by bankers and university graduates being granted two votes in parliamentary elections.[11]
Instead, they embraced fact-based media reporting—only newspapers in
their day—in hopes of creating an informed electorate resistant to being
misled by fabulists. With the recent uprising by his western neighbors
in mind, for example, prominent Massachusetts delegate Elbridge Gerry
warned the Constitutional Convention that voters were being "daily misled . . . by the false reports circulated by designing men," whom he allitera-
tively labeled "pretend patriots."[12] And Madison warned in *Federalist 63*
that voters must become alert in order to reject what today we call fake
news—he termed it "artful misrepresentations by interested men."[13] In
addressing the Constitutional Convention, Madison was explicit, warning that ill-informed, misled voters "will become the tool of opulence and
ambition, in which case . . . property and individual liberty will not be
secure in their hands."[14]

An electorate armed with factual information was central to the framers' vision for the First Amendment and indeed to the success of the new nation. Here is the single most powerful sentiment that Madison expressed of all the dangers that confronted the new nation: "A popular government, without popular information, or the means of acquiring it, is but a prologue to a farce or a tragedy; or perhaps both. Knowledge will forever govern ignorance; and a people who mean to be their own governors must arm themselves with the power which knowledge gives."[15]

Madison and his fellow framers viewed the choice starkly. A democracy whose voters are misinformed or otherwise lack factual information and thus "the power knowledge gives," will assuredly be a troubled nation, destined to become a farce or worse. Abraham Lincoln, America's greatest president, shared the founders' obsession with the centrality of facts to a democracy: "I have faith in the people. They will not consent to disunion. The danger is, that they are misled. Let them know the truth and the country is safe."

The Low Quality of American Democracy Is Documented by the Income Bias

The low quality of American democracy reflects the failure of lawmakers and the Supreme Court to honor and operationalize the second and third imperatives set forth by the framers. They have failed to corral political corruption or to seek an electorate armed with facts. These failings are long-standing, but have become considerably more pronounced in recent years. Above all, the embrace of *pay-to-play*—decriminalizing the buying of lawmakers' votes—by the Supreme Court is the primary reason that American democracy is of low quality.

The most credible and objective proof is provided by what political scientists refer to as the *income bias*, examined in chapter 2. Income bias describes a society where public policy outcomes reflect elite preferences rather than broadly held preferences. The income bias explains why American wages in the key manufacturing sector are $10 an hour lower than in other wealthy democracies, why America lacks employer-paid maternity or annual leave, why America has the lowest minimum wages and why America alone among the rich democracies elects huckster populists. It also captures the array of policies responsible for the decline in the share of national income received by middle- and working-class Americans in the bottom half from 20 percent in 1980 to 12 percent in 2014. That income has been redirected upward. The share accruing to the top 1 percent rose from 11 percent when Ronald Reagan took office to 20 percent by 2014.[16] (Overall, the top 20 percent or so of workers—so-called knowledge workers—have enjoyed some gains in real wages in recent decades, although the gains are highly skewed to the top 5 percent and especially the top 1 percent.)

The income bias is a consequence of a skein of Supreme Court rulings explored in chapter 3 that have placed the industrial-scale buying of public officials' votes at the center of American democracy. Beginning with *Buckley v. Valeo* (1976), pay-to-play has been empowered by the Court. The narrow majority of Supreme Court justices responsible for the *Buckley* genre believe that the buying of lawmaker votes is some sort of free enterprise variant of democracy where (to paraphrase Stanford economist Tibor Scitovsky) what voters receive depends on how much each of them spends on politics—a rather stark abandonment of James Madison, the framers, and of *originalism*. (Scitovsky was a pioneer in marrying the study of happiness and economics, writing, "Consumer sovereignty in a free enterprise economy is a plutocracy, the rule of the rich, where each consumer's influence on what gets produced depends on how much he spends.")[17] Thus, while America adheres to many of the practices of other wealthy democracies in conducting its elections, its ballot boxes are de facto stuffed by judicially empowered elites. For their part, lawmakers honor the preferences of the wealthy donor class for the same reason robber Willie Sutton focused on banks—"Because that's where the money is."

The transformation of the US economy wrought by the *Buckley* era is widely acknowledged; here is how prominent hedge fund manager Jeremy Grantham put it: "Steadily increasing corporate power over the last 40 years has been . . . the defining feature of the US government and politics in general."[18]

Writing in June 2017, in the wake of Associate Justice Neil Gorsuch's confirmation to the Supreme Court, the conservative Grantham explicitly credited the Supreme Court for this transformation: "Corporate power, however, really hinges on other things, especially the ease with which money can influence policy. In this, management was blessed by the

Supreme Court, whose majority in the *Citizens United* decision put the seal of approval on corporate privilege and power over ordinary people. Maybe corporate power will weaken one day if it stimulates a broad push-back from the general public . . . I suggest you don't hold your breath."[19]

Corralling Aristotelian oligarchs more effectively has enabled the quality of democracy in other wealthy nations to forge ahead, leapfrogging well beyond the United States. In comparison, America is a low-quality democracy lacking voter sovereignty, with policy outcomes commonly unreflective of middle-class or majoritarian preferences. Indeed, in the eyes of the late dean of American political scientists, Robert Dahl, that characteristic calls into question whether the United States should any longer be viewed as a democracy. In his book *Polyarchy*, Dahl asserted that "A key characteristic of a democracy is the continuing responsiveness of a government to the preferences of its citizens, considered as political equals."

The low quality of America's democracy is responsible for rising economic inequality in recent decades, characterized by wage stagnation and the decline of collective bargaining among blue- and most white-collar workers. Political inequality has begotten economic inequality with flat wages while there have been handsome and rising returns on capital. That further begets political inequality, trapping most Americans in what French economist Thomas Piketty calls an "endless inegalitarian spiral." This spiral unsurprisingly has nurtured cynicism, bringing the inestimable value of democracy itself into question: 32 percent of surveyed Americans now express support for an authoritarian government.[20] They have grown disaffected with the foundational values of democracy that are responsible for the remarkable international spread of human rights, prosperity, and middle classes since the nineteenth century. Frankly, it's stunning that so many Americans are discontented with the only device in history proven capable of disrupting mankind's dismal default setting.

Even before the 2016 election, pay-to-play had caused America to be viewed as the most corrupt of all wealthy economies. The global scold Transparency International, surveying internationally in 2015, ranked America as only sixteenth best in controlling public corruption, its governance more corrupt in recent years than Barbados or Uruguay, and on a par with Chile, Qatar, and the Bahamas.[21] Gallup surveys have found that government corruption is perceived to be more widespread in the United States than in nations such as Belize, Estonia, Malta, or Slovakia.[22]

These assessments are evidenced by two of the last five elections, in which popular-vote losers were elevated over winners to become US president. In the 2000 presidential election, five Supreme Court judges overruled the majority decision of 104 million American voters to elevate a member of their own political party. If the two preceding sentences were not associated with this country, most Americans reading them would instantly consider such a nation to be a corrupt, faux democracy.

Accountability for the Income Bias

The Supreme Court is responsible for pay-to-play, supplanting votes with dollars as today's political medium of exchange. But responsibility for policies that reflect the income bias itself is shared in different degrees by lawmakers from both political parties. Democrats shoulder some of the blame, but scholars hold Republicans considerably more accountable—a consensus that is also reflected in much of this book.

Democrats

Democratic Party officials arrogantly overlook concerns of its traditional noncollege white voter base, as argued by scholars such as University of California Hastings College law professor Joan C. Williams and pollster Stanley Greenberg.[23] Infatuated with market fundamentalism, too many left-leaning economists have given only lip service over the past three decades to the Democratic Party's traditional focus on the economic plight of America's working and middle classes. For decades as wages stagnated, they have refused to advance the seasoned systemic innovations used by other wealthy democracies—requiring employers to share productivity gains with employees—that have produced steadily rising real wages. The innovation accomplishing that outcome is German-style codetermination, where employees comprise half of corporate boards of directors (discussed further in chapter 1). This innovation yields the most proficient version of capitalism in the world for avoiding American-style wage stagnation or sending jobs offshore. Yet that potent and time-tested upgrade of corporate governance is ignored despite being for decades the norm for "contemporary corporate governance" in other wealthy democracies across northern Europe.[24] The nation's most progressive Democratic politicians, such as Senators Bernie Sanders and Elizabeth Warren, are in the dark. That has left the Democratic Party with a meek, ersatz wage agenda—with feet of clay on their signal issue. Moreover, both the Clinton and Obama administrations were complicit in job offshoring that has seen imports rise from 6.2 percent of nonenergy manufacturing inputs in 1984 to 16.4 percent in 2010.[25]

Secretary Hillary Clinton suffered from a drop compared to President Obama in turnout among (unenthusiastic) minorities whose wages have stagnated. And she lost white noncollege voters by a 39 percentage point margin—voters fired by populist anger with flat wages, job offshoring, and the perception that Democrats coddle Wall Street millionaires, minorities, and immigrants at the expense of "real" Americans. In exit polling, 80 percent of white noncollege voters in 2016 said their personal economic situation was worse or no better after eight years of the Obama administration.[26] This inattention to Americans of modest means was repaid in kind in November 2016.

Republicans

Democrats have been inattentive to middle-class wage stagnation, but Republican leaders have become overtly hostile to higher wages. And wages will assuredly continue to stagnate during the inept and erratic Trump administration. More responsive than Democrats to the donor class, the GOP aggressively pursues a small-government agenda that features profit maximization through deregulation and wage suppression. The party of Lincoln, Teddy Roosevelt, and Eisenhower is now committed to the narcissistic agenda of many of America's most affluent families, who are covetous of wealth stratification. That commitment has produced America's first ideologically pure political party, its lawmakers willing, for instance, to strip health care from tens of millions of working-class families to fund tax cuts for their donors. Thomas Mann of the progressive Brookings Institution and Norman Ornstein of the conservative American Enterprise Institute explained the consequences of this transformation in 2012: "We have no choice but to acknowledge that the core of the problem lies with the Republican Party . . . The GOP has become an insurgent outlier. It has become ideologically extreme; contemptuous of the inherited social and economic policy regime; scornful of compromise;

unpersuaded by conventional understanding of facts, evidence and science; and dismissive of the legitimacy of its political opposition."[27]

Fake News

The furtherance of the donor class agenda has been enhanced by the emergence of fake news as a potent GOP political tool. The misrepresentation of facts for partisan gain or profit is as old as humankind. It has been exacerbated in recent years, most dramatically by conservatives on talk radio, at partisan organizations such as Fox News, and on social media platforms by cyber entrepreneurs, polemists, political partisans, and Kremlin propagandists. Importantly, weaponized fake news proved politically effective for Republicans in 2016. By Election Day, for instance, two-thirds of voters supporting candidate Donald Trump believed the unemployment rate rose under Obama (it fell by more than one-half to near full employment by 2016). Only 17 percent of Republicans believed that Obamacare reduced the number of Americans without health insurance to the lowest in history.[28] And two-thirds of Trump supporters also believed that the election machinery in America can be rigged, enabling three or four million illegal votes to be cast for former Secretary Clinton.

The GOP exacerbated its afactual narrative by demonizing mainstream fact-based reporting. Channeling Joseph McCarthy and President Richard Nixon from December 1972,[29] for instance, candidate Trump routinely asserted that "the press is the enemy," attacking factual journalists as "enemies of the American people."[30] The disconcerting outcome was that by the end of 2016, barely one-third of Americans retained faith in factual, mainstream journalism.

The GOP prospered by polarizing America. Immediately before the GOP theology fully embraced pay-to-play in 1994, only 21 percent of party members surveyed by the Pew Research Center had a "very unfavorable view of Democrats." The transformation since is stunning, with that figure nearly tripling to 58 percent by 2016.[31] Democrats' distrust of Republicans has grown as well. Only 21 percent of Americans now believe the nation is united.[32] And political scientists document that the share of swing voters has declined by half since the 1990s to barely 5 percent today.[33] The Republican Party's success with fake news in engineering distrust and polarization has diminished the moderate middle of American politics, rendering compromise based on an agreed body of facts less likely.

The framers primarily rested their aspirations for the new nation on public officials free from bribery and an electorate well-armed with facts. America today is failing to fulfill those hopes. The challenge before us now is to divine how America can avoid becoming the farce or even the tragedy feared by James Madison.

———— ☆ ————

America Is a Low-Quality Democracy

THE LOW QUALITY OF American democracy reflects denial of majoritarian rule, an eventuality sought by many of America's wealthiest. Stout majority rule in other wealthy democracies has translated into larger government sectors funding an expansive array of public services. Alarmed by this powerful postwar evolution, a number of conservative American billionaires have contrived in recent decades to deny voter sovereignty and rule by majority. Their names, tactics, and strategies have been extensively documented by researchers such as Jane Mayer, Nancy MacLean, Kim Phillips-Fein, and Steven M. Teles.

The chapters in this section examine how they have exploited Supreme Court rulings embracing pay-to-play to achieve success. Their tawdry accomplishment is measured in the redirection upward of the gains from growth since the Reagan administration—leaving wages stagnant and lowering opportunity while darkening hopes and the American dream for most (chapter 1). Their accomplishment is documented by the Income Bias (chapter 2) resulting from their exploitation of pay-to-play (chapter 3) centered on the successful suborning of the Republican Party (chapter 4).

CHAPTER 1

Faux Democracy: America's Decline to History's Dismal Default Setting

[American] economic inequality has followed through to political inequality and democratic government is bereft of power and capacity.[1]

—Stein Ringen, Oxford Professor Emeritus, 2014

The main question confronting us today is not really about capitalism in the 21st century. It is about democracy in the 21st century.[2]

—Joseph Stiglitz, *The Great Divide*

The hollowing out of middle income households is a US-only phenomenon.[3]

—*The Financial Times*, December 2016

POLITICAL DECISIONS DETERMINE WHO receives the fruits of capitalism. High-quality democracies spread those fruits broadly. The low quality of American democracy is at the heart of America's middle- and working-class economic stagnation. Flat wages and rising income disparity are eroding the spirit of community, enthusiasm, and optimism just as they did during the Great Depression when Franklin Roosevelt affirmed that "necessitous men are not free."

A Majority of Americans Believe the American Dream Is Dead

The US economy has been misfiring for most Americans for over a generation—wages have been flat, millions of quality jobs exported, and economic mobility has declined. The decline in economic opportunity is so pronounced that the phenomenon is common fodder for leading European newspapers. The *Financial Times* in August 2017, for instance, headlined "Five Charts Show Why Millennials Are Worse Off Than Their Parents."[4] Indeed, 54 percent of US respondents to the 2013 Economic Values Survey cited by Brookings Institution economists believe the American Dream of opportunity as originally defined by James Truslow Adams is dead: "Hard work and determination are no guarantee of success."[5] Their pessimism is fact-based. Upward mobility for youths has fallen sharply since the 1980s. Some 92 percent of Americans born during the 1940s, for instance, earned more than their parents in inflation-adjusted or real dollars. Fewer than half of those born in the 1980s have done as well.[6]

With wages today scarcely better for most people than earned by their parents, optimism about the future has rightly suffered. Surveys document that decades of wage stagnation have caused Americans to grow pessimistic about the future for their children. Only 21 percent of respondents to a *Wall Street Journal*/NBC News survey in 2014 believed their children would live better, a record low in polling. The share stood at 54 percent in 1980 before Ronald Reagan launched today's era of inequality.[7]

Some workers have realized higher wages, but an overwhelming majority has suffered stagnant or real wage declines. Even many of the better educated younger workers today earn no more than did younger workers with less education in 1980. And overall, census data show that the real median income of young workers aged twenty-five to thirty-four was 5.5 percent lower in 2016 ($35,000) than in 1975 ($37,000).[8] True, household incomes rose until 1999, but that reflected women working longer hours. Since then, overall family incomes have fallen. As documented in an analysis prepared for the National Bureau of Economic Research in April 2017, weak wages have caused lifetime earnings for an entire generation of Americans to flat-line or fall. And no improvement is expected by the authors of this authoritative analysis: "Partial life-cycle profiles of income observed for cohorts that are currently in the labor market indicate that the stagnation of lifetime incomes is unlikely to reverse."[9]

Since Ronald Reagan, birth status has come to dictate life's opportunities for too many, hardening American social classes. Importantly, despite eight years of a Democratic White House, the ability of labor unions to raise wages has been the weakest since the 1920s. Economists at the International Monetary Fund have concluded that this factor alone is responsible for about one-half of the erosion in net US income equality between 1980 and 2010.[10]

Dwindling opportunity and flat wages explain why two-thirds of respondents to a Public Religion Research Institute survey in 2015 believed that "one of the big problems in this country is that we don't give everyone an equal chance in life."[11] The ensuing despair has bled into the social fabric for Americans of modest means, who are experiencing rising opiate abuse and suicide rates and falling marriage rates.

Wage Rates and Economic Mobility, Here and Abroad

In contrast to America, voter sovereignty translates to economic policies that create prosperous middle-class societies in higher quality democracies. The outcome is that economic mobility is more robust there, with youths readily earning more than their parents did at the same age. Their superior performance begins at an early age with abundant public prenatal care, expansive child care, early prekindergarten, quality health care, and inexpensive, quality education—kindergarten through college. Investment and job up-skilling is higher as well, causing workforce skill levels in northern Europe and Australia to now exceed those of the United States.[12] Unsurprisingly, productivity levels in nations such as Belgium, Denmark, and France now surpass America's.[13]

The beneficence of these policies for low- and middle-income cohorts is exemplified by Germany. Real wages there at lower income levels rose steadily during the 1990s at more than 1 percent annually, even outpacing earnings growth at the top of the income scale. That trend slowed during the 2007 economic crisis. But real wage growth at low- and middle-income levels has since returned to the long-term trend of around 1 percent per year.

How do the real earnings of lower wage workers in Germany and across western Europe keep pace with income growth at the middle and top? German economists explain:

> [T]his development is also likely a result of changes linked to the collective bargaining policy. In the hospitality sector, for example—an industry with particularly low wages—collective-agreement wages increased between 2010 and 2015 (by 16.7 percent in the East and 9.9 percent in the West). Although not all employees are subject to a collective bargaining agreement, the tariff increases may have also had an influence on the wages of companies that were not bound by the agreement. Trade unions were increasingly successful in claiming and enforcing sectoral [widespread] collective agreements . . .[14]

The contrast with America is dramatic. Hourly pay adjusted for inflation in Germany has increased nearly 30 percent since 1985.[15] Labor compensation as a share of national income has actually increased in Germany since the 2007 recession, rising from 47.6 percent to nearly 51 percent.[16] And the gains continue today. In fact, the average 2.5 percent real wage gains reported by the Federal Statistics Office for German workers in 2015 alone matched the *cumulative* rise in median real American weekly wages between 1979 and 2015.[17] More broadly, real wages rose an average of 1.4 percent in the twenty-eight European Union (EU) countries in 2015 and 1.7 percent in 2016.[18]

These steady gains have enabled real salaries abroad adjusted for purchasing power to leapfrog American wages. In the capstone manufacturing sectors in eleven wealthy democracies, wages and benefits are now more than $10 per hour higher than in the United States, according to the US Bureau of Labor Statistics.[19] Service sector wages have risen steadily at nearly the same pace.[20] Even so, despite notably higher wages, higher quality democracies outcompete America. Germany is the most competitive economy on earth, its manufacturing sector is robust, wages are high and rising, and unemployment in 2016 was at a twenty-five-year low. Similar outcomes are commonplace across western Europe, where GDP grew faster in 2016 than in America despite their higher wages.[21] Burger King employees in Denmark earn $20 per hour (versus $9 in the United States), receive five weeks' paid vacation, overtime bonus pay, national health insurance, paid maternity and paternity leave, and have a pension plan.[22]

This striking contrast between falling American and rising western European economic opportunity and wage performance is reinforced by international economic mobility statistics; they measure how readily males in various nations can improve their economic situation through education and diligence. At this writing the most recent assessment is from May 2016 by Miles Corak of the University of Ottawa, published by the Stanford Center on Poverty and Inequality.[23] He and his colleagues concluded that America has devolved into a low-mobility society where parental status is increasingly the determinant of lifetime economic prospects: Intergenerational earnings mobility of Americans is lower than in *every* nation of northern Europe. American economic mobility is just one-half that of Australia and Canada. The anemic rewards from education and hard work for American men is little better than for contemporaries in Chile or Argentina, where widespread wage stagnation and rising inequality also chill economic opportunity.

Higher wages also mean the quality of life for most families in northern Europe is superior, with secure retirements, longer vacations, and necessities such as quality public education, child care, college, and health care more broadly available and affordable. Specific economic policies enacted in response to middle-class demands are responsible for the success of these countries and for their higher economic mobility, especially policies linking wage increases to rising productivity. That linkage is the black box behind their success in widely broadcasting rising incomes.

Economic outcomes similar to Europe today were commonplace in America during the post–World War II decades, ending only with the arrival of the Reagan era and pay-to-play. Between 1947 and 1972, real wages in America rose steadily with improving productivity, which increased 97 percent over this period while real median pay rose 95 percent.[24] This postwar boom temporarily created history's greatest middle class—now eclipsed by northern Europe. Many men and women could control their own economic futures in an opportunity society where striving frequently produced a secure and rewarding life for college and high school graduates alike. By 1968, income disparities were the lowest in American history, as measured by a standard used by economists, the Gini coefficient.[25]

During this era, real wages rose because lawmakers both heard and heeded popular sentiment for rising family prosperity, creating a high-quality American democracy.

Labor Unions and Economic Growth, Here and Abroad

Northern European lawmakers and citizens view labor unions as existential allies in the struggle to fend off the default setting of capitalism. In contrast, too many Americans—particularly billionaires, GOP lawmakers, and the Republican majority on the Supreme Court—reject labor unions and their role as antibiotics for the inequalities that are woven into capitalism's DNA. Unions are the backbone of the northern European model of dynamic economies with robust social protections that deliver steady real income growth up and down the income ladder. This union-friendly mindset, reflected in public policies, is why corporations in northern Europe widely broadcast prosperity. Wages there rise faster than inflation, roughly in line with productivity growth. Collective bargaining is why the bottom 90 percent of workers across western Europe and in Oceania

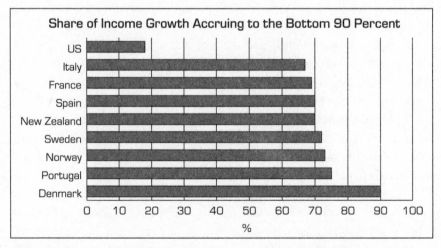

Chart 1.1 Share of income growth accruing to the bottom 90 percent, 1976–2007.

"Focus on Top Incomes and Taxation in OECD Countries: Was the Crisis a Game Changer?" Organisation for Economic Co-operation and Development, May 2014, chart 3, www.oecd.org/social/OECD2014-FocusOnTopIncomes.pdf

have received a far greater share of the gains from economic growth than have Americans since the Reagan era (chart 1.1). For example, the bottom 90 percent of Danish employees have received 90 percent of all income growth between 1976 and 2007, while during the same period, the bottom 90 percent of Americans received only 18 percent.

As concluded by the *Financial Times* in December 2016, after examining the wealthy democracies: "The hollowing out of middle income households is a US-only phenomenon."[26]

Comparing American and European Work Effort

Unemployment rates are higher in some EU nations than the United States, but that primarily is an artifact reflecting the millions of discouraged Americans who no longer are counted in the labor force. In Europe, by contrast, higher wages encourage men and women to work. Indeed, Americans find it startling to learn that more Europeans than Americans work. Specifically, a higher proportion of both European men and women twenty-five to fifty-four years old—the cohort central to middle-class family prosperity—work than their counterparts in America. The data from the US Council of Economic Advisors is unequivocal. Some 12 percent of twenty-five- to fifty-four-year-old American men were neither seeking work nor employed in 2014, for instance. That figure was only 7 percent in France and Spain and 4 percent in Japan.[27] Higher European workforce participation translates to fewer of the pathologies unfortunately growing common in the United States, such as addiction and suicide, explored by Robert Putnam in *Bowling Alone,* as well as by Angus Deaton, Ann Case, and other sociologists. Importantly, the International Monetary Fund has concluded that the strong collective bargaining institutions, codetermination, and other practices responsible for steadily rising wages in other wealthy democracies like Germany are costless: They do not slow productivity or GDP growth.[28]

The Reagan Administration Launched the Age of Political and Economic Inequality

Today's age of rising political and economic inequality was ushered in by the 1980 election of Ronald Reagan. An analysis by the Economic Policy

Institute found that 70 percent of all income growth from 1935 to 1980 went to the bottom 90 percent of households, while 7 percent went to the top 1 percent. Since 1980, however, real wages have barely risen, despite per capita production rising 80 percent,[29] with the top 1 percent garnering 72 percent of all income growth.[30] By receiving much of new income growth, the share flowing to the 1 percent grew to exceed 22 percent of all national income in 2012, compared to 11 percent in 1944.[31]

Former American central bank (Federal Reserve) chairman and conservative Ben Bernanke notes that the wage stagnation, declining economic mobility, and the weaker workforce participation of our era reflects a failure of public policy beginning with Reagan: "The Reagan revolution heralded a more constrained approach to economic policy . . ."[32] Bernanke explains the ideological "errors and omissions" of Reagan were repeated by both the Clinton and George W. Bush administrations, which failed

> to expand job training and re-training opportunities, especially for the less educated; to provide transition assistance for displaced workers, including support for internal migration; to mitigate residential and educational segregation and increase the access of those left behind to employment and educational opportunities; to promote community redevelopment, through grants, infrastructure construction and other means; and to address serious social ills through addiction programs, criminal justice reform and the like.

The outcome of Bernanke's "Reagan revolution"—ending the steady postwar rise of real wages—has created a second Gilded Age. The original nineteenth-century version was described by the American Populist Party platform of 1892: "The fruits of the toil of millions are boldly stolen to build up colossal fortunes for a few, unprecedented in the history of mankind; and the possessors of those, in turn, despise the republic and endanger liberty. From the same prolific womb of governmental injustice we breed the two great classes—tramps and millionaires."[33]

Other wealthy democracies have continued to broadcast income growth widely since the 1980s because their citizens have retained political leverage; their voters are sovereign. An example of this is the minimum wage. Unlike the United States, the proportion of low-wage workers in Germany, for instance, is stable.[34] That is because, also unlike the situation in the United States, rising poverty induced the German government to institute a nationwide minimum wage and to increase it regularly to €10 per hour in 2017. In contrast, the "Reagan revolution" ushered in decades of stagnant wages (the real minimum wage has declined), job offshoring, widespread acceptance of greed in corporate executive suites, a spread in employment contracts containing noncompete and mandatory arbitration clauses, and a surge of independent contracting. Weaker unions are a key factor in US wage stagnation, and the combination of pay-to-play and hostility to collective bargaining has caused the share of union jobs to be the smallest since 1916, a hundred-year low. The American middle class is paying a high price for weaker unions: The Bureau of Labor Statistics reports that union members had annual earnings of about $49,000 in 2013, compared to $38,600 for comparable nonunion workers.[35]

Certainly, rapid technology change and globalization have contributed a bit to wage stagnation. But the continued growth of real wages in northern Europe affirms that the policies of Reaganomics are primarily responsible for US wage stagnation. After all, the high-wage economies of northern Europe experienced the same technology transformation as America in recent decades. Moreover, they are even more involved in international trade. Yet real wages there have continued to increase.

The most important reason is that voters, not political donors, are sovereign. Their political architecture favors majoritarian rule. Pay-to-play is explicitly rejected (as reviewed in detail in chapter 10). Lawmakers have naturally responded to satisfy those sovereigns. They have installed works councils in corporations (employee groups performing the equivalent of midmanagement duties in US firms), shareholder approval ("say-on-pay") for CEO and director compensation levels, and, importantly, codetermination to reform corporate governance. Codetermination requires that employees sit on corporate boards of larger domestic firms in order to ensure a middle-class rather than an elitist firm mission. Those laws are sweeping, applicable also to foreign investors. For instance, the $200 million invested by American private equity firm KKR in the Nuremberg-based GFK in April 2017 included the appointment of three new corporate board members.[36] They displaced existing shareholder representatives, leaving the original power of employees' representatives unaffected.

Employee representatives on corporate boards would upgrade governance at American firms. Employee representatives naturally focus on long-term prosperity, which results in greater investment, R&D, and higher wages. That different focus is a major reason that corporate prosperity in northern Europe translates to family prosperity. To put it in Aristotelian terms, their political systems produce more equitable economic outcomes because their "landless" are kings.

That is not America, and foreign observers know it, exemplified by German journalist Marc Hujer writing in *Der Spiegel*: "During the last few decades, . . . [America] has been a country in which the rich have become richer, and the poor poorer, and in which the middle class seems to be disappearing and, with it, the sense that everyone shares in rising prosperity."[37] And here is former Australian Treasurer Wayne Swan, quoted in the *Brisbane Times*, "Don't let what has happened to the American economy happen here. Don't let Australia become a down-under version of New Jersey, where the people and communities whose skills are no longer in demand get thrown on the scrap heap of life."[38]

In Australia, Canada, and northern Europe, the policy preferences of a majority of citizens are implemented by responsive lawmakers. The sovereignty of voters is responsible for their superior economic performance, with income disparities far smaller than in the United States. Indeed, the United States has the most severe income disparity of any wealthy democracy—more skewed than Greece or Portugal and comparable to that of authoritarian Turkey.[39]

America's Shrinking Middle Class

The median weekly wage of a full-time American worker in the all-encompassing nonfarm business sector in 2016 was a bare 3.3 percent ($11) higher than in 1979, after adjusting for inflation.[40] This stagnation began in the 1980s and has been exacerbated by today's gig economy, where many employee–employer relationships are impersonal and transactional. The number of "nonstandard jobs"—temporary, on-call, independent contractor gigs, or workers supplied by outside contractors—has risen 70 percent since 2006 to 24 million, now comprising one in six jobs.[41] They are popular with employers, enabling them to dodge benefit and other employee costs such as Social Security or Medicare taxes. Thus "nonstandard" translates to lower wages—7 percent less for janitors, 14 percent less for educators, up to 24 percent less for security guards, and

9 percent less in retailing, according to economists.[42] Combine that with job offshoring, weak labor unions, and the migration of jobs to the non-union American South, and the consequence is new American jobs that are disproportionately insecure and low wage. Indeed, Harvard economist Lawrence F. Katz and Alan B. Krueger of Princeton have concluded that a whopping 94 percent of employment growth since 2007 has been in nonstandard categories.[43]

Data show that new jobs created in recent decades have consistently paid less than the old ones they replaced. More than 40 percent of the 8.5 million jobs lost in 2008 and 2009, for instance, had median wages above $20 an hour. But only 30 percent of jobs created through February 2014 were comparable.[44] The international Organisation for Economic Co-operation and Development (OECD) has concluded that the United States has the largest share of low-wage jobs of any wealthy democracy.[45]

The outcome of Reaganomics is exemplified by the average wage of $12 per hour at America's largest employer, Walmart. In contrast, the average pay at General Motors—America's largest employer in the 1960s—was $35 an hour in today's dollars.[46]

These trends have reduced the American middle class, as documented by the Pew research organization.[47] According to an April 2016 analysis, the share of American adults between 2000 and 2014 living in middle-income households declined in 203 of 229 metropolitan areas examined.[48] And a Pew study one year later found that the share of American adults living in middle-income households dropped nearly 5 percent between 1991 and 2010.[49] Contrary to the views of conservatives at the American Enterprise Institute and elsewhere, households falling out of the middle class account for most of that decline.[50]

Americans know it. A detailed Pew survey in 2014 (see chart 1.2) found for the first time ever that the share of Americans who consider themselves below middle class nearly equaled the share self-identifying as middle class. One in six Americans who considered themselves middle class in 2008 have since fallen out, causing a 40 percent jump in the share of Americans who self-classify as below middle income. Moreover, the ranks of those who consider themselves above middle income (not shown) have also declined from 22 percent in 2008 to 16 percent in 2014.

This subjective assessment is supported by objective international data. America now has the smallest middle class of any wealthy democracy,

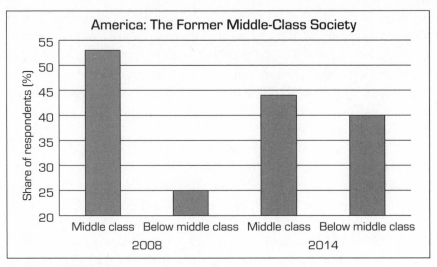

Chart 1.2 Self-defined by respondents.

Rakesh Kochhar and Rich Morin, "Despite Recovery, Fewer Americans Identify as Middle Class," Pew Research Center, January 27, 2014, www.pewresearch.org /fact-tank/2014/01/27/despite-recovery-fewer-americans-identify-as-middle-class/

using global OECD standards. Measured by the share of households with disposable incomes between one-half and twice the national average, America's middle class is smaller than every nation in western Europe and even Russia. It is comparable to the size in Uruguay and is scarcely larger than in developing nations with notably skewed income distributions such as Egypt, Mexico, Brazil, and South Africa.[51]

Beginning in the Reagan presidency, the income garnered by the top 5 percent of American households grew faster than in every other democracy while the income accruing to the middle class grew the least. That has caused America to drop near the bottom of wealthy democracies in providing equal economic opportunities. In 2011, for instance, the German Bertelsmann Foundation ranked America twenty-eighth of the thirty-one highest income democracies, providing less economic opportunity than considerably less affluent nations such as Ireland, Poland, Portugal, and Slovakia. It only ranked ahead of Chile, Mexico, and Turkey—nations with far lower per capita incomes and weak investments in education and other public goods integral to upward mobility. Notably, these other low opportunity nations share the US pay-to-play political systems and thus are low quality democracies.[52] In a separate analysis three years later in 2014, officials with the United Nations Development Program also placed the United States only twenty-eighth in its prominent Inequality-adjusted Human Development Index measuring citizen overall well-being.[53]

Low-Quality American Democracy as Described by Aristotle

The market economies of Aristotle's day intrigued him with their promise of expanding prosperity, and he devoted considerable attention to the pivotal role that politics play in determining market outcomes. He observed that over time, markets produce economic inequality and a class of predatory elites he termed oligarchs. Unless corralled, they deploy their economic power to subvert the political process, inevitably leading to a reduction in the quality of democracy and in turn more severe economic inequality. So powerful was this insight that Aristotle made it his measure of the quality of democracy.[54] As noted earlier, his key test was the extent to which preferences of the landless are reflected in policy outcomes: "What differentiates oligarchy and democracy is wealth or the lack of it. The essential point is that where the possession of political power is due to the possession of economic power or wealth, whether the number of persons be large or small, that is oligarchy, and when the unpropertied class have power, that is democracy."[55]

Aristotle's *Politics* and humanist *Ethics* explored this theme and were inspirations to political revolutionaries of the seventeenth and eighteenth centuries, including Thomas Hobbes, Thomas Jefferson, and John Locke.[56] And his seminal principle linking democracy and economic outcomes has been repeatedly affirmed in America since the colonial era. Drawing on experience during the Gilded Age, for instance, Supreme Court Justice Louis Brandeis concluded that Americans "may have democracy or may have political power concentrated in the hands of a few, but can't have both."[57]

In recent years, econometricians have explored the Aristotelian theme in unprecedented detail. Using gigantic digitalized statistical bases, they have developed a data-rich understanding of the economic character and historic evolution of cultures.[58] Economists Daron Acemoglu of the Massachusetts Institute of Technology and James Robinson of Harvard document that past societies have rarely been uplifting for the 99 percent, virtually always subject to relentless predation by elites. In *Why Nations Fail*, they conclude that political elites always connive to extract economic surplus, and economic elites always connive to control politics. Thus, de facto indentured men, women, and children, dehumanized as prey, analogized to beasts of burden and tribal others, have been a large proportion of nearly all societies throughout history. There were only four relatively brief epochs before the political revolutions beginning in seventeenth-century Europe where the grip of elites was considerably if temporarily eased and innovative, entrepreneurial "new men" could emerge: in the ancient Greek city-states beginning with Corinth; Republican Rome prior to Caesar; the thirteenth-century Venetian Republic; and the handful of innovative textile centers that emerged in fifteenth- and sixteenth-century Europe in circumstances conducive to entrepreneurship.

The Quality of Politics Determines Economic Outcomes

Like Aristotle, Acemoglu and Robinson conclude that the political nature of a society is the major determinant of how the gains from growth are allocated. They and others, such as historian Yuval Harari, explain that the default setting of history is for predatory, exclusive economic *and* political systems to go hand-in-hand.

Periods of high-quality democracy, as in postwar America until the 1980s, or Europe today, are rare and tenuous. They are continuously under threat from Aristotelian oligarchs, as noted by Oxford professor Stein Ringen: "Democracy is not the default. It is a form of government that must be created with determination and that will disintegrate unless nurtured."[59] Political and economic equality are unnatural states, achieved and sustained only through a relentless, vigorous struggle against long odds, as summarized by OECD officials: "Equitable societies with large middle classes are not the natural outcome of market forces. Equity, rather, is created by society, by institutions—the laws, policies and practices—that govern the society, its economy and in particular its labor markets."[60]

Nobel laureate Joseph Stiglitz notes that elites design "the rules of the game to ensure this outcome; that is, through politics."[61] The Greeks called this plutocratic bias of market economies *diaploki*, the consequence of an incestuous relationship between powerful economic and political actors. Martin Wolf of the *Financial Times* explains "this outcome is 'rule by affluent vested interests,' or quite simply, plutocracy."[62]

In the modern era, this predatory, extractive default setting began to give way only in the wake of the remarkable seventeenth-century revolutions in politics (and the later revolution in technology when James Watt had perhaps the single most transformative scientific insight in human history: Compressed steam pushes back). More equitable income distributions and expanding middle classes began to emerge on the heels of political tumult as political revolutions in Britain and Europe slowly gained traction. Most notably, the British Glorious Revolution of 1688 affirmed the principle that legislatures rather than monarchs rest at the center of governance. This transition was neither peaceful nor linear, instead achieved as a consequence of revolution, regicide, great depression, or war. As inclusive or pluralistic governing systems with diffused political power emerged, popular pressure for the development of more inclusive economic systems featuring social safety nets and labor rights grew. In America, Acemoglu and Robinson note that rising suffrage produced a "gradual virtuous circle" of political and then social and economic reforms. "The political changes were unmistakably toward more inclusive political institutions and were the result of demands from empowered masses."[63] The capstone democracy model that emerged only slowly across western Europe, Britain, Oceania, and North America is a fragile, historical aberration from the natural state of mankind.

Creating Political Equality

Countries such as America that desire greater economic equality must first craft institutions that promote and sustain political equality. The post–World War II governments of nations such as Denmark and Germany created high-quality democracies featuring political equality and voter sovereignty. The ensuing public policies created opportunity societies characterized by strong wage growth, universal health care, collective bargaining, quality daycare, stakeholder corporate governance, quality schools, routine job up-skilling, inexpensive higher education, and the like.

Codetermination and High-Quality Democracy

High-quality democracies diffuse economic gains and increase economic opportunity with policies that link de facto growth in real wages to labor productivity growth. The institution at the center of this process is codetermination. By requiring that employees sit on corporate boards of larger domestic firms, codetermination ensures a middle-class corporate culture. It is a culture that is also focused on long term firm prosperity, rising real wages, and little if any job offshoring. It's a concept that is sixty years old, and has been adopted by nineteen of the twenty-seven EU nations (not counting the departing UK). In Germany, for instance, employees occupy half of the seats on boards of directors at the six hundred largest firms.[64]

The prowess of codetermination is affirmed by the German economic performance. Its impact on job offshoring was documented in October 2016 by the international consulting firm EY (Ernst & Young) using data from the blue-chip firms comprising Germany's DAX 30 stock index. The study period was 2011 to 2015. These firms are global household names such as Adidas, BMW, Daimler, and Merck, all with codetermination governance systems. EY analysts found that the increase in sales made abroad (either exports or produced abroad) by these firms (28 percent) considerably exceeded their creation of foreign jobs (8 percent). The difference was satisfied by adding jobs at home to produce exports. That explains why German employment increased at these huge firms domestically by a greater amount than their rise in domestic sales.[65] This outcome reflects the impact of employees sitting on these corporate boards, attentive to long-term firm prosperity, investment as well as expanding domestic employment.

These policies are the precise opposite of policies pursued by many larger American firms, who grow by offshoring higher wage US jobs to low-wage nations. For example, a *Wall Street Journal* analysis by David Wessel covering the period from 2000 to 2009 found that American multinational firms eliminated a net of 2.9 million domestic jobs while adding a net of 2.4 million jobs abroad.[66] A second study by Martin A. Sullivan on behalf of the nonpartisan Tax Analysts think tank confirmed that data. It found that US multinationals cut a net 1.9 million domestic jobs during this period while adding a net 2.35 million jobs abroad.[67] The lesson: Codetermination prevents job offshoring. It ensures that corporate job growth occurs at home rather than in low-wage nations abroad.[68]

Handelsblatt editor Frank Specht quotes German president Joachim Gauck as describing codetermination as "an important cultural asset," because of its centrality to middle-class prosperity in capitalism.[69]

American Ignorance of Codetermination

The responsiveness of lawmakers to voter preferences explains why higher quality democracies achieve steadily rising real wages. Laws and institutions such as those in Germany produce outcomes that are the antithesis of American-style wage suppression.[70] Yet, Americans are simply unaware that the northern European variant of capitalism produces larger and more affluent middle classes, with superior future prospects as well. European economists such as Thomas Piketty regularly explore the profile and dynamics of these superior-performing democracies and their economies. But his American counterparts are mostly mum.[71] Progressive American economists, many liberal organizations, and mainstream media economic journalists have kept American voters in the dark (no public shaming, but you know who you are). Only a handful of American industry and labor experts write about the superior living standards in northern Europe, including Scott N. Paul writing in the *New York Times* in December 2016: "We're not Germany, with its high-wage, high-export and stable manufacturing sector . . ."[72] But only rarely are the higher living standards of middle-class Europeans and their greater workforce participation even noted in the US media. Few economic journalists and academic economists in the United States are informed about works councils and codetermination, with exceptions such as Olivier Blanchard at MIT (born in France), Larry Fauver at the University of Tennessee, Michael Fuerst at the University of Miami, and Barry Eichengreen at the University of California, Berkeley. It is ironic that the most thorough analysis clarifying that shareholders in codetermination firms earn higher returns than shareholders in firms lacking codetermination has been conducted by two American economists, Fauver and Fuerst.[73]

Low-Quality American Democracy: The Income Bias

Stagnant wages since the Reagan revolution signal that American democracy is of lower quality than in northern Europe, with US policy outcomes reflecting the preferences of higher income Americans, producing what political scientists call the income bias.

Surveys reveal that voters realize their votes are outweighed by donors, including respondents to the November 2015 survey, noted earlier, by the Public Religion Research Institute. Some 64 percent, for example, believe their "vote does not matter because of the influence that wealthy individuals and big corporations have on the electoral process." Some 79 percent (including 63 percent of Republicans) believe American capitalism "unfairly favors the wealthy."[74] Only 5 percent believe the government looks after the interests of the middle class.

Americans also realize that the income bias has grown more severe of late. Pew polling in 2015 found that 76 percent of Americans believe money has a greater influence on politics and elected officials "today than in the past"; only 22 percent see little difference. And 74 percent believe that elected officials "don't care what people like me think." That figure is up from 55 percent in 2000.[75]

Four factors are primarily responsible for the income bias. The first is the corporate culture that emerged during the Reagan presidency, drawing on the narcissistic free-market philosophy of the Russian émigré and atheist Alisa Rosenbaum (Ayn Rand). This culture embraces Rand's "rational selfishness" philosophy, urging corporate officials to set aside biblical teachings in favor of their own pecuniary self-interest. The Randian revolution marked abandonment by executive suites of the postwar model of stakeholder capitalism, in which corporations had been managed to benefit employees and local communities as well as shareholders. It demonized the collective bargaining responsible for high wages and prioritized behaviors designed to facilitate the seizure of windfalls by senior executives armed with stock options. Share buybacks, uneconomical leveraged buyouts or mergers, and corporate inversions are other manifestations of this syndrome. Stock options became widespread, with executive remuneration tied to next quarter's earnings per share. The consequence was a sharp focus by CEOs on self-aggrandizement attained by raising short-term quarterly profits, achieved by allowing cash flow to fall to the bottom line—cash flow that had previously been devoted instead to R&D, wages, and investment. The reduction of corporate cash flowing to investments in order to show greater current income explains why privately held firms (where CEOs are tightly monitored) invest at a stunning 2.5 times the rate of public US companies (10 percent of assets vs. 4 percent).[76]

A second factor contributing to the income bias is a willingness of wealthy conservatives to aggressively invest in politicians in order to further their philosophy of small government. They have donated and spent billions of dollars on the GOP to further their agenda of boosting profits through wage suppression, deregulation, and greater market concentration, while also seeking to lower taxes at the expense of spending on public R&D, innovation, education, and the like.

A third factor is a transformation of the Republican Party in the early 1990s that was initiated by then-Congressman Tom DeLay and Speaker of the House Newt Gingrich. DeLay believed that accumulating political power necessitated an expansive pandering by the GOP to affluent donors, especially corporate interests and wealthy staunch conservatives. Gingrich, as quoted by E.J. Dionne Jr., explained to Republicans, "You're fighting a war. It's a war for power."[77]

Fourth is the decriminalization of political bribery that marks the *Buckley* pay-to-play era since 1976, to be discussed in chapters 3 and 8. The Supreme Court ruling in *Buckley v. Valaro* and similar decisions including *Citizens United* has transformed the currency of American democracy to, well, currency, rather than votes.

These four factors explain why numerous lawmakers have come to favor the agenda of donors rather than the preferences of the broader public, with a profound impact on the quality of American democracy. As quoted in the *New York Times,* Trevor Potter, a former Republican member of the Federal Election Commission admits, "It just takes a random billionaire to change a race and maybe change the country."[78] Acemoglu and Robinson explain that "Inclusive institutions . . . can also reverse course and become more extractive because of challenges during critical junctures."[79] Two such critical junctures were President Nixon's four Supreme Court appointees, responsible for the original *Buckley* ruling, followed more than a decade later by the three simpatico appointees by Ronald Reagan. America's economic inequality comes from the political inequality ushered in by the era of pay-to-play and the other three factors.

As noted earlier, Piketty describes this etiology as producing an "Endless Inegalitarian Spiral," portraying the decades since Reagan this way: "We subsequently see a rapid rise in inequality in the 1980s until by 2000 we have returned to a [1910–1930] level on the order of 45–50 percent of national income [flowing to the top 10 percent]. The magnitude of the change is impressive: . . . [an] unprecedented explosion of very elevated incomes . . . The egalitarian pioneer ideal has faded into oblivion, and the New World may be on the verge of becoming the Old Europe of the twenty-first century's globalized economy."[80] This theme is also reflected in numerous recent works by other economists including Robert Reich and Joseph Stiglitz.[81]

Recall that Aristotle's test of the degree of democracy is the extent to which the economically powerful are constrained, with preferences of the landless reflected in policy outcomes. As we see next, Aristotle's maxim in the context of the US economy is the precise question that political scientists Martin Gilens and Benjamin Page set out to test in their path-breaking 2014 research that has convincingly documented the income bias.

CHAPTER 2

Documenting Low-Quality American Democracy: The Income Bias and International Evidence

The essential point is that where the possession of political power is due to the possession of economic power or wealth, whether the number of persons be large or small, that is oligarchy . . .[1]

—Aristotle, *Politics*

[America features] democracy by coincidence, in which ordinary citizens get what they want from government only when they happen to agree with elites or interest groups that are really calling the shots.[2]

—Martin Gilens and Benjamin Page,
Perspective on Politics, March 2014

Financial support from wealthy individuals and companies ensures political success. While the US system remains democratic in form because freedom of speech and association is preserved and elections are free, in essence it is becoming a plutocracy.[3]

—Branko Milanovic, World Bank, March 2013

THE BIG-DATA ANALYSES EXAMINED in this chapter provide compelling evidence that American democracy is of a low quality; Public policy outcomes do not reflect the wishes of a majority of citizens. Indeed, independent scholars analogize the stratification of contemporary US political outcomes with the behaviors evident during the end times of the first democracies in ancient Greece. Here is Stein Ringen: "In Athens, democracy disintegrated when the rich grew super-rich, refused to play by the rules and undermined the established system of government. That is the point that the United States . . . [has] reached. Both these governments came up against concentrations of economic power that have become politically unmanageable."[4]

Recently, scholars have examined the money–politics nexus in America, bringing to bear digital databases of unprecedented size and detail.[5]

Documenting an Income Bias

In his 2012 book *Affluence and Influence,* Princeton political scientist Martin Gilens merged decades of data on federal legislative votes, with survey data on both political donations and voter preferences parsed by respondents' incomes. Gilens found a statistical correlation between federal policy outcomes and the policy preferences of higher income citizens; in contrast, policy outcomes had no correlation with preferences of other income classes:

> Money—the "mother's milk" of politics is the root of representational inequality . . . Under typical circumstances, the middle class has no more sway than the poor when their preferences diverge from those of the affluent . . . The associated pattern of policy influence and political contributions offer at least one highly plausible explanation for the inequality in policy responsiveness to different economic strata . . . This representational inequality was spread widely across policy domains, with a strong tilt toward high-income Americans on economic issues, foreign policy and moral/religious issues . . .[6]

Moreover, Gilens found that this income bias has become stronger during the decades since 1980:

My expectation was that representational inequality had grown in the US along with the growth in economic inequality. I did find evidence of this pattern in the steadily rising responsiveness to the well-off—but not to other income levels—over the four decades covered by my data . . . In recent decades the responsiveness of policy makers to the preferences of the affluent has steadily grown, but responsiveness to less-well-off Americans has not.[7]

Like other research on the nexus of money and politics, the study by Gilens was indicative, but statisticians found his evidence only suggestive, a correlation. However, a more expansive and meticulous second analysis by Gilens, published in 2014 with coauthor Northwestern University political scientist Benjamin Page, definitively documented for the first time evidence of an income bias. Their seminal analysis found a strong statistical *causal* relationship between the policy preferences of top earners and federal policy outcomes. The odds of the relationship they revealed occurring randomly are quite remote, making their analysis historically significant—a smoking gun. The evidence is compelling:

America's claims to being a democratic society are seriously threatened . . . Multivariate analysis indicates that economic elites and organized groups representing business interests have substantial independent impacts on US government policy, while average citizens and mass-based interest groups have little or no independent influence . . . When the preferences of economic elites and the stands of organized interest groups are controlled for, the preferences of the average American appear to have only a minuscule, near-zero, statistically non-significant impact upon public policy.[8]

Gilens, Page, and their research assistants evaluated 1,779 contentious Congressional votes over more than two decades beginning in 1981. Those policy votes were carefully matched with contemporary public opinion surveys on the same topics. The survey data were differentiated by respondent incomes, segregated into three income ranges—the tenth percentile of family incomes (mean income $12,200 in 2012), fiftieth percentile

($51,000), and ninetieth percentile ($146,000). The policy preferences of various interest groups such as unions and business lobbyists were also evaluated separately in the study. This encompassing analytical approach and huge data set enabled Gilens and Page to determine the likelihood that a particular policy outcome would be realized based on the specific preferences held by various income groups.

They found that economic elites (and separately, business lobby organizations) have dominated American policy outcomes since the 1980s:

> Until very recently it has not been possible to test theories [of policy dominance] against each other in a systematic, quantitative fashion . . . We have been able to produce some striking findings. One is the nearly total failure of the "median voter" to influence policy . . . In the United States, our findings indicate, the majority does *not* rule—at least not in the causal sense of actually determining policy outcomes. When a majority of citizens disagrees with economic elites and/or with organized interests, they generally lose.[9]

You have just read the definition of income bias. Even more compelling, their statistical analysis occurred before the *Citizens United* ruling (discussed in chapter 3) or the surge into politics in recent years of private money, corporate money, and independent expenditures by political action committees (PACs) and super PACs.

Americans enjoy the trappings of democracy, including free elections; but they are only trappings. The most powerful political science analysis of our era has concluded that average Americans have little or no influence on government policy outcomes. There are certainly instances when the policy preferences of middle- and low-income citizens are reflected in policies. But Gilens and Page conclude that such occasions occur only in the happy coincidence when high-income voters share those preferences. When preferences of top-income earners conflict with those of low- or middle-income citizens, lawmakers consistently ignore the latter two groups.

The inconsequential nature of average Americans' political clout is depicted graphically in chart 2.1, one of the most important in this book. If only 10 percent of top earners favor a particular policy outcome, the odds of that outcome occurring were found to be less than 10 percent. However, as the share of top earners favoring that outcome rises to 90 percent, the odds of that outcome becoming law increase by about 45 percentage points (to better than 50 percent in total). In contrast, as the share of average Americans (the 50th income percentile) favoring a policy outcome rises from 10 percent to 90 percent, the odds of that outcome improved by less than 4 percentage points.

Gilens and Page note: "Not only do ordinary citizens not have uniquely substantial power over policy decisions; they have little or no independent influence on policy at all . . . When a majority—even a very large majority—of the public favors change, it is not likely to get what it wants . . . [elites are] calling the shots."[10]

Gilens and Page also teased out the influence of organized groups, including mass organizations such as the American Association of Retired Persons (AARP) or labor unions, on public policy outcomes. They found that business groups such as the Chamber of Commerce hold considerably

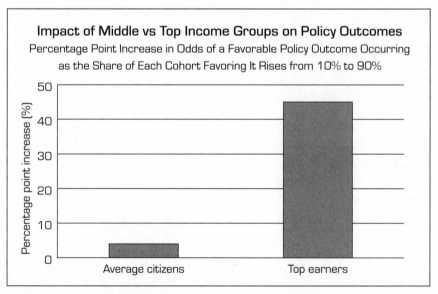

Chart 2.1 Top earners dictate federal policy outcomes

Martin Gilens and Benjamin I. Page, "Testing Theories of American Politics: Elites, Interest Groups and Average Citizens," *Perspective on Politics*, September 2014, doi: 10.1017/S1537592714001595

more sway in Washington than even enormous groups like AARP and unions whenever their agendas conflicted: "These business groups are far more numerous and active; they spend much more money; and they tend to get their way . . ."[11] Lee Drutman, a donations expert at the nonpartisan New America Foundation, concluded in 2015 that the business community outspent such mass membership groups by a whopping 34:1 margin. This advantage was up from 22:1 in 1998.[12] Campaign donations or the promise of them, rather than membership numbers, is the decisive factor; trade unions and groups like the AARP have vastly larger memberships than business groups, but the latter contribute vastly more money, the key determinant of influence.*

The political impotence of average Americans has consequences because their policy preferences differ from those of higher income households or from corporate groups such as the Chamber of Commerce. The preferences of average families include higher wages, environmental protections, stronger worksite labor protections, consumer protections, higher taxes on corporations instead of families, and an end to job offshoring. But their preferences are mostly ignored. Gilens and Page concluded that "empirical support for majoritarian pluralism looks very shaky, indeed."[13]

Evidence of the Income Bias in Federal Tax and Spending Programs

Further analytic verification of the income bias is provided by a separate study prepared under the auspices of the nonpartisan Washington-based Center on Budget and Policy Priorities. Arloc Sherman, Robert Greenstein, and Kathy Ruffing utilized detailed budget and tax data from 2010 and 2011 in an analysis concluding that federal programs viewed comprehensively redistribute income *upward* rather than downward.[14] The large national entitlement programs like Social Security, Medicare,

---

*Other big-data researchers have also concluded that lawmakers respond primarily to opinions of the wealthy and to business groups such as the Chamber of Commerce. See for example, Kay Scholzman, Sidney Verga, and Henry E. Brady, *The Unheavenly Chorus* (Princeton, NJ: Princeton University Press, 2012), xxiv, 8. See also, Christopher Howard, *The Welfare State Nobody Knows* (Princeton, NJ: Princeton University Press, 2007), 198.

Medicaid, and food stamps redistribute income downward, disproportionately favoring lower income households. Yet when tax policies and
all individualized federal spending policies are added to the data, their
impact swamps entitlement flows, yielding an upward net redistribution
by government.

Most of this upward redistribution is due to large tax benefits, called
tax expenditures by budgeteers, whose benefits disproportionately accrue
to higher income households. Examples include charitable donation and
home mortgage tax deductions. The researchers concluded that about
30 percent of all income redistributed via entitlements and tax expenditures by the federal government goes to the top-earning 20 percent of
households (see chart 2.2). For every dollar redistributed to the poorest
20 percent of Americans by the federal government, $1.35 is redistributed
to the highest earning 20 percent.[15]

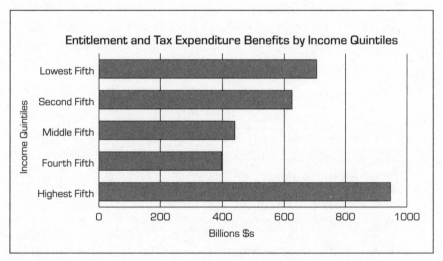

Chart 2.2 2010 (budget) and 2011 (tax expenditures). Entitlement spending represents 60 percent of federal budget outlays; excluded are federal
programs with diffused benefits including defense, general programmatic
spending, and civil service. Business and other tax benefits of a diffused
nature were also not included.

Eduardo Porter, "A Nation of Too Many Tax Breaks," *New York Times*, March 13, 2012,
www.nytimes.com/2012/03/14/business/a-nation-with-too-many-tax-breaks
-economic-scene.html?_r=1&ref=business

Policy Preferences of Ordinary Americans Closely Mirror Those in Other Democracies

Preferences of most Americans are largely ignored by lawmakers. Even so, ordinary Americans share the same hopes and aspirations as citizens of peer nations. Quite naturally, they seek to improve their lives and favor government policies that address such hopes. There are no comprehensive studies like those of Gilens and Page that assess causal linkage transnationally between preferences, incomes, and policy outcomes. There are, however, databases that provide evidence of correlation. The most comprehensive is another big-data analysis by College of William & Mary professor Christopher Howard using statistics from the International Social Survey (ISSP), a respected survey that documents citizen attitudes from Europe, the United States, Britain, and Canada. Reproduced from Howard's 2008 statistics, chart 2.3 displays the degree of support among US and foreign respondents for greater spending on government programs like health care or education. Americans were *more* supportive of additional government spending for social services and for education than respondents in these other wealthy democracies. And they were nearly

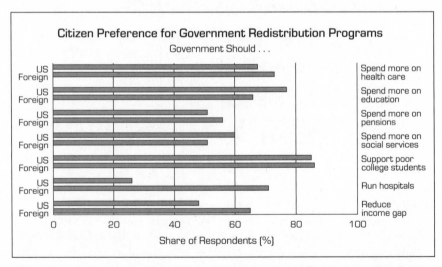

Chart 2.3 Citizen preferences in Canada, Germany, Italy, Norway, Sweden, and Britain compared to the United States.

Christopher Howard, *The Welfare State Nobody Knows* (Princeton, NJ: Princeton University Press, 2008), table 6.1.

as enthusiastic about increased government spending in the other areas surveyed, except running hospitals and reducing income gaps.

Other surveys document similar support among US citizens for such public goods. A March 2013 survey of public attitudes found that 53 percent of US respondents believed it is a duty of government to provide government jobs if necessary to provide employment for all those willing to work.[16] A separate June 2013 survey of rural Americans by the Center for Rural Affairs found that more than 80 percent of respondents supported more government spending for infrastructure, preschooling, and job retraining.[17] Some 66 percent of respondents in a *New York Times*/CBS News survey in May 2015 believed the gap between rich and poor is widening and that the distribution of wealth should be more even.[18]

Weak American Efforts to Ameliorate Economic Inequality

Americans have the same strong preferences for government income redistribution as citizens in peer nations, but government policy outcomes abroad better reflect aspirations of average citizens, defining them as higher quality democracies.

The most comprehensive international indicator of economic policy outcomes are OECD statistics documenting the extent to which government tax and income policies change domestic income distributions. All thirty-four OECD member nations utilize tax and spending programs to redistribute income downward, drawing from the affluent to improve the lot of the less fortunate.

In nearly every instance, such practices reduce the *ex-ante* market (prior to government redistribution) income disparities, although the magnitude varies greatly as we now see.

Utilizing OECD data, Drew DeSilver of the Pew Research Center measured the intensity of government redistribution policies through their impact on Gini coefficients. This statistical measure of income distribution noted earlier was developed before World War II by an Italian, Corrado Gini.[19] On the Gini scale of 0 to 1, zero value means that all citizens have the same income while a value of 1 denotes that one person receives all income. The figures in chart 2.4 are the changes in Gini coefficients as a consequence of government tax and transfer policies. The value shown for each nation is the net difference between the Gini coefficient calculated using *ex-ante* market (pregovernment) incomes and the Gini coefficient calculated *ex-post* after accounting for the impact of government income redistributions. For example, the depicted US figure is .119; that is the difference between the 2010 market-income (pregovernment redistribution) Gini coefficient of .499, and the Gini coefficient of .380 measuring income disparities with federal government taxes and transfers included (postgovernment redistribution). For comparison, the German tax and income transfer programs reduced its *ex-ante* market-income Gini coefficient by .206 points or by nearly twice as much as US policies.

The US market-income (pregovernment) Gini figure of .499 is easily the most skewed of any wealthy democracy, reflecting the relatively large American income disparity. Even so, the American income redistribution effort is paltry compared to peer nations. In fact, only three nations (South Korea, Switzerland, and Chile) have weaker redistributive outcomes (not shown) than the American .119. Chile makes virtually no effort to redistribute income. And both South Korea and Switzerland have weaker

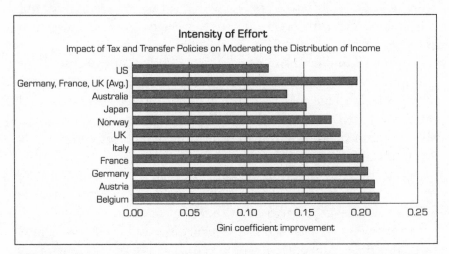

Chart 2.4 Change in Gini coefficients (reduction in income disparities) as a consequence of federal taxes and transfers; 2010 data except Japan 2009 and Chile 2011.

Drew DeSilver, "Global Inequality: How the US Compares," Pew Research Center, November 19, 2013, www.pewresearch.org/fact-tank/2013/12/19 /global-inequality-how-the-u-s-compares/

efforts because the *ex-ante* market (pregovernment) income disparity in each nation is dramatically more equal than in the United States: The market-income Gini coefficient values for South Korea and Switzerland respectively were .342 and .372, in contrast to .499 for the United States. In fact, income is more equally distributed in Korea and Switzerland *before* government redistributive policies are applied than are American incomes *after* government redistribution (.380 as detailed momentarily).

The relatively weak government redistribution effort means the *ex-post* American income disparity is significantly more unequal or skewed than in other OECD nations. The post-redistribution US Gini coefficient of .380 is about 30 percent larger than values of the other large democracies of Germany (.286) or France (.303), as reproduced in chart 2.5. These are simply huge differences, emblematic of large middle-class economies, unlike the United States. In fact, America has the most skewed income disparity after government redistribution programs of all OECD nations aside from Brazil, Chile, and Mexico. It most closely resembles that of authoritarian Turkey.[20] As noted, these outliers share American-style pay-to-play political systems.

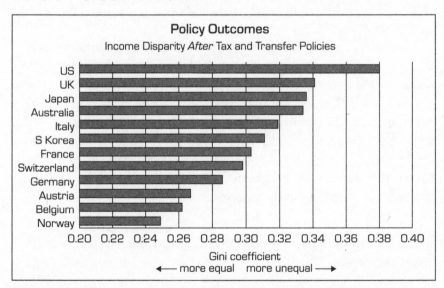

Chart 2.5 Gini coefficients after federal government taxes and transfers.
Drew DeSilver, "Global Inequality: How the US Compares," Pew Research Center, November 19, 2013, www.pewresearch.org/fact-tank/2013/12/19 /global-inequality-how-the-u-s-compares/

DeSilver did not address whether government redistribution policies extract a penalty by slowing economic growth, a contentious issue not resolved until 2014, the year after his analysis was published. Until then, despite lacking evidence, conservative American economists, including the late Arthur Okun, had asserted that government redistribution policies slow growth and diminish economic efficiency. The flood of digitized international statistics in recent years enabled economists at the International Monetary Fund in 2014 to apply rigor to that question. They found the trade-off imagined by Okun and others between redistribution and growth to be mythical: "The best available macroeconomic data do not support such a conclusion."[21] The considerable redistribution conducted by higher quality democracies such as Belgium, Austria, and Germany does not reduce GDP or productivity growth. Indeed, American evidence suggests that redistributional programs can aid growth and employment by reducing inequality. A 2016 analysis by economists at the World Bank concluded that the increase in inequality from falling American household incomes between 1998 and 2013 reduced consumer spending by over 3 percent. The widening income disparities accounted for an overall decline in US consumer spending of about $400 billion annually, slowing both GDP and job growth.[22]

The impact of economic inequality on US social indicators has also been examined. In *The Spirit Level*, for instance, public health scholars Kate Pickett and Richard Wilkinson teased out the impact of rising inequality on life expectancy, teen motherhood incidence, and the like. They concluded that a number of social pathologies such as infant mortality, addiction, suicides, and mental illness grow worse as income disparity rises. Other data suggest these pathologies—already evident among Black Americans—have become especially evident of late among economically stressed white working-class Americans.

Ronald Reagan: When American Income Disparity Began to Skew

As noted earlier, American income disparity is an international outlier, the most exaggerated of the wealthy democracies. We have seen how this profile emerged in the 1980s, when most gains from growth began to flow upward, with political scientists James Druckman and Lawrence Jacobs confirming that the Reagan administration initiated this sea change.[23] Its policies, noted in chapter 1, produced a sharp reversal of the economic outcomes common during postwar decades.

The shift in distribution of the gains from growth that began during the Reagan administration has produced the grandest income redistribution in world history. Compared to income shares in 1980, the amount now being redistributed each year from wages to profits is comparable in magnitude to two-thirds of the annual export earnings of the Organization of Petroleum Exporting Countries (OPEC). Widening income disparity has also caused wealth disparities to skew: Back in 1989, the Federal Reserve reported that the top 3 percent of households held 44.8 percent of all US wealth; that share increased steadily to 51.8 percent in 2007 and to 54.4 percent in 2013.[24] A handful of Americans have grown startlingly wealthy. The six Walmart heirs alone, grown wealthy on inexpensive Asian imports and low wages, are worth as much as the bottom 41 percent of US households.[25] According to economists Emmanuel Saez and Gabriel Zucman, the wealthiest 16,000 Americans are each worth $110 million or 1,100 times the American average. In 1979, they were worth about 220 times the average.[26]

The Income Bias Originates with Republicans

Both Democratic and Republican lawmakers bear responsibility for the income bias and resulting failure of national policies to ameliorate rising income disparities or prosper middle- and working-class Americans. Bipartisan inaction has long protected the carried interest tax loophole, for instance, saving high-income hedge fund managers billions of dollars annually in taxes.[27]

But scholars have grown convinced that Congressional Republicans are vastly more culpable for laws benefiting the wealthy and in derailing laws and regulations intended to aid the middle class. The scope of their actions is broad, ranging from resisting higher wages (overtime pay or minimum wages) and protecting extravagant levels of pharmaceutical profits to rejecting reforms that would punish Americans and other global tax evaders who use secret offshore accounts.[28] Indeed, Republican lawmakers in states such as Missouri go so far as to preempt local efforts to improve wages, stripping counties and communities of the ability to raise minimum wages within their jurisdictions. Even some conservatives assign most of the blame for these and other behaviors that widen income disparities to Republicans. Prominent Republican and conservative Christopher Caldwell of the *Weekly Standard*, for instance, in September 2014, acknowledged the "[economic] inequality for which Republicans are rightly given much of the blame."[29]

There's plenty of evidence that supports Caldwell's assertion. A 2008 analysis by Vanderbilt University political scientist Larry Bartels concluded that GOP lawmakers (senators specifically) are considerably more responsive to the agenda of high-income Americans than to middle-class preferences. In contrast, Democratic Party senators were found to be most responsive to the middle class, displaying considerably less of an income bias. Bartels drew on voting statistics from the 101st, 102nd, and 103rd Congresses (1988–1994) to assess how the voting behavior of senators tracked the preferences of various income classes. The ideological votes he evaluated involved employer versus employee rights (raising the minimum wage, enforcing civil rights in the workplace) and shifting federal funds from defense to the antipoverty programs Head Start and low-income energy assistance. Lawmakers from both parties tend to give little weight to the opinions of lower income constituents. But Bartels identified a sharp partisan divide in the responsiveness of senators to the agendas of middle-income versus upper income groups. And the differences he identified persisted even between senators from different parties who represent the same state or states with similar ideological profiles.[30] Bartels found that Republicans paid no more attention to the opinions of middle-class constituents than to opinions of the poor—which is to say none (chart 2.6). In contrast, Democratic senators were most attentive to middle-class opinions: "For Republican senators, there is no evidence of responsiveness to middle-income constituents, much less low-income constituents. The views of high-income constituents, however, seem to have received a great deal of weight from Republican senators on these four issues . . . more than four times as much as for Democrats . . . Democrats seem to have responded at least as strongly to the views of middle-income constituents as to the views of high-income constituents . . ."[31]

Republican Party indifference to middle- and lower-income voter preferences has continued in recent years. They have enjoyed majorities

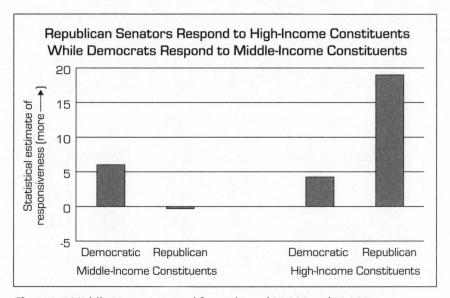

Chart 2.6 Middle income ranged from about $35,000 to $70,000.

Larry M. Bartels, *Unequal Democracy* (Princeton, NJ: Princeton University Press), fig. 9.4.

in the Senate since 2010 and in the House of Representatives since 2014. Yet during that time, Congressional Republicans have been loath to enact policies on a host of issues that benefit the middle class—policies that enjoy huge popular support, including higher minimum wages, providing employees advance notice of work schedules, mandating paid sick leave, or raising taxes on high incomes to sustain Social Security (chart 2.7). Such policies are commonplace in higher quality democracies. They are popular with Americans as well, including many Republicans, but clash with the priorities of higher income donors.

Such policies also clash with a Republican imperative that emerged during the Obama administration to deny Democrats legislative successes. For instance, GOP Senate leader Mitch McConnell was rather infamously overheard declaring in 2009: "The single most important thing we want to achieve is for President Obama to be a one-term president."[32]

That strategy signaled to donors that the GOP was committed to meeting their small-government agenda while resisting Democrats' wage, tax, and spending increases. Not a single Republican member of the House

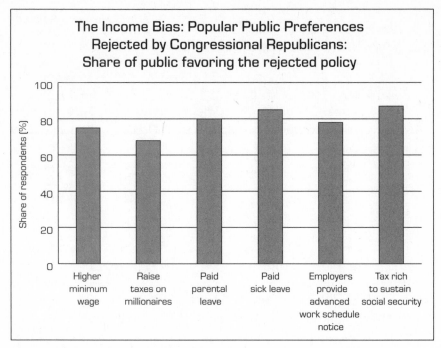

Chart 2.7 Popular public preferences rejected by Congressional Republicans.

Noam Scheiber and Dalia Sussman, "Inequality Troubles Americans Across Party Lines, a Poll Finds," *New York Times*, June 4, 2015 (work schedule); Harold Meyerson, "The Next Debate Topic," *Washington Post*, August 27, 2015 (tax on millionaires, Social Security); and Robert P. Jones, Daniel Cox, Betsy Cooper, and Rachel Lienesch, "Anxiety, Nostalgia and Mistrust," *American Values Survey*," Public Religion Research Institute, November 17, 2015 (minimum wage, paid sick leave, paid parental leave), www.publicreligion.org/site/wp-content/uploads/2015/11/PRRI-AVS-2015.pdf

of Representatives voted for the Obama administration's economic stimulus law in early 2009 that averted a deeper recession. Subsequently, they forced federal spending cuts using contentious negotiating tactics including a government shutdown in October 2013, the threat of another shutdown in September 2015, and additional threats that included contriving a default on the national debt. In a government whose architecture demands cooperation and collaboration for legislative success, polarization and gridlock became routine. Other scholars join Thomas Mann and Norman Ornstein in blaming Republicans. Robert Kaiser in his book *Act of Congress*, for instance, describes McConnell's partisanship in these terms: "Refusing to cooperate with the Democratic president took precedence over legislating . . . He ruled out bipartisanship because the term itself implied a truce in, or even an end to, the partisan wars. McConnell was no peacemaker . . . He never hid his desire to prevent Obama from winning politically useful victories."[33]

Congressional Republicans' gridlock tactics from 2010 through 2016 reduced the government's share of Gross Domestic Product (GDP) spending by 2015 to the lowest in nearly a decade[34]—reduced further by the Trump administration budgets. Discretionary federal government spending in 2016 was lower than in 2005, adjusted for inflation, including an 11 percent drop in education spending in real terms.[35] Important R&D spending has been reduced dramatically: Only 18 percent of grant applications could be funded by the National Institutes of Health in 2015, compared to 32 percent in 2000.[36] And although President Obama raised taxes on higher incomes, Congressional Republicans have succeeded in reducing the overall American tax burden: Data from the thirty-four richest democracies collected by the OECD document that the US total tax-to-GDP ratio declined from 28.2 in 2000 to 26 in 2014, nearly the lowest (31st) among them. That decline contrasts with the other democracies, whose average ratio rose slightly over this period to 34.4.[37] Moreover, tax loopholes abound, leading the *Sydney Morning Herald* by 2016 to a headline "US Overtakes Caymans as Tax Shelter for Rich."[38]

The small-government agenda of the GOP benefited its wealthy donors, but weakened the recovery from the 2008 recession. The government sector actually subtracted from growth in 2013 and 2014. It added nothing to growth in 2015 and little in 2016 or 2017 either.[39]

The GOP chokehold on fiscal policy placed undue reliance on monetary policy alone to spark growth. Then Republicans promptly took aim at monetary policy as well, seeking to browbeat independent Federal Reserve Board (Fed) officials into withdrawing monetary stimulus. Indeed, GOP members of the House of Representatives in June 2016 ignored salient issues including wage stagnation, widening income disparities, and job offshoring to question Fed Chair Janet Yellen whether the Fed was solvent. Economists were stunned (the Fed can create money at will).[40]

These GOP strategies presumably pleased donors but reveal how far today's Republican Party has strayed from its 1850s roots. It has become a party hostile to the hopes of Lincoln for an activist government expanding economic opportunity to meet the aspirations of average Americans. It has become obsessed with fulfilling its donor class agenda, relentlessly pressing for partisan advantage regardless of circumstance, as powerfully explained by Mann and Ornstein: "The clear implication [of McConnell's strategy] was that if default brought economic hardship and the president and Democrats got blamed, that would be fine. That kind of calculus—putting partisan advantage ahead of problem solving, with the stakes for the country sky-high—was not politics as usual, at least not as we have seen it practiced through several generations of party leaders."[41]

Because of the riches on offer from public policies, politics is always and everywhere a tough business. The Republican Party's Machiavellian strategy of slowing the recovery in order to diminish a political opponent is not unprecedented; President Grover Cleveland was victimized by similar tactics in 1892. But its intensity and duration is testament to the powerful impact of pay-to-play on American democracy. One of the most consequential indicators is Senate Republicans' refusal to seat President Obama's nominee Merrick Garland in 2016, which derailed a potentially progressive majority on the Supreme Court for the first time in forty years. Indeed, billionaires, including Sheldon Adelson and Joe Ricketts spent well over $10 million on TV ads in support of the new justice, Neil Gorsuch, whose 2017 confirmation has cemented pay-to-play for perhaps decades to come.[42]

The income bias is grounded in pay-to-play. The next chapter examines its roots in the decriminalization of pay-to-play by conservative Supreme Court justices since 1976.

CHAPTER 3

The *Buckley* Era: Constitutionally Shielding Vote Buying

The unlimited giving to parties and to candidates really pushes us more toward a plutocracy. They say it's free speech, but someone can speak 20 or 30 million times and my cleaning lady can't speak at all.[1]
                                   —Warren Buffett, CNN, April 3, 2015

There was no history, logic, or reason given to support that [corporate personhood] view . . . The purpose of the [Fourteenth] Amendment was to protect human rights—primarily the rights of a race which had just won its freedom.[2]

  —Supreme Court Justices Hugo Black and William O. Douglas, in dissent, *Wheeling Steel Corp.,* 1949, quoted in Torres-Spelliscy, 2014

CHARLES AND DAVID KOCH were the founding funders of the libertarian Cato Institute and have donated about $30 million to it over recent decades.[3] They got their money's worth in Ilya Shapiro, a researcher there, who made the following statement, which reads like the donor class credo, at a Senate Committee hearing in 2010: "To the extent that 'money in politics' is a problem, the solution isn't to try to reduce the money . . . but to reduce the scope of political activity the money tries to influence. Shrink the size of government and its intrusions in people's lives and you'll shrink the amount people will spend trying to get their piece of the pie or, more likely, trying to avert ruinous public policies."[4]

There you have it: Public goods are the problem, not private money purchasing the votes of public officials.

Elections still determine who leads America. But the American political system has undergone a seminal deterioration in the past generation due to the income bias, with much of the blame centered on a transformed Republican Party. The Democratic Party has retained its postwar sizable core of moderates whose share (35 percent) matches the share of moderates (34 percent) nationwide.[5] In contrast, both progressives and moderates have been culled from the Republican Party in recent decades. The influence of pay-to-play is largely responsible for that party shrinking by one-quarter and morphing into a near-uniformly conservative entity. The agenda of the donor class to cosset the wealthiest Americans has de facto become the GOP's agenda.

The emergence of a political party unduly influenced by a conservative donor class resembles events in the GOP a century ago during the Gilded Age. In his 1913 book, *The New Freedom*, President Woodrow Wilson expressed alarm about the economic power increasingly wielded by the robber barons of his era. He had in mind Cornelius Vanderbilt, John Pierpont Morgan, and especially John D. Rockefeller—the latter controlled 88 percent of American oil production and was soon (1916) to be the world's first billionaire. Some wealthy conservatives of today exhibit behavior similar to plutocrats such as Vanderbilt, who lived above the law, routinely buying the votes of Congress and judges: "What do I care about the law? Hain't I got the power?"[6]

Buckley v. Valeo

Today's reprising of the Gilded Age is rooted in the Warren Burger Supreme Court decision *Buckley v. Valeo*, 424 US 1 (1976). The Court concluded that limits on independent spending by individuals to benefit politicians were unconstitutional and also found that limits on candidate electioneering spending were unconstitutional. Limits on donations directly to campaigns remain constitutional. The decision began a process of decriminalizing vote buying* that continues today. *Buckley* and subsequent similar rulings (the *Buckley* genre) have produced an era where dollars rather than votes are determinant in American democracy. The rulings have induced numerous American politicians to (correctly) conclude, as Gilens and Page document, that their career prospects are maximized by pandering to affluent contributors.

Prior to the *Buckley* era, party elites—officials, lawmakers, consultants, donors, corporate CEOs, activists, and media figures—selected nominees for both the Democratic and Republican Parties. Elite endorsements were more predictive of nominating contest outcomes than money, media attention, celebrity, or polling results. The *Buckley* era changed that dynamic, elevating donors to outweigh traditional elites in party matters—at least with Republicans. Democratic lawmakers have failed to support policies ending wage stagnation in recent decades, but as previously noted by Larry Bartels, they display primary sympathy for middle-class aspirations. They seem less reliant than Republicans on wealthy donors, enjoying ready access to millions of small donors, and display an income bias infrequently. Recall that the Obama administration reregulated the financial sector, bailed out the auto industry, enacted Obamacare, created a consumer finance watchdog agency, and raised tax rates on the very highest income earners to 1990s levels.

In contrast, on the Republican side, what *New York Times* journalist Nicholas Confessore terms the "conservative donor class" has edged aside other elites to join the grassroots as the party's power brokers.[7] This transformation is the result of a perfect storm of events that included the following elements: a clutch of staunchly conservative and politically savvy wealthy donors covetous of small government; the decision by Tom DeLay in the early 1990s to partner with these conservatives; a sizable core of small-government social conservatives among the GOP grassroots; the 2008 election of a Black Democratic president favoring big government activism; and, beginning in the 1990s, the culling of moderates from the GOP.

---

*As used herein, "vote buying" does not refer to candidates bribing voters. It refers to political donations, contributions, and independent spending in support of politicians or political parties.

Another major contributing factor to the increased donor influence on Republicans was the emergence of a conservative-themed media complex featuring Fox News and talk radio (made possible by President Reagan's repeal of the Fairness Doctrine, discussed further in chapter 13). The most important factor was the emergence of a clutch of politically active, wealthy conservatives—an eventuality empowered by *Buckley.* As a consequence, the postwar inclusive and pluralistic American political system morphed into an "extractive, exclusive" one in the lexicon of Acemoglu and Robinson.

Nineteenth-Century Darwinians Decriminalized Political Bribery

When the Burger Court concluded that acquiring the allegiance of public officials with cash is a variant of constitutionally protected free speech, it adopted the game-changing notion that individuals are entitled to spend whatever they can afford to buy the votes of public officials. This purchase of political speech furnishes an individual with a metaphorical sound truck to outshout his or her neighbors.

This novel jurisprudence is grounded in a conjuration, a misinterpretation regarding the nature of speech rights provided by the First Amendment. The Burger justices' error was their conclusion that the right to free speech addresses the *amount* of speech as well as the traditional interpretation that it addresses the *content* of speech. Critics of *Buckley* contend that everyone is entitled to their own soap box and street corner, but not to rent a sound truck. This seminal distinction was noted by Justice John Paul Stevens writing a concurring opinion in *Nixon v. Shrink Missouri Government PAC* (2000): "The right to use one's own money to hire gladiators, or to fund "speech by proxy," . . . [is] not entitled to the same protections as the right to say what one pleases."[8]

The *Buckley* conjuration also lacks precedent. Political scientist Robert E. Mutch in 2014 quotes Harvard law professor Laurence Tribe explaining that *Buckley* "was obviously not grounded on prior constitutional authority."[9] And Harvard law professor Cass Sunstein terms the entire *Buckley* genre "an adventurous interpretation of the Constitution."[10] The founding fathers, the framers, numerous states, and all prior Supreme Court rulings had criminalized virtually all campaign contributions as political bribery—vote buying. Congress repeatedly agreed beginning in 1867, notably including the Tillman Act during Theodore Roosevelt's presidency in 1907 (banning corporate donations), Taft-Hartley in 1947 (banning independent expenditures on behalf of candidates, parties, or political issues) and the 1974 amendments to the Federal Election Campaign Act (1971) in the wake of the Watergate scandal.

The original intent of the founding fathers at the Second Continental Congress in 1776 and the constitutional drafters in 1787 was a government free of influence peddling and corruption. They were strongly opposed to the buying of lawmakers' votes, as explained by James Madison: "My wish is that the national legislature be as uncorrupt as possible."[11] In *Federalist 52*, he urged that members of Congress avoid dependence on donors or favor seekers.[12] George Mason explained the framers' stark concern in these terms: "If we don't provide against corruption, our government will soon be at an end."[13] The framers worried so much that they placed twenty or so broadly drawn, specific anticorruption clauses in the Constitution itself.[14]

Importantly, the framers adopted the broadest possible definition of acts that constituted "corruption." They were political sophisticates and aware that *any* campaign contribution was corrupting. They were informed by the prowess of British monarchs using the Royal Treasury to purchase Royalist fidelity among the parliamentarians of their day. Central to the context of contemporary pay-to-play is the framers' unequivocal belief that such "Royal Treasury" largesse represented political vote buying regardless of whether the recipient would have supported the Palace otherwise—or whether there was an evident quid pro quo. The framers sweepingly viewed all acts of providing and accepting donations as inherently corrupting. Harvard law professor Lawrence Lessig in 2011 quotes British historian J.G.A. Pocock's clarification of this important point:

> The King's ministers were not attacked for sitting in Parliament, but they were attacked for allegedly filling Parliament with the recipients of government patronage. For what was universally acknowledged was that if the members of the legislature became dependent upon patronage, the legislature would cease to be independent . . . Corruption on an eighteenth-century tongue . . . meant not only venality, but disturbance of the political conditions necessary to human virtue and freedom.[15]

The founding fathers and the framers would surely reject Justice Anthony Kennedy's naïve assertion in 2009 that "The fact that speakers may have influence over or access to elected officials does not mean that these officials are corrupt."[16] They would instead nod in agreement with Jack Abramoff, a lobbyist jailed in 2006 for bribery, who summarized the lesson of his years of buying votes in Congress this way: "When somebody petitioning a public servant for action provides any kind of extra resources—money or a gift or anything—that affects the process."[17]

Buckley and *Citizens United*

Buckley not only rejects the intent and concerns of the founding fathers and the framers but also contradicts the iconic conservative Barry Goldwater, who argued even before the *Buckley* era that "Senators and representatives . . . can scarcely avoid weighting every decision against the question, 'How will this affect my fund-raising?'[18] . . . The role of money is way out of line. It's strangling us. The influence of money distorts everything. Government of and by the people, for example, is waning . . . Our nation is facing a crisis of liberty if we do not control campaign expenditures. Unlimited campaign spending eats at the heart of the democratic process."[19]

Ironically, *Buckley* was promulgated in the wake of the Watergate break-in and corruption scandal that induced enactment of the most comprehensive legislation ever in US history to criminalize political bribery. The 1974 amendments to the Federal Election Campaign Act (FECA) established strict limits on donations and campaign spending, mandated *only* public funding of presidential elections, and established the Federal Election Commission to police campaign finance. These aggressive FECA expansions were the high watermark in America's struggle to corral vote buying and improve voter equality. The pinnacle of American political equality embodied in the FECA amendments lasted only two years.

Since 1976, *Buckley* has been affirmed and expanded by rulings of bare majorities of the subsequent Rehnquist and Roberts Supreme Courts. The *Buckley* genre has grown to now include *First National Bank of Boston v. Bellotti* (1978), *Citizens United v. Federal Election Commission* (2010), and *McCutcheon v. Federal Election Commission* (2013). The genre also includes the *SpeechNow.org v. Federal Election Commission* ruling in 2010 permitting unlimited donations; although issued by the District of

Columbia Circuit Court of Appeals, it was based on *Citizens United* and was favorably reviewed by the conservative Republican majority on the Roberts Court, hereinafter Roberts Republicans.

Lacking precedent and defying original intent, the original *Buckley* ruling and the Roberts Court ruling in *Citizens United* featured legal legerdemain. *Citizens United* redefined "natural persons" to include, well, unnatural persons, drawing on the mischief first conjured in *Santa Clara* (discussed later) by the Morris Waite Supreme Court in 1886. Inanimate legal artifices such as corporations cannot vote, attend church, speak, read, pray, or hold office; nor are they natural persons as defined by Chief Justice John Marshall two centuries ago: "[A corporation is] an artificial being, invisible, intangible and existing only in contemplation of law."[20] Former Fed chairman Ben Bernanke agrees: "A financial firm is of course a legal fiction; it's not a person."[21] And so does Goldwater, drawing the line quaintly at flesh and blood: "Financial contributions to political campaigns should be made by individuals and individuals alone."[22]

The root of the *Buckley* genre is nineteenth-century social Darwinism: the 'fittest' anointed by the market should not be hobbled by the 'unfittest' (read on) in the theocratic terms favored by the likes of William Graham Sumner. A pioneering nineteenth-century sociologist at Yale, Sumner gave aid and comfort to plutocrats of the day, providing a veneer of scholarship in his 1883 book *What Social Classes Owe to Each Other* for their rampant pay-to-play during the Gilded Age: "Let it be understood that we cannot go outside of this alternative: liberty, inequality, survival of the fittest; not-liberty, equality, survival of the unfittest."[23]

In their bodies of work bearing on economic and political concerns, the conservative majorities of the Burger, Rehnquist, and Roberts Courts have dusted off Sumner's nineteenth-century notion, ruling repeatedly to crown his "fittest." They have mimicked the Melville Fuller Court justice, David Brewer, who wrote in *Pollock v. Farmers' Loan and Trust Co.* (1895), that civilization's "unvarying law . . . [is] that the wealth of a community will be in the hands of a few."[24]

They have explicitly rejected Aristotle, not to mention James Madison, Barry Goldwater, and prominent contemporary scholars such as the late Robert Dahl.[25] They have disenfranchised the powerless and protected the propertied, gilding the donor class just as historian Lawrence Goldstone suggests that the Waite and Fuller Courts bequeathed legitimacy to robber barons of their day: "Social Darwinism had given the capitalist class a great gift: the ability to consider itself virtuous while acting in blatant self-interest. In the 1780s, slaveholders brandished their Bibles; in the 1880s, Andrew Carnegie brandished *Social Statistics*."[26] And in the 1980s, conservative billionaires brandished *Buckley*.

The courts of the *Buckley* era have exalted the *fittest* by creating a novel constitutionally shielded category of speech—a category that can only be purchased. Thus it is the preserve of those Americans whom the late Justice Scalia believed "best represent the most significant segments of the economy." Justice Kennedy drew on Scalia's full quote to explain his own rationale for providing constitutional protections for political vote buying by the *fittest*: "The censorship [donation limit] we now confront is vast in its reach. The government has muffle[d] the voices that best represent the most significant segments of the economy."[27]

Kennedy's Darwinian definition discounts the fact that many Americans consider average families, firefighters, financial sector regulators, military personnel, teachers, nurses, and the like to best represent the "most significant segments" of the American economy, not plutocrats who buy legislators' votes.

As noted by Justice Stevens, the Roberts Republicans decriminalized vote buying by conflating constitutional protections for speech content with its volume. Abruptly, money in support of politicians became protected speech. Chief Justice Roberts asserted that the Court "must give the benefit of any doubt to protecting rather than stifling speech."[28] This novelty was reasserted in the Court's subsequent ruling, *McCutcheon v. Federal Election Commission* (2014), which further eased limits on political giving. Millionaire Shaun McCutcheon, the prevailing party in that suit, unintentionally if aptly described the Roberts Republicans' theology this way: "I would think everybody would be for more money in politics like I am, because we're just spreading speech."[29] And that theology was famously synthesized earlier in the *Buckley* era by the Ford administration solicitor general, Robert Bork: "money can sometimes be the equivalent of speech . . . money is a proxy for speech."[30]

Given the nearly two-century legal precedent criminalizing vote buying and the fear of the corrosive impact of pay-to-play by the founding fathers, the framers, and iconic conservatives such as Goldwater, those whom Kennedy and Scalia viewed as "the most significant" Americans were doubtless agog at their good fortune with *Buckley*.

Today, in other rich democracies, wealthy elites tend not to dominate government because voters and courts agree with the American founding fathers and framers that vote buying corrodes democracy. Wealthy citizens in these other nations enjoy stout constitutional minority protections against majoritarian rule. But unlike in America, such minority protections do not include the right to bribe lawmakers and buy favorable government policies.

Globally, that makes America an outlier among the wealthy democracies, along with Mexico and Brazil, where half the legislature is under investigation for graft or worse.[31] However, even Brazil and Mexico outlaw corporate political donations.[32] The United States is singular in its system of pay-to-play and its decriminalization of vote buying by corporations. American CEOs are permitted to lavishly fund political favorites using shareholder and investor money without permission. The only recourse of disgruntled investors is to sell their shares.

Santa Clara: Corporations Are People, Too. No, Really . . . Trust Me

The uniquely American ability of CEOs to tap corporate treasuries to bribe lawmakers is rooted with one Roscoe Conkling. A powerful politician who narrowly lost the 1876 presidential nomination to Rutherford B. Hayes, Conkling was among the top two or three most influential Republicans of the day. In 1882 he represented the rail baron Leland Stanford before the Waite Supreme Court in *San Mateo v. Southern Pacific Railroad*. Stanford was seeking to roll back local nuisance taxes on his holdings—specifically, property taxes imposed by San Mateo County, California. Hoping to be rewarded with a large paycheck from a grateful Stanford, Conkling devised a strategy that included conjuring from thin air an expansive concept of corporate personhood that, in a peculiar twist of American history, brought about *Citizens United* more than a century later.

As a former Congressman, Conkling was uniquely positioned to make his case. Back in 1868, he had been an original member of the Congressional committee that debated and approved the Fourteenth

Amendment. That amendment enshrined equal protection and legal rights for Black males under the Constitution in the wake of the Civil War. It was a pillar of Reconstruction, providing protections against their harassment by state and local officials. But Conkling had something else entirely in mind, an audacious, contrived addendum to that amendment. Conkling baldly asserted to the Waite Court that he and his committee colleagues had also meant for the amendment to extend protections to the legal artifice of corporations. Bothersome discriminatory local taxes and other regulations on railroads were thus unconstitutional. He knew Chief Justice Morrison Waite and some of his Supreme Court colleagues would be sympathetic because they were former railroad attorneys.

Conkling's bogus claim of such intent by the drafters of the Fourteenth Amendment was ludicrous. As constitutional historian Howard Jay Graham explained, "[t]his part of Conkling's argument was a deliberate, brazen forgery."[33] Contemporaneous evidence was never offered to support Conkling's assertion, because none existed. Indeed, the only proof offered in 1882 by Conkling himself was his own spare, hand-written ruminations. A considerable body of US corporate jurisprudence had evolved by 1882, but none granted these artifices the legal rights enjoyed by persons of flesh and blood.

The definitive published record of legislative action in 1868 during deliberations on the Fourteenth Amendment itself was called the *Congressional Globe*. It contained no reference even to a debate on granting personhood to corporations, much less a Congressional or committee vote on such a profound and controversial—not to mention bizarre— extension of the Fourteenth Amendment. In a profession that cherishes debate, minutiae, and records, none existed. As University of California Los Angeles law professor Adam Winkler wrote in 2012, "no independent evidence to support his claim has ever been uncovered."[34]

Conkling was untroubled by his factual vacuum because he knew his audience. Historian James MacGregor Burns explained events this way:

> There was little evidence to back up Conkling's claim, but neither did anyone contradict him—most of his colleagues on the framing committee were dead.[35] Americans might have mused that corporation

heads packed the [Supreme] Court as much as presidents. Exerting their overpowering influence on the White House and Congress, an astonishing number of railroads and other industries put their people on the Supreme Court. All of Grant's appointees . . . including Chief Justice Waite were railroad attorneys.[36]

Presidents filled the Supreme Court with industry straw men to thank their grandest contributors. And the grandest of all were railroad proprietors. In the early Gilded Age, railroads were the central American industry, consuming vast quantities of steel, men, and capital to connect far-flung America. It was today's IT, auto, internet and aircraft sectors rolled into one spectacularly wealthy industry with irresistible political power to match. Malcolm Gladwell has concluded that the second and fourth richest persons in all of human history derived their wealth one way or another from the American railroads of this era: Andrew Carnegie and William H. Vanderbilt.[37] Like most billionaires, they were economic Darwinians—and so were the justices appointed at their behest to the Waite and successor Fuller Supreme Courts.

The Waite and Fuller Courts' justices routinely favored powerful economic interests while displaying hostility to human rights, to the emerging middle class, or to labor rights. Appallingly, they even refused to apply the constitutional protections explicitly provided in the Fourteenth Amendment to prevent the mayhem, hanging, and vote suppression by Southern state and local officials that were rampant during the Jim Crow era. The Equal Justice Initiative documented 4,075 lynchings through the 1940s, worse than one every week since the end of Reconstruction seventy years earlier.[38]

As events transpired, the personhood of corporations was not an issue in the *San Mateo* ruling. But the payoff for Conkling's mendacity was realized in January 1886 when the Waite court heard another Southern Pacific case, this one involving taxes imposed by Santa Clara County. With no discussion, personhood for corporations entered into American statutes with the *Santa Clara* ruling. Without debate, Chief Justice Waite peremptorily asserted that he and his colleagues believed corporations to be "persons" like African-American men and thus were also covered by the Equal Protection Clause of the Fourteenth Amendment. "We are all of the opinion that it does," he concluded, credentialed solely by Conkling's spurious contention nearly four years earlier.[39]

Corporate personhood is without precedent—it is immaculate jurisprudence. The Waite Court's unsolicited and undebated assertion of corporate personhood is not supported by historical documents or prior jurisprudence. Silent Congressional records belie Conkling. Indeed, that silence includes the voluminous debates by legislators in the many states as they discussed ratification of the Fourteenth Amendment in 1868. That silence included Conkling himself and every one of his Congressional colleagues then or in the years thereafter. Political scientist Howard Jay Graham noted in the *Yale Law Review* in 1938 that what he rather generously labeled Conkling's 1882 "misquotations" of the record "are difficult to reconcile . . . in view of the absence of corroborating statements by other members of the Joint Committee, and since Roscoe Conkling himself appears to have said nothing publicly for sixteen years" until *San Mateo*.[40] Moreover, the chief drafter of the 1868 Equal Protection Clause of the Fourteenth Amendment was committee member John Bingham from Ohio. He frequently discussed and interpreted the amendment in years following, even noting in the *Congressional Globe* that it made the entire Bill of Rights enforceable against the states on behalf of African-American men. Never a hint of corporate personhood from him, either.[41]

Indeed, the vacuous foundation of the Conkling/Waite corporate personhood contrivance is responsible for its dismissal by two of the most respected twentieth-century Supreme Court justices, William O. Douglas and Hugo Black. They concluded that there was a good reason why Bingham, Conkling, and all the others involved in the Fourteenth Amendment neither wrote nor spoke regarding inclusion of corporations: because it simply was pure chicanery. Writing in *Wheeling Steel Corporation v. Glander* (1949), they concluded: "There was no history, logic or reason given to support that view," by the Waite court. "There was no suggestion in its submission [for states' ratification] that it was designed to put negroes and corporations into one class and so dilute the police power of the states over corporate affairs." Douglas and Black noted that various Supreme Court justices of the era had even explicitly rejected corporate personhood.[42]

Finally, there is the actual language of the Fourteenth Amendment that makes it clear that only human beings are persons: "All persons born or naturalized in the United States, and subject to the jurisdiction thereof, are citizens . . . No state shall . . . deprive any person of life, liberty, or property, without due process of law . . ." As Douglas and Black noted regarding Conkling's assertion, "'Persons' in the first sentence plainly includes only human beings, for corporations are not 'born or naturalized.' Corporations are not 'citizens' within the meaning of the first clause of the second sentence. It has never been held that they are persons whom a State may not deprive of life . . ." Moreover, Douglas and Black noted the antithetical reasoning it takes to construe that the amendment includes corporations: "It requires distortion to read 'person' as meaning one thing, then another within the same clause and from clause to clause . . ."[43] If corporate personhood had been created as Conkling averred, it is simply the best-kept secret in all of American history.

CHAPTER 4

The Donor Class Buys
Itself a Political Party

[American plutocrats] have become rich enough to buy themselves a party.[1]

—Paul Krugman, *Conscience of a Liberal*, 2007

Economic and geographic segregation have immunized those at the top from the problems of those down below. Like the kings of yore, they have come to perceive their privileged positions essentially as a natural right.[2]

—Joseph Stiglitz, June 2014

THE POLITICAL PREFERENCES AND personal agendas of the stupendously wealthy in America matter a great deal. Most of America's richest individuals are highly active politically, and their vast resources give them a disproportionate influence on US politics. Harvard political scientists Vanessa Williamson and Theda Skocpol, the former president of the American Political Science Association, note that

Wealth and income have become so amazingly unequal in the United States that a few hundred billionaire families have the means to push their own worldview in civic and political affairs . . . When it comes to

setting agendas for public discussion and policy debates—encouraging
entire convoys of organizations or office holders to move in one direction or another—the super-duper wealthy in America today can make
quite a difference. At the very highest levels of wealth and disposable
income, resources are so stupendous that the personal outlooks, even
quirks, of the super-rich matter."[3]

In 2012, for instance, 388 of the wealthiest Forbes 400 made political
contributions.[4] Their agendas matter because their generosity has come to
dominate campaign contributions and political/issue advertising. In 1980,
the richest one-tenth of one percent (0.1 percent) of donors contributed
less than 10 percent of all campaign contributions. In 2012, their share
was greater than 44 percent.[5] In 2016, their share reached two-thirds of
donations to Congressional candidates and it dominated contributions in
hundreds of state contests.[6] Their political preferences matter because the
"personal outlooks, even quirks" of these politically active multimillionaires
and billionaires are shared by few other Americans; as noted in chapter 2,
they are disdainful of middle- and lower-class priorities. In this chapter,
we'll see how they have adopted the GOP to implement their agenda. Even
so, their agendas are so uniquely self-serving that they are often at odds
with the preferences of their fellow Republican Party members.

Affluent political donors have favored the Republican party since the
Gilded Age, transforming the party of Lincoln into a refuge for the privileged. That bias eased for a generation before Reagan during the postwar
decades, when moderate Republicans ascended. Indeed, the party's collaboration and cooperation with Democrats were instrumental in the rise
of the great American middle class and the resurrection of civil rights.
Since Reagan, however, that trend has dissipated; the Gilded Age bias has
reappeared. That trend accelerated in the early 1990s when Congressional
Republicans sought political ascendency by formally adopting a pay-to-play
strategy to lure wealthy donors. Both the GOP's agenda and power and influence within the party itself were explicitly linked by former Congressman
Tom DeLay's "K-Street Project" to servicing wealthy donors.

This shift to transactional politics is evident in the evolution of GOP
party platforms. In 1992, for example, the GOP had advocated limits on
soft money donations and favored elimination of corporate and union

PACs. But by 2004, it had reversed course, deciding that any funding restrictions violated the First Amendment.[7] To appease the donor class, GOP moderates had to accept a small-government agenda that conflicted with their postwar support of Medicare, capital gains taxes, and stronger public schools. Moderates began abandoning the party. Others were culled from leadership positions in a process managed by officials including Newt Gingrich, or defeated in primaries.

This shift to transactional politics has been rewarded by corporate America and by the *fittest*. Cornell University economist Jin-Hyuk Kim found that only twenty of the S&P 500 Index firms during the period 1998 to 2004 donated primarily or exclusively to Democrats while *tenfold* more (206) primarily or exclusively contributed to Republican lawmakers.[8] Among the 200 best compensated CEOs in 2016, the nonpartisan Center for Responsive Politics notes they gave $6.50 to the GOP for every dollar going to Democrats, "a clear propensity to support Republicans."[9] Moreover, among the wealthy, some 158 families accounted for nearly half of all contributions to the 2016 presidential race made during the critical money-primary season in 2015, with nearly all (138, or 87 percent) supporting Republicans.[10] Very few wealthy donors follow the lead of George Soros or environmental advocate Tom Steyer, who favor Democrats.

The rightward shift with the departure of moderates is reflected in a Pew Research Center finding that the share of Republicans viewing government as an "enemy" increased nearly 60 percent between 1996 and 2015. By contrast, the share of Democrats viewing it as an enemy changed little—and the share viewing it as a friend rose nearly 20 percent.[11] An example of this transformation is the issue of renewable energy that moderate Republicans such as former Senator Chuck Percy of Illinois in the past supported. No longer. Beginning in 2010, the *fittest* led by the Koch brothers spent tens of millions of dollars in primary contests on behalf of climate deniers. Their lobbyist Tim Phillips explained the consequence: "After that, [renewable energy] disappeared from Republican ads. Part of that was the polling, and part of that was the visceral example of what happened to their colleagues who had done that . . . It told the Republicans that we were serious, that we would spend some serious money against them."[12]

Culling of moderates from Republican ranks was important because it set the stage for the Tea Party. That, in turn, enabled opportunistic donors to unduly influence these staunchly conservative GOP grassroots that came to dominate party primary elections and conventions.

Tea Party Grassroots: The Donor Class's Disproportionate Influence on the GOP

Using the formulation devised in 1982 by political economist Mancur Olsen (*The Rise and Fall of Nations*), the donor class has emerged as the pinnacle "distributional coalition" in American politics. Most of its members have far more at stake than you or me from specific public policies, and thus are willing to spend mightily to influence those specific policies—think fossil fuel industry moguls, hedge fund managers, or pharmaceutical firm CEOs. Most are small-government aficionados and some have spent years shaping public opinion, as Nancy MacLean detailed in *Democracy in Chains* (2017) or Jane Mayer of the *New Yorker* noted in 2016. Families like the Scaifes, Coors, Ricketts, and Kochs "were among a small rarefied group of hugely wealthy, archconservative families that for decades poured money, often with little public exposure, into influencing how the Americans thought and voted."[13]

As 2009 unfolded, some of these activist donors seized the moment offered by the emergence of the Tea Party to rather dramatically increase their influence within the GOP, described here by Skocpol and Williamson:

> A vast network of policy-oriented right-wing intellectual organizations, generously funded, has been strategizing and writing for many years, awaiting the moment when political and electoral winds might shift just enough, to allow their ideas to find a larger place on the mainstream agenda . . . National organizations, such as Freedom Works and Americans for Prosperity [both belonging to the Koch brothers], suddenly saw fresh opportunities to push long-standing ideas about reducing taxes on business and the rich, gutting government regulations, and privatizing Social Security and Medicare.[14]

By dint of wallet, wealthy donors began to dramatically enhance the reach of those social conservative GOP grassroots activists. The Kochs "were among the original financiers of the Tea Party movement," explain

New York Times journalists Sheryl Gay Stolberg and Mike McIntire.[15] Journalist Jurek Martin of the *Financial Times* adds: "It is the Kochs and their ilk who have fueled the Tea Party engine . . . Radical Washington institutions with mellifluous and innocent-sounding names—Freedom Works, Americans for Prosperity and the National Taxpayers Union—have thrived under their largesse."[16]

Their support was matched by the conservative media mogul Rupert Murdoch, owner of Fox News, who sought a niche to distinguish his network from the mainstream broadcast behemoths ABC, CBS, and NBC. Commentator Frank Rich considers Murdoch's March 2009 directive that his media empire publicize the Tea Party to be as instrumental as Koch cash in its rise: "The Kochs surely match the in-kind donations the Tea Party receives in free promotion 24/7 from Murdoch's Fox News . . ." Fox has been a right-wing mouthpiece and echo chamber in the years since, routinely and more recently relentlessly peddling conspiracies and half-truths that observers today would term fake news. Here is *New York Times* journalist Nick Corasaniti: "The network has provided a strategic path for Republican politicians and candidates with a message: To raise an issue, set an agenda or change the talk around a charged topic, go to Fox News."[17]

Skocpol and Williamson explained the lure of Tea Partiers to the decidedly upscale donor class:

> Alignment with Tea Party activists is the latest elite maneuver in the war against taxes and associated push to dismantle costly popular social programs like Medicare and Social Security . . . Now the anti-tax mantra would have some popular oomph behind it, enthusiastic backing from the ranks of ordinary middle-class conservatives attending Tea Party rallies and meetings. Indeed the Tea Party erupted at just the right moment to cut Obama and the Democrats off at the pass in the never-ending war to reduce regulations on business and free the US wealthy from having to pay taxes to sustain social supports for their fellow citizens. That is how the situation looks to right-wing interests . . . GOPers loyal to ultra-right agendas can roll back government spending, smash unions that are politically aligned with Democrats, and—above all—block tax increases on the privileged.[18]

Studying the mechanics of intraparty Republican politics in light of the rise of the Tea Party, the donor class quickly mastered its vulnerability: The departure of moderates had left staunch conservatives disproportionately influential in party primaries. The Tea Party appellation has become unpopular even among conservatives in recent years. Even so, Pew surveys have found that 49 percent of those who *always* vote in GOP primaries are self-identified Tea Partiers or their ideological mates. More than 50 percent who voted in the GOP 2012 primaries were evangelicals.[19] When combined with other self-identified conservatives, right-wing voters have come to represent fully 75 percent of those who always vote in GOP primaries.[20]

The donor class has magnified the rightward shift of the GOP by further culling remaining moderates in recent election cycles. Journalist Joe Rothstein explains what occurred during 2010 in North Carolina: "James Arthur 'Art' Pope, [is] an extraordinarily wealthy North Carolina native who has invested tens of millions of dollars in buying legislative and Congressional seats and as many statewide offices as his fortune (mostly inherited) can buy."[21] Many of the eighteen moderate state senators and delegates across North Carolina swept from office in 2010 by Pope's cash were moderate Republicans. The process was described this way by one of the defeated: "They spent nearly a million dollars to win . . . [my state Senate] seat. A lot of it was from corporations and outside groups related to Art Pope. He was their sugar daddy."[22]

In 2012, Koch money helped defeat eight moderate Republican state senators in Kansas primaries. In Arkansas, conservative donors spent millions of dollars ousting moderates in a state where politicians traditionally spent a few thousand dollars, as noted by Democratic state Senator Robert Thompson in November 2012: "If any outside group comes in and spends $10,000, that's a big chunk of what the candidates are going to spend."[23]

In *Fighting For Common Ground*, former Senator Olympia Snowe of Maine, a moderate Republican, writes that her party's grassroots with Tea Party sympathies hold "the most extreme views within our party . . . [seeking to] 'purify' it by defeating moderates."[24] Her Congressional history of collaborating with Democrats attracted a chorus of boos at the state Republican convention in Bangor in early 2012, causing her to end her reelection bid.[25] Only in a few instances of overreach, such as Kansas governor Sam Brownback in 2016, has the culling been reversed.

Donor class spending pushed the GOP rightward even when their favored candidates didn't prevail in primaries. The threat of an intraparty contest or a sizable negative advertising buy can be enough. Senators Ron Wyden and Lisa Murkowski in December 2012 noted that Congressional voting "is often colored by the prospect of facing $5 million in anonymous attack ads if a member of Congress crosses an economically powerful interest."[26]

Gerrymandering has also helped conservatives triumph over moderates, and as a result a sizable number of general election outcomes are increasingly determined by sparsely attended primaries in one-party legislative districts. Indeed, gerrymandering has caused the number of actual competitive elections for Congress to become minuscule: The Cook Report, for instance, found only thirty-two races out of 435 in 2016 were decided by a margin of 10 percentage points or less, compared to at least 123 races in 1992, 1994, and 1996.[27] It is the same story in state elections. Some 71 percent of candidates in the November 2015 state election ran unopposed for the Virginia House of Delegates, heavily gerrymandered by the GOP.[28] Not a single incumbent legislator was defeated. Careful to preserve their careers, those same legislators in mid-February 2017 vetoed placing a voter referendum on redistricting reform on the Virginia November 2017 ballot.[29] These dark corners of American politics were conceived explicitly to strengthen one-party rule. The consequence is to facilitate the *fittest* agenda by enabling (immoderate) voters in primaries rather than in general elections to dictate who serves in Congress.

The Koch Apparatus

A number of wealthy families such as the Mercers—part owners of the white supremacist website Breitbart—were important in the Trump and GOP victories in 2016; the Adelsons alone donated more than $40 million to Donald Trump and the GOP. But the Koch brothers stand out for their heft, their skill as political tacticians, and the vast scope of their political activities, which equal or exceed the reach of the Republican Party itself. They have emerged as a highly effective and sophisticated third force in American politics alongside the two political parties. Kenneth Vogel explained in *Politico*: "The Koch political operation has become among the most dominant forces in American politics, rivaling even the official

Republican Party in its ability to shape policy debates and elections."[30] In 2012, the Koch apparatus of four hundred mega-donors spent about $400 million supporting the GOP—more than double the spending in opposition by the ten largest labor unions.[31] Although they refused to contribute to the narcissistic Donald Trump, they marshaled a reported $750 million during the 2016 election cycle to support down-ballot conservatives, funding 1,600 full time, year-round staff in 107 offices across thirty-eight states.[32] Their network has spent over $1.5 billion since the mid-2000s to identify and support conservative Republicans, with a preference for electable libertarians.[33]

Former Obama White House official Chris Lahane spelled it out: "[The Koch brothers] have effectively acquired the Republican Party and repurposed it."[34] Skocpol and Williamson explain that the goal of the Kochs and other conservative moguls is to "remake the Republican Party into a disciplined, uncompromising machine devoted to radical free-market goals."[35] The income bias, the attacks on Obamacare, tax cuts, deregulation of environmental and labor rules, and the decline in the share of GDP attributed to government spending are evidence that these billionaires have largely succeeded in seizing the agenda of the GOP. Certainly, many thoughtful Republicans believe they have, including the commentator Ross Douthat who acknowledges that "the party's basic orientation . . . [has become] a tool of moneyed interests."[36]

A prediction made by commentator Frank Rich in 2010 has been realized: "Yet, inexorably the Koch agenda is morphing into the GOP agenda, as articulated by current Republican members of Congress . . . Their program opposes a federal deficit, but has no objection to running up trillions in red ink in tax cuts for corporations and the superrich . . . [while it] opposes the extension of unemployment benefits . . ."[37]

The *Fittest Fifty*

Not all Republicans or even all conservatives are pleased with this turn of events. South Carolina GOP Senator Lindsey Graham in April 2015 lamented the role being played by a few dozen wealthy donors in his state's presidential primary, arguing, "basically fifty people are running the entire show."[38]

In honor of social Darwinians such as William Graham Sumner, the conservative donor class is henceforth in this book referred to as the *fittest fifty*. A close contender was the *fittest 100* because the Center for Responsive Politics found that the top 1 percent of Super PAC contributors in 2012 were responsible for two-thirds of their donations. That is a universe of about one hundred people and their spouses.[39] Also considered was the *fittest 195*, because the Brennan Center for Justice noted in 2016 that about 60 percent of the $1 billion in campaign spending channeled through super PACs in the five years since *Citizens United* had come from 195 people.[40]

Pin Money

"It's just one quarter's dividend." That's how billionaire hedge fund manager Bill Ackman described the relatively trivial cost of funding a political campaign, even for a presidential primary aspirant.[41] Ready examples include Bill Marriott's support of Mitt Romney; Foster Friess and Rick Santorum; Harold Simons and Rick Perry; Norman Braman and Marco Rubio; Robert Mercer, the Wilks brothers, and Ted Cruz. The list grows longer with each election.

A candidate's political appeal, stage-presence, and campaign organization are vital elements in a competitive political contest, but so is money. That makes the *fittest fifty* indispensable to aspiring politicians in both parties—rare exceptions being aspirants such as Dr. Ben Carson, Donald Trump, or Bernie Sanders who mobilized small donors. Controversial or prominent figures such as Trump, who are able to garner massive free media exposure, are also less reliant on the *fittest fifty*. Indeed, MediaQuant concluded that Donald Trump benefited from an astounding $4.6 billion in free cable and broadcast coverage during 2016, garnering considerably more exposure than Secretary Clinton.[42] Even so, Trump received lavish donations from multimillionaires and billionaires Sheldon Adelson, Ronald Cameron, Betsy DeVos, Harold Hamm, Bernard Marcus, Rebekah Mercer, Linda McMahon, Steven Mnuchin, Wilbur Ross, Anthony Scaramucci, and Peter Thiel, among others.[43]

At the presidential level in November, the breadth of popular support for major candidates neutralizes any advantage of political money, as noted by researchers such as Thomas Frank, Jane Mayer, and journalists like Steven Pearlstein and E.J. Dionne Jr.[44] However, that parity disappears when it comes to down-ballot races. Support from the *fittest fifty* has been instrumental to the success in recent years of the GOP at the state level, especially during off-year elections. A very modest dump of campaign cash by national standards—$10 million or $20 million—has proved sufficient for quick-witted local conservatives to capture entire state governments. In fact, well-funded Republicans captured a near-majority of state governments in 2010, building on grassroots energized by criticism of big government, Democratic elitism, and Obamacare. That brought control of the 2011 redistricting process in those states, with the resulting gerrymandering enabling Republicans to solidify their hold on the House of Representatives.

Low turnout and frustration with Democrats were powerful factors in the Republican ascendency beginning with the 2010 election. But donations from conservatives unleashed by the Supreme Court's *Citizens United* ruling in January 2010 were also important. Kenneth Vogel explained its impact this way: "It changed the mind-set of big donors and big-money operatives. Perhaps more importantly, it introduced the idea that a single ultra-donor, or a well-connected consultant with the ears of a handful of mega-donors, could fundamentally shift a campaign for the US presidency, not to mention a handful of Senate or governors' races or dozens of House seats."[45]

The centrality of *Citizens United* to this political success is confirmed by an elaborate analysis by Tilman Klumpp, Hugo Mialon, and Michael Williams. They examined the ruling's specific impact, utilizing as a control group those states that had previously prohibited corporate political spending. They concluded that new corporate contributions to GOP candidates in state-level races in 2010 and 2012 increased the Republicans' odds of winning individual elections by an average of 4 percentage points. Their findings drew on data from 29,698 state House races and 8,517 state Senate races in forty-nine states. Importantly, in the swing states of Michigan, Minnesota, North Carolina, and Ohio (plus the red states of Montana and Tennessee), GOP odds improved by a minimum of 10 percentage points. And they increased by 7 percentage points in Texas, Colorado, Iowa, Wisconsin, and Wyoming. Moreover, *Citizens United* was found to reduce the number of citizens donating to campaigns. It also reduced the number of candidates willing to run as Democrats.[46]

The hundreds of millions of dollars contributed to this and more recent GOP electoral successes did not jeopardize fortunes of the *fittest fifty*. An extreme example is the casino owners Miriam and Sheldon Adelson. Their contributions and political/issue advertising in 2012 alone was *greater* than the combined contributions from *all* donors in twelve of the smaller states like Delaware, Idaho, and Maine.[47] They squandered some $91.8 million boosting Newt Gingrich and others during the 2012 election cycle,[48] yet their wealth *increased* by $14.4 billion in 2013.[49] Most US billionaires were lukewarm to candidate Trump in 2016, but spent lavishly on behalf of other candidates. Even so, like the Adelsons, the aggregate wealth of American billionaires in 2016 increased (a total rise of $77 billion according to the *Bloomberg Billionaires Index*) far beyond their outlays.[50]

It's just pin money. The *Wiktionary* defines pin money as "an amount not particularly significant . . . for routine expenses or incidentals." You know, cash spent on whatnots—including the wardrobe pins for Henry VIII's wives. The Kochs spent less than 1 percent of their fortune in the 2016 election cycle. Chicago hedge fund billionaire Kenneth Griffin spent more money on the Rauner race for Illinois governor than every member of 244 labor unions.[51] He can afford it because his after-tax income is $68.5 million *a month*.[52] None of these billionaire donors is less wealthy after their contributions; they remain as rich as Croesus. Just pin money. The process at work is explained by French economist Thomas Piketty, noting that size effects enable even the most extravagant to live well on a tiny portion of their income, the balance saved and reinvested to grow even more.[53] That process is exemplified by a handful of Florentine families who have managed to sustain wealth since 1427. Four of the five families with the highest incomes in 2014 were in the top 3 percent of earners there in 1427, according to research by Guglielmo Barone and Sauro Mocetti: "Those who earn the most among current taxpayers were already at the top of the socioeconomic ladder there six centuries ago."[54]

I Pledge Allegiance to the *Fittest Fifty*

Adopting the *fittest fifty* agenda has transformed Republicans to be the first uniformly conservative party in American history. GOP lawmakers are certainly subject to other powerful influences in crafting policy, including tightly focused and organized interest groups such as the gun lobby, right-to-life advocates, the Chamber of Commerce, staunch conservatives such as the Freedom Caucus, and the like. But when it comes to economics, the income bias documents that shrewd GOP lawmakers have adopted the *fittest fifty* agenda of small government and wage suppression as their own. Maintaining this fealty has been awkward at times. In 2017, most Congressional Republicans sought to strip health insurance from twenty million working-class Americans to fund $300 billion in tax cuts for the *fittest*. And on global warming since 2010, they have been required to suspend reason, evidence, and critical thinking to avoid offending the Koch brothers. The *New York Times* investigative reporters Carol Davenport and Eric Lipton explain: "Koch Industries and Americans for Prosperity started an all-fronts campaign with television advertising, social media and cross-country events aimed at electing lawmakers who would ensure that the fossil fuel industry would not have to worry about new pollution regulations."[55]

Put differently, timorous Republican lawmakers since 2010 have urged voters to ignore the ocean lapping at living rooms in Miami and Norfolk—move on, nothing to see here! As Stuart Stevens, a GOP strategist, acknowledges, "the Republican Party has greatly changed."[56]

Mann and Ornstein argue that the GOP has been tarnished by its pursuit of the *fittest fifty* agenda they described as an "unabashed ambition to reverse decades of economic and social policy by any means."[57] Their tactics (reliance on a drumbeat of fake news, polarizing voters, and shutting down the government twice, for instance) are indicative of a political party that has fallen out of the historic American political mainstream: "It is as if one of the many paranoid fringe movements in American political history has successfully infected a major political party . . . What used to be seen as loony is now broadly accepted or tolerated."[58]

Falling unduly under the spell of the *fittest fifty* has also placed the GOP well on the fringe among all political parties in the higher quality democracies. In 2012, Paul Quinn, a legislator from the conservative New Zealand National Party, explained the consequences to visiting American Fulbright scholars: "I will explain to you how our system works compared to yours: You have Democrats and Republicans. My Labor opponents would be Democrats. I am a member of the National Party, and we would be . . . Democrats as well."[59]

Moreover, pursuit of the *fittest fifty* agenda represents a de facto disavowal of the Republicans' Lincolnian roots as the party of opportunity for average Americans. That is particularly evident in Republican Party support of wage suppression. Indeed, the *fittest fifty* and executive suites have made the advocacy of higher wages a third rail of internal Republican Party politics. GOP lawmakers have logically responded by opposing higher minimum wage laws, independent contractor reforms, collective bargaining, overtime pay reform, paid parental leave, or preventing wage theft through stricter enforcement of wage and overtime regulations. Hostility to these pillars of middle-class prosperity is a bizarre position for any political party in a democracy, but flows naturally from the GOP's allegiance to the *fittest fifty*.

GOP Lawmakers Prioritize the *Fittest Fifty* Agenda Over Party Faithful

Finally, adoption of the *fittest fifty* agenda has caused GOP lawmakers to ignore the major economic policy preferences of party grassroots beyond just higher wages. The results of a CBS/*New York Times* survey from 2015 are informative: Some 85 percent of Americans, including 77 percent of Republicans, support requiring corporations and other employers to provide paid sick leave for employees, for instance (chart 4.1). Similar proportions of GOP party members also support paid parental leave and raising taxes to buttress Social Security—policy preferences studiously ignored by Republican lawmakers.

The disconnect between the preferences of the GOP grassroots and party lawmakers has forced the latter to adopt a bait-and-switch strategy. Action on hot-button issues such as Obamacare, traditional marriage, or abortion rights has been promised. But progress has been fitful even in 2017 with the GOP in full control of the federal government. (Conservative intellectuals such as Ross Douthat argued that the party is burdened by a weak, uninformed, erratic, and disinterested President.)[60] In quite sharp contrast, the *fittest fifty* agenda of wage stagnation, deregulation, and tax cuts has been quite successfully pursued by GOP lawmakers. This allegiance to elite donors is especially evident on fortifying the legalities of pay-to-play, exemplified by the Senate Republicans' refusal during 2016 to even consider the Obama nomination of Judge Merrick Garland to the Supreme Court. Democratic Senator Jeff Merkley explains: "The thing the Republican leadership feared most was that an Obama [Supreme Court]

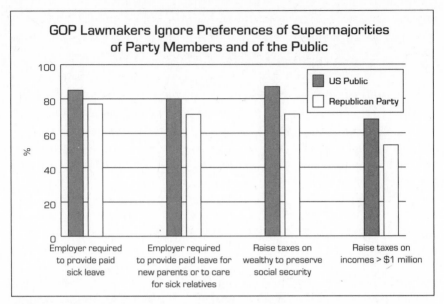

Chart 4.1 Share of respondents favoring noted policy. CBS News/*New York Times* survey (paid leave, tax on million-dollar incomes) and National Academy of Social Insurance (Social Security), 2012.

Noam Scheiber and Dalia Sussman, "Inequality Troubles Americans Across Party Lines, a Poll Finds," *New York Times*, June 4, 2015; and Harold Meyerson, "The Next Debate Topic," *Washington Post,* August 27, 2015.

nominee would rule against the huge influx of 'dark' money into political campaigns that is corrupting our system of government. They feared this outcome more than any other because it is that dark money, a vast amount of which came from the Koch brothers and their organization, that has played a huge role in putting the Republicans in the Senate majority."[61]

Pursuing policy outcomes in disagreement with majoritarian economic preferences and their own grassroots has positioned the contemporary Republican Party well out of the American mainstream. Even so, this pattern may persist for many years until a progressive Supreme Court recriminalizes vote buying, thereby providing the freedom for lawmakers to end the income bias if they choose. That eventuality is the focus of section 2.

SECTION 2

Reducing the Role of Money to Improve the Quality of American Democracy

THE *BUCKLEY* GENRE HAS lowered the quality of American democracy, placing wealthy conservative families at the center of American politics. The *fittest fifty* mimic the canny pigs in George Orwell's *Animal Farm,* dominating politics in order to disproportionately glean economic gains. Here is David Cay Johnston reflecting on the *Buckley* era: "The system today is not promoting prosperity based on individual enterprise and thriftiness. It is instead working, as all socialist redistributional schemes do, to enrich and benefit those who have access to the levers of power. In America, that is the political donor class."[1]

This section examines the characteristics of the *Buckley* genre beginning with the overt partisan character of the Supreme Court. It includes the Court's rejection of political equality, which is the global gold standard for democracy, as well as its rejection of the founding fathers' and framers' deep concerns over vote buying. The section concludes with a review of how the GOP's embrace of pay-to-play has diminished faith domestically and abroad in the American versions of both democracy and capitalism.

CHAPTER 5

The Roberts Republicans: A Partisan Court of Sumner Darwinians

The Supreme Court is not an ordinary court but a political court, or more precisely a politicized court, which is to say a court strongly influenced in making its decisions by the political beliefs of the judges.[1]

—Chicago Federal Appeals Court Judge Richard A. Posner,
March 2016

There's just such a control of government by the wealthy that whatever happens, it's not working for all the people; it's working for a few of the people.[2]

—Stanley Greenberg, Pollster, August 2011

T HE RISE OF THE *fittest fifty* is rooted in an unprecedented partisan divide on the Supreme Court. Beginning with the Burger Court, justices appointed by Republican presidents have outvoted mostly Democratic appointees to rule repeatedly in suits involving the political system in favor of William Graham Sumner's *fittest*. The preferences of higher income Americans, financiers, and CEOs have always been important to public officials. Many are employers, entrepreneurs, and community leaders who can create jobs. They are traditionally important cogs in society, and their concerns warrant attention. But a cultlike devotion to the *fittest* among justices has come to characterize the *Buckley* era.

Ideological divides within the Supreme Court aren't new. But law professors Neal Devins of William & Mary, Lawrence Baum of Ohio State University, and Richard Hasen of the University of California, Irvine, document that the Roberts Court's partisan split is unprecedented.[3] Its Republican appointees have proven far more eager than Democratic appointees to accommodate the GOP's allies in moneyed circles, especially after Justice Samuel Alito replaced the centrist Justice O'Connor in 2006. Jeffrey Rosen writing in the *New York Times Magazine* in March 2008 concluded that the ensuing partisan divide "was no accident. It represents the culmination of a carefully planned, behind-the-scenes campaign over several decades to change not only the courts but also the country's political culture."[4] A wide partisan gap now separates Democratic and Republican justices on the key issues of voting rights and pay-to-play that bear directly on the equality and the sovereignty of voters and thus the quality of American democracy. The 2017 appointment of Justice Neil Gorsuch ensures that the Roberts Republicans can muster majorities to continue cosseting the already comfortable by disenfranchising Democratic voters and continuing to legitimize political bribery.

A judicial partisan divide is widely acknowledged. "Today's Republicans are essentially saying the court is nothing but another political body," is how a *New York Times* editorial described it.[5] The increasingly political nature of Federal courts is exemplified by the refusal of GOP senators to consider the nomination of Merrick Garland or numerous other Obama judicial nominees once they regained a majority in the 2014 elections. Republican senators confirmed only 28 percent of judicial nominees during the last two years of the Obama administration. That provided President Trump with well over one hundred federal judgeships to fill upon taking office, sufficient to notably tilt federal courts to the right.[6] In contrast, 67 percent of George W. Bush appointees in his last two years were confirmed by the then-Democratic majority in the senate, leaving Barack Obama with only fifty-three vacancies to fill.[7] Between vacancies and mandatory retirements, President Trump is likely to appoint nearly one-half of appellate seats by 2020, the powerful courts immediately below the Supreme Court that decide thousands of cases annually.[8] That prospect greatly pleases Google, Chevron, and the *fittest fifty*—including the Scaife family foundation, Sheldon Adelson, the Kochs, and the Mercers—who have donated tens of millions of dollars to the Federalist Society and the Judicial Crisis Network managing this methodical and successful transformation to a partisan Republican Federal judiciary.

The transformation has succeeded, as noted earlier, because majorities of the Burger, Rehnquist, and Roberts courts accountable for the *Buckley* genre have ignored nearly two centuries of precedent. Their logic perhaps draws from the sentiments of conservatives such as Ed Whelan. He is president of the Ethics and Public Policy Center that provided guidance to Republican senators who refused to debate or vote during 2016 on Merrick Garland. Whelan argues that adherence to original intent needs to be situationally rejected, that is, "supplemented . . . when that methodology fails to yield a sufficiently clear answer to a constitutional question."[9]

The leading American conservative jurist and retired federal appeals court Judge Richard Posner has argued that such malleable principles have tarred the Roberts Court in particular as "a politicized court, which is to say a court strongly influenced in making its decisions by the political beliefs of the judges."[10] The late Justice Scalia, for instance, asserted "originalism" as justification for his refusal to recognize new rights for Americans such as marriage equality. Yet, his perception of originalism was sufficiently malleable to extend religious rights to corporations, to permit corporations to buy legislators' votes, and to permit GOP officials to shrink Black voting rights despite the Fourteenth Amendment.

Chief Justice Roberts objects to Posner, insisting any partisan bias of his court is merely impressionistic, colored by the increasingly politicized confirmation process: "Judges are not politicians, even when they come to the bench by way of the ballot."[11] This assertion is belied by a number of rulings by Roberts Republicans that constitutionally embraced state laws that disproportionately suppress the votes of Democrats. *Crawford v. Marion County, Indiana Election Board* in 2008 shielded spurious voter ID laws, while *Shelby County v. Holder* in 2013 weakened the Voting Rights Act.

The Roberts Court's Embrace of Democratic Voter Suppression

Voter purges and voter ID laws imposed by Republican state election officials in the wake of *Crawford* reduced the Black and Latino franchises in nearly every Southern state (and others like Iowa, Kansas, and Wisconsin), creating the greatest suppression of minority voters since Jim Crow. That is why Posner has concluded that *Crawford* is "[w]idely regarded as a means of voter suppression rather than of fraud prevention."[12] In Texas, for instance, *Crawford* permitted GOP state officials to reinstall de facto poll taxes with rules burdening some voters with the need to travel hundreds of miles to obtain newly demanded IDs. The potential disenfranchisement is huge: a federal court in Texas found that 608,470 registered voters lacked the IDs that *Crawford* required.[13] They tend to be poor, elderly, and minorities who vote disproportionately for Democrats.

In Iowa, new voter ID laws enacted by GOP officials in 2017 potentially exclude 11 percent (260,000) of eligible voters. As elsewhere, minority voters trending Democratic were targeted. In Blackhawk County (Waterloo), for instance, Blacks comprise 27 percent of eligible voters without requisite IDs, but comprise only 10 percent of county eligible voters. The GOP also eliminated same day registration and the ballot option of party-line voting despite acknowledging that voter fraud was nonexistent: Not one case of voter impersonation occurred among the 1.6 million votes cast in 2016, for instance.[14]

These suppression tactics proved highly effective. Voter turnout rose 1.3 percent from 2012 to 2016 in states not imposing voter ID restrictions. In contrast, turnout in states including, Mississippi, Texas, Virginia, and Wisconsin that imposed new voter ID laws in the wake of *Crawford* and *Shelby* fell 1.7 percent. Moreover, these suppression laws proved to be artfully crafted, disenfranchisement falling most heavily among minorities leaning Democratic. Turnout in counties where Blacks comprised up to 40 percent of voters rose 0.8 percent in 2016 in states without voter ID restrictions. In contrast, turnout in such counties in states with new voter ID laws fell 2.5 percent in 2016. The drop was an even larger 5 percent in counties with new ID laws where Blacks comprised more than 40 percent of voters.[15] In Wisconsin, state voter ID restrictions by Republican lawmakers contributed to a 41,000 drop in turnout between 2012 and 2016 in mostly minority Milwaukee. Statewide, a study by Priorities USA found that turnout dropped by 200,000.[16] That almost certainly flipped the state to Donald Trump in 2016, whose winning margin was just 22,748. It is reminiscent of Gore-Bush in 2000. While the Supreme Court famously and inappropriately stopped the Florida recount, that count was only necessary because 12,000 predominantly Black voters had been erroneously purged by Republican officials.[17]

Crawford and the *Buckley* genre share a disregard by Republican Supreme Court jurists of prior jurisprudence or sustentative law, an absence of factual grounding, and a justification in each instance by the introduction of novel legal arguments lacking underpinning in established legal doctrine.

In *Citizens United,* for instance, the Roberts Republicans could not cite a single precedent involving First Amendment speech rights of for-profit corporations.[18] Not one. In its *Buckley* genre rulings, the Burger, Rehnquist, and Roberts courts could not cite a single precedent in the canons of American law where vote buying had previously been constitutionally shielded or decriminalized. Not one. And in *Crawford,* the Roberts Republicans could not identify one instance of voter identity fraud in the entire history of Indiana. Not one.

In-person voter fraud is virtually nonexistent, an awkward fact for Roberts Republicans.[19] Their insistence that state officials enacting voter ID laws are nonetheless meeting the spirit and letter of the Constitution would have made the nineteenth-century Justice Joseph McKenna proud (read on).

Of course, the *Buckley* genre is not the first skein of Supreme Court rulings embracing voter inequality grounded in contrived, dubious, or fallacious legal thinking. The Jim Crow era of Supreme Court decisions stripping constitutional protections for Black Americans began with the *Slaughterhouse* ruling in 1873. Justice John Marshall Harlan later charged that his predecessors favoring Jim Crow utilized sham legal reasoning to justify this and subsequent rulings weakening the Fourteenth Amendment.[20] Similarly, the Roberts Republicans' support for sham voter ID laws in *Crawford* rather precisely mimics the Fuller Court's *Williams v. Mississippi* (1898) ruling; it held that election officials in Mississippi were not attempting to disenfranchise its 907,000 Black voters with literacy tests. Justice Joseph McKenna's majority opinion at the time asserted:

"The constitution of Mississippi and its statutes do not on their face discriminate between the races, and it has not been shown that their actual administration was evil; only that evil was possible under them."[21] Justice McKenna and the Fuller Court's writ included Alabama, where delighted elites rushed to draft a new 1901 constitution to ensure "white supremacy in this state . . . [against the] menace of Negro domination." It barred voting by anyone convicted of crimes involving "moral turpitude"—the definition of that term was left to local voting registrars.[22] And it included Louisiana where only 1,700 out of 700,000 eligible Blacks were permitted to vote in 1900; by 1904, only 1,342 were even allowed to register.[23] Much of Justice McKenna's opinion stood as writ on Black (and immigrant) voting rights until the 1960s.

How evil was the Fuller Court's writ? Most telling is that Adolph Hitler sought to normalize the racist Nazi Nuremberg Laws that presaged the Holocaust by analogizing them with the Jim Crow era, including its weekly lynchings. As Yale law professor James Whitman has noted, *Mein Kampf* lauds Jim Crow. And Nazi propagandists later touted to Germans the precedent of America's "racist politics and policies . . . [featuring] special laws directed against the Negroes, which limit their voting rights, freedom of movement and career possibilities." Whitman quotes one Nazi who wrote, "What is lynch justice, if not the natural resistance of the *Volk* to an alien race that is attempting to gain the upper hand?"[24]

The pernicious *Crawford* and *Shelby County* rulings have compromised the Roberts Court's prestige and authority. Their ancestry is the poisonous tree of the racist *Williams* ruling. All three decisions empowered discrimination among voters by partisan state electoral officials. Adding to their discomfiture is a failure to remove the last vestiges of Jim Crow. The Roberts Republicans permit the disenfranchisement of Democratic-leaning citizens in states like Alabama where 20 percent of Blacks are denied the vote as felons, many convicted for noncrimes including—yes, moral turpitude.[25] The consequence is dramatized by Virginia Democratic Governor Terry McAuliffe who—despite apoplectic Republican lawmakers—restored voting rights to 156,000 former felons in recent years, helping turn a red state purple.[26] University of Texas law professor Justin Driver summarizes: "An undesirable consequence of the court's partisan divide is that it becomes increasingly difficult to contend with a straight face that constitutional law is not simply politics by other means, and that justices are not merely politicians clad in fine robes."[27]

Indeed, Supreme Court reporter Robert Barnes notes that virtually all Supreme Court justices of late are the product of a highly politicized process: "The thing that separates all the smart lawyers who would like to become federal judges from the ones who actually *become* judges is most often political connections. Involvement in ideological causes, political campaigns and conservative or liberal organizations acts as a sieve. It separates out those who are chosen by the political elite for lifetime appointments."[28]

The Roberts Republicans Embrace the Fittest

The court's partisan divide has been documented by legal journalist Adam Liptak of the *New York Times*. Over the long sweep of American history, only two of the 382 most important court rulings between 1790 and 2010 broke along party lines. Since 2010, however, at least seven such important rulings have broken along partisan lines, including rulings on voting rights, campaign finance, mandatory (customer, client, and patient) arbitration, immigration, and strip searches.[29] That partisan divide has since expanded to also include union agency fees in *Friedrichs v. California Teachers Association* (2016).

Partisanship is also evident in Roberts Republican rulings involving major economic interests, corporate behavior, or clashes between economically upscale and downscale citizens. As summarized by David Cay Johnson in his book *Free Lunch*, the Roberts Republicans take from the many to cosset the few, while stripping grievances voiced by the many of judicial standing.[30]

A landmark 2013 statistical analysis by professors Lee Epstein, William Landes, and Judge Posner examined votes by the thirty-six Supreme Court justices who had served during the prior sixty-five years. The five Republican appointees sitting on the Roberts court in 2013 were among the ten justices during that period whose rulings most closely hewed to business positions. And the two most obsequious of all thirty-six justices are Roberts and Alito.[31] Judge Neil Gorsuch will very likely make a triumvirate. The Roberts Republicans have rejected the founding principle of their Republican Party as asserted by Abraham Lincoln in 1859: "Labor is prior to, and independent of capital . . . Capital could never have existed without labor . . . labor is the superior—greatly the superior—of capital."[32]

Specific examples abound. Roberts Republicans have ruled that corporate officials need not obtain shareholder approval for corporate political donations (*Knox v. Service Employees International Union, Local 1000*). Yet, union officials are required to obtain prior approval of political donations from each individual member. Interestingly, this right for CEOs to divert investor or shareholder money to ingratiate and gain political access is viewed askance by many in the American business community itself. A 2012 survey of that sector by the Corporate Reform Coalition found 71 percent of respondents supported requiring firms to "only spend money on political campaigns if they get approval from their shareholders first."[33] The same proportion of self-identified Republican respondents agreed.

Other Roberts Court rulings favoring the *fittest* include:

- *Gross v. FBL Financial Services* (2009)—Firms are largely impervious to age discrimination lawsuits.[34]
- *Walmart v. Dukes* (2011) and *AT&T Mobility v. Concepcion* (2011)— Corporations are permitted to restrict access to the courts by aggrieved customers, patients, or employees, instead insisting on arbitration. That is, firms can sue employees, patients, clients, and customers in court, but simultaneously force those possibly victimized by corporate actions into arbitration, blocking their access to the justice system for class action suits.[35] In the year following these rulings, there was a doubling of firms banning class action lawsuits in their user agreements with employees, customers, and others.[36]
- *Janus Capital Group v. First Derivative Traders* (2011)—Immaculate fraud. Use of a shell entity by mutual funds prevents prosecution of the funds for defrauding clients (by completing some buy-or-sell-orders on behalf of favored clients at the expense of other clients).[37]
- *Comcast v. Behrend* (2013)—Comcast was shielded from prosecution for overcharging its Philadelphia customers by $875 million.[38]
- *RJR Nabisco Inc. v. The European Community* (2016)—Tobacco firms smuggling cigarettes to Europe and participating in international money laundering enterprises cannot be sued by European nations or the European Community.[39]

As the scope of these rulings indicates, the Roberts Republicans have been quite energetic in providing a broad constitutional shield for the actions of the *fittest fifty* and corporations. That reflects in part the fruits of a deft legal stratagem pursued by a variety of private attorneys funded by the *fittest fifty*. Led by corporate enthusiasts such as James Bopp Jr., a host of Republican groups have become serial filers of lawsuits cosseting the powerful, many alleging violation of ephemeral or mythical corporate First Amendment rights. Their model is to run suits en masse past the Roberts Republicans to see what sticks, court conservatives opportunistically picking and choosing cases to hear.

The Roberts Republicans have also been proactive on their own initiative. Most notably, they demanded an unusual reargument of the initial March 2009 *Citizens United* case in order to justify their eventual ruling that went considerably beyond the original complaint. As former Justice John Paul Stevens explained: "Five justices were unhappy with the limited nature of the case before us, so they changed the case to give themselves an opportunity to change the law."[40]

Exemplified by *Crawford* and the *Buckley* genre, rulings that have transformed the architecture of American politics have been instituted by Republican jurists on a foundation of sand. In the fullness of time, they are likely to be reversed. Just ask the CEO of Dow Chemical. Shortly after the death of Justice Scalia, that firm abruptly paid $835 million to settle a long-standing price-fixing conviction in a class action suit. Until then, they had every reason to believe the Roberts Republicans would intervene and overturn the Appeals Court verdict against them—just as they had done in other similar instances.[41]

CHAPTER 6

Rejection of Political Equality by the Constitution

The Constitution was designed to reverse the democratic trajectory of American politics.[1]

—Historian Matthew C. Simpson, September 2016

Jefferson saw that Hamiltonianism would concentrate power in the hands of the business leaders and financiers that it primarily served, leading inevitably to an American plutocracy . . . Jefferson's fears were not misplaced. In modern America, concentrated wealth controls politics and government.[2]

—Historian John Ferling, *Jefferson and Hamilton*

BEGINNING IN ANCIENT ATHENS, philosophers pondered the contours of a democratic republic. The ideal that emerged was self-government by citizens who enjoy political equality—equal influence—and voter sovereignty—elected representatives who enact policies that accurately reflect popular preferences. Attaining such equality, featuring rule by Aristotle's "unpropertied," came to be understood by Jean-Jacques Rousseau, John Locke, Charles-Louis Montesquieu, and other political philosophers as the quintessential feature of a representative democracy. More than a decade before the American Revolution in 1762, Rousseau had concluded that a self-governing democracy within a republic structure is dependent on public opinion being fairly heard because that "is the general will; and the will must speak itself or it does not exist . . ."[3] Rousseau argued that when a nation's public opinion is not fairly heard, or when representatives substitute their own judgment for public sentiment in crafting policy outcomes, that nation fails the test of being a self-governing democracy. Representatives must both hear and heed citizens as equals.

The founding fathers certainly reached the same conclusion in 1776, as reflected in their preamble to the Declaration of Independence. Yet in 1787 at Philadelphia, the framers rejected political sovereignty and equality, diminishing their moment in history. The further rejection of political equality that emerged during the *Buckley* era was simply part of a pattern established in colonial times in which America's leaders cosseted the comfortable at the expense of Sumner's unfit.

Another of the founding fathers' revolutionary ideals fared much better—the historically unprecedented expansion of the franchise noted earlier. Many of the founders also sought the abolition of slavery, as Heritage Foundation historian Matthew Spalding notes: "In the wake of independence, state after state passed legislation restricting or banning the institution."[4] In Massachusetts, for example, the soaring language of the Declaration of Independence reproduced in the state constitution was the explicit judicial foundation for its 1783 abolition of slavery.[5] Even so, that aspiration fell to the vision of one grand nation of thirteen states—a vision of the framers that enabled slave states to reject abolition.

Shays' Rebellion: Political Inequality Becomes a Core Constitutional Value

Recall from the Introduction that Shays' Rebellion caused colonial elites to wrestle with the implications of a broadly enjoyed voter franchise. The rebellion itself was short-lived. An armed protest in western Massachusetts by indebted small farmers run afoul of creditors after borrowing to pay taxes was quickly suppressed by the militia. It produced few casualties (eight deaths including two looters) and a few debtors were freed from prison. But Shays' Rebellion was a supremely pivotal moment in American history, because shortly after their protest was put down, the farmers found success through the ballot box. As 1787 arrived, they refused reelection of the Massachusetts governor, inducing state lawmakers to soon enact much of their agenda—debt forgiveness, progressive taxes, and easy money (printing) laws.

The lawmakers' response demonstrated that voters could exercise their sovereignty to trump the influence of elites. Colonial creditors, attorneys, merchants, slave owners, and wealthy landowners were stunned by the spectacle of Massachusetts lawmakers acting like, well, politicians. Historian John Ferling explained the elites' angst: "This was not the American Revolution that they had imagined . . . they sought the means of removing important decisions from popular control . . . the most conservative Americans . . . grew steadily more agitated about what a Massachusetts merchant called 'plebian despotism and the "fangs" of the citizenry.' "[6]

Anxious elites mobilized swiftly in the heat of the moment to secretly debate ways and means of ending political equality and voter sovereignty. Their solution was a Constitutional Convention of selected attendance that convened within weeks in Philadelphia. Their goal was to unwind the quality of democracy empowered by the Second Continental Congress in 1776 and its outgrowth, the Articles of Confederation. Historian Joseph J. Ellis cites James Madison's "critical assessment of the popularly elected state governments" as a reflection of his and many of his fellow Philadelphia delegates' fear of political equality and voter sovereignty.[7]

Certainly, there were other nagging issues of moment requiring revisions to the Articles. A federal structure was needed for the new nation, including a system for selecting a president and creating federal taxing authorities to sustain law, order, national defense, and credit reform. But an important—perhaps the most important—motivation for the framers' abrupt rewrite of the nation's founding document in Philadelphia that summer was the danger they perceived from the emerging high-quality colonial democracy. Their intention to roll back the Articles was made clear by the fact that only six of the nation's fifty-six founding fathers were invited to or attended the Constitutional Convention.

The Constitutional Architecture: A Faux Democracy

The framers' overreaction in the wake of Shays' Rebellion produced a governance architecture that has denied political equality to Americans in the centuries since. Historian Matthew Simpson summarizes: "The proposed government was less democratic than either the Articles of Confederation or the individual state constitutions. For example, the president would be chosen by an Electoral College rather than by citizens themselves; senators would be appointed by state legislators; the smallest states would have as many senators as the largest . . . The constitution was designed to reverse the democratic trajectory of American politics."[8]

The rejection of political equality and sovereignty is exemplified by the Electoral College and, of course, the issue of slavery. Nearly half (twenty-five) of the delegates were slaveholders; several of them owned more than 200 slaves. The new constitution established the primacy of federal authority in many matters. Congress, not the states, henceforth was the determinant legal authority on a number of issues, including slavery. Thus, slave owners demanded that the newly empowered Congress be prevented from ever abolishing slavery. If their demand went unaddressed, the delegates from slave states appeared determined to create their own separate nation, perhaps in league with France or Spain. There is a misimpression among historians that the slavery issue pitted large states against small. Not true. James Madison provides clarity on this point: "The states were divided into different interests not by their difference in size, but principally from their having or not having slaves . . . It did not lie between the large and small states, it lay between the Northern and Southern."[9]

To preserve the union, the framers accepted a constitutionally guaranteed right for Americans to hold human beings in bondage in perpetuity. That right was guaranteed by creation of a second legislative body (the Senate) that gave vote parity to each state—a malapportioned, undemocratic provision that granted slave states a veto in perpetuity over all laws.

The framers also created a constitution centered on selective individual liberty, with white and a handful of Black male voters (and a few women) of means comprising the electorate. The expectation in this new construct was that lawmakers would routinely substitute their own judgment for the will of elite voters, voter sovereignty rejected. Ferling notes Hamilton's support for this elite bias: "Hamilton emphasized the preservation of order and stability, the protection of those who had reached society's summit, and the means of restraining those who had not . . . He was convinced that social stability required the presence of a strong central government dominated by those at the top of a hierarchical society."[10]

This history explains why, despite its provenance in the Declaration of Independence, America has had an erratic and ultimately unsuccessful courtship with the concept of political equality. At Gettysburg, Lincoln termed political equality the nation's "sheet anchor."[11] It is true that most women, Native Americans, and Americans of color have come to enjoy the franchise. Yet, the income bias and the resurgence of state-sponsored disenfranchisement by the GOP of late are evidence that voter sovereignty and political equality remain only aspirational in America. Indeed, without seminal reforms to pay-to-play and to the US Senate, the nation's electoral system, and the Electoral College, noted in later chapters, they are unobtainable.

The political revolutions of eighteenth- and nineteenth-century Europe produced four seminal pillars of democratic governance: acknowledgment of the supremacy of individual human rights (including the abolition of slavery), government based on the political equality of each citizen, representatives who fairly hear and fairly heed voters, and the shackling of economic elites and monarchs who dominated previous societies. Aside from rejecting the British monarchy, the American Constitution lacks all four pillars.

In stark contrast, voter equality and sovereignty has become the global gold standard for a genuinely democratic society by other wealthy democracies over the past century. Operationally, that gold standard means the absence of dependence corruption, as noted by Harvard law professor Lawrence Lessig—lawmakers craft outcomes for the broad public good rather than on behalf of donors. Robert C. Post, dean of the Yale Law School, calls this desideratum a state of "electoral integrity," where elections are sufficiently fair and free of taint that they accurately reflect public sentiment—where each vote is fairly heard and is weighted equally with its neighbor by representatives.

Political inequality is deeply embedded in America's constitutional DNA. But realizing the goal of political equality in America means acknowledging the distinction between the Constitution and original intent. The latter is a separate, prior, and more foundational standard.

And laws or Supreme Court rulings such as the *Buckley* genre that affirm, promote, or shield political inequality do not necessarily comport with original intent. In any case, as was argued earlier, there is no ambiguity regarding the founding fathers and framers' position on political bribery writ large; they greatly feared the pathologies incited by vote buying. And modern research on those pathologies has fully credentialed their fears, as we will next see.

CHAPTER 7

Political Bribery Decriminalized: Vote Buying as "Free Speech"

There is only scant evidence that independent expenditures ever ingratiate.[1]

> —Justice Anthony Kennedy, Majority opinion in
> *Citizens United*, 2010

In the last nine years, six [*Buckley* genre] Supreme Court decisions have wreaked havoc on the nation's campaign finance laws, opening the door to super PACs and corporate spending, creating new channels for wealthy donors and candidates to influence elections, and weakening programs meant to lower barriers for ordinary Americans to run for office.[2]

> —Brennan Center for Justice,
> New York University Law School, 2016

FRANK CAPRA'S GREATEST FILM was *Mr. Smith Goes to Washington.* Andy Barr is no Mr. Smith.

As a newly elected member of Congress in 2012, Andy Barr really hit the ground running. Before he had even been sworn in, Andy, a former lobbyist from Kentucky, had a decidedly odd fundraiser for a freshman Congressman. It was cosponsored by a powerful K Street lobbyist whose clients included financial firms like Bank of America and MasterCard

International. It was held at the upscale Charlie Palmer Steak house, within sight of the Capitol, a decidedly glitzy setting for soliciting campaign contributions for a new Congressman. The crowd was heavy on financial industry lobbyists including powerful donors like the American Bankers Association and PNC Bank.[3]

How did the neophyte Andy earn such a celebrated welcome to Washington? It turns out that Andy is a very lucky young man. The forty-year-old freshman Republican had won a coveted appointment to the House Financial Services committee. There was intense bank industry pressure to jump Barr over more than a hundred more senior GOP members of Congress covetous of that slot, and the GOP leadership wilted. The industry had obviously concluded Barr was theirs. And Andy? Well, he may not appreciate the complexities of banking, but he certainly knows the secret of success in Washington. The Financial Services Committee controls banking regulations, making it the primo spot on Capitol Hill for attracting campaign cash from the richest of all US industries. Andy may be clueless about CDOs (collateralized debt obligations), but not about the key to a long career in the *Buckley* era of American politics.

You might think of folks like Andy as public servants. But the donor class thinks of politicians like him as an investment, and Andy was an asset who was positioned to yield a bonanza return of fruitful votes for years to come. One donor explained Barr this way for *New York Times* journalist Eric Lipton: "It's almost like investing in a first-round draft pick for the NBA or NFL. There is a potential there. So we make an investment, and we are hopeful that investment produces a return."[4]

Andy soon made his investors look clever, providing a quick return on their initial outlay of $151,200 in campaign donations. Although he campaigned as a fiscal prude, Congressman Barr committed to donors by his first April in office to sponsor a financial industry tax loophole law that would deepen the deficit by $500 million annually. Even better, the promising rookie introduced legislation to unwind a portion of the Dodd-Frank reregulation law that prohibits financial institutions from lending to unqualified home buyers. The ambitious young man either didn't know or didn't care that such predatory subprime loans were a major cause of the Great Recession a few years earlier.

Congressman Barr is far from being alone in trading away the public interest and common sense in exchange for cash. Another promising investment by banking industry lobbyists is Congresswoman Ann Wagner of Missouri. In appreciation for their contributions, she sponsored legislation to derail the Obama administration "fiduciary rule" protecting consumers; it required life insurance and financial brokers selling financial products to put their clients' interest ahead of their own. Such protections are commonplace in every other wealthy democracy. The (Obama) White House Council of Economic Advisers found that Americans pay $17 billion annually in excess broker commission because brokers put their own financial interests first. Even so, the Trump administration protected the scam by financial advisors, torpedoing the reform proposed by the Obama administration just as Wagner and the financial industry wanted.[5]

Barr and Wagner are part of a wave of politicians with, well, Randian views toward public service who have entered politics over the last two decades. They are willing to spend four hours daily in a cubical for half the week phoning strangers for money. Their most receptive targets are upper income Americans across the nation and corporate officers hoping to influence lawmakers to enhance profits by lowering taxes, suppressing wages, and the like. And their soulmates are Roberts Republicans.

Decriminalizing Vote Buying

The Roberts Republicans contend the vast bulk of political contributions and third-party independent expenditures on behalf of lawmakers are "not corruption . . . [but] embody a central feature of democracy."[6] In their view, a donation reciprocated by an explicit quid pro quo (say, a government contract) constitutes corruption. But, donations to acquire as yet unspecified future benefits from the same lawmaker—such as a supportive vote on favored legislation—are instead "a central feature of democracy." Fordham Law professor Zephyr Teachout argues that this definitional legerdemain is "bedeviled by problems and confusion. Subsequent [judicial] decisions are unclear about the meaning of 'explicit' and how the *quid pro quo* requirement is defined . . . Nearly twenty-five years later it is still not clear exactly what kind of campaign exchange constitutes a violation . . ."[7]

The decriminalization of cash given to or spent on behalf of politicians ignores the intent of donors to buy votes; donors always and everywhere intend to influence the recipient's viewpoint. That is why Judge Posner describes the "legislative system [as] one of quasi-bribery."[8] The late Democratic Senator Russell B. Long was more, well, measured in his assessment: "Almost a hairline's difference separates bribes and contributions."[9] Justice Kennedy dismissed those sentiments, asserting in the majority opinion of *Citizens United* that "There is only scant evidence that independent expenditures ever ingratiate."[10]

There was one Republican Supreme Court justice during the *Buckley* era who disputed Kennedy and the Roberts Republicans. In her opinion in *McConnell v. FEC* (2003), then-Justice Sandra Day O'Connor wrote:

> We [have] recognized a concern not confined to bribery of public officials, but extending to the broader threat from politicians too compliant with the wishes of large contributors . . . [M]any of the deeply disturbing examples of corruption cited by this Court . . . were not episodes of [quid pro quo] vote buying, but evidence that various corporate interests had given substantial donations to gain access to high-level government officials . . .
>
> Justice Kennedy's interpretation of the First Amendment would render Congress powerless to address [these] more subtle but equally dispiriting forms of corruption. Just as troubling to a functioning democracy as classic *quid pro quo* corruption is the danger that officeholders will decide issues not on the merits or the desires of their constituencies, but according to the wishes of those who have made large financial contributions valued by the officeholder. Even if it occurs only occasionally, the potential for such undue influence is manifest.[11]

"There Is Only Scant Evidence That Independent Expenditures Ever Ingratiate"

This Kennedy quote, a pillar of the *Buckley* genre, collapses under close scrutiny. Both independent expenditures and campaign contributions have repeatedly been demonstrated to induce favorable voting by legislators—the process responsible for the income bias. University of Chicago law professor Nicholas A. Stephanopoulos notes: "There is near consensus in the empirical literature that politicians' positions more accurately reflect the view of their donors than those of their constituents."[12] Moreover, business donors occasionally misspeak by publicly revealing that contributions are intended to buy votes. The National Association of Homebuilders Political Action Committee (BUILD-PAC), for instance, ceased donating to Congress for a period in 2008, in a pique at congressional failure to reciprocate its donations by increasing housing subsidies. Its criticism inadvertently leaked to the press, causing campaign finance expert Kenneth Gross to note: "This highly visible carrot-and-stick approach to the use of PAC contributions displays a disquieting nexus between lobbying and political contributions."[13] A second exposé occurred three years later in New York State. A trade association solicited $10,000 from each of its members; the plea explained, "Our future ability to adopt favorable legislation, stop terrible legislation or modify legislation to limit the pain to our industry is directly tied to our continued positive relationship with all the leaders in Albany."[14]

Anecdotal evidence is buttressed by donors such as then-candidate Trump, who described the political contributions he made in the course of his career as investments: "When I need something from them two years later, three years later, I call them."[15] This process of investing in politicians, as practiced by Trump and by bankers donating to Barr or Wagner, was generalized by professors Jennifer Brown, Katharine Drake, and Laura Wellman in the *American Accounting Association* journal this way in 2015: "Proactive firms build relationships with policymakers through continued campaign support, with the expectation of gaining some economic benefit."[16]

Indeed, if contributions or independent expenditures on behalf of politicians did not influence them, they would not occur. It would simply be foolish for corporations or billionaires to donate to politicians, much less to both candidates (as some do). In particular, worldly and canny billionaire campaign contributors such as Sheldon Adelson and the Koch brothers would be fools. Whatever you may think of CEOs or the *fittest fifty*, they are not fools. They view spending on politicians such as Barr like any other investment; a return is expected, as explained by lobbyist Theresa Kostrzewa in September 2015: "Donors are demanding a lot these days, man, and they want answers and they want results . . . Donors consider a contribution like, 'Well, wait, I just invested in you. Now I need to have my say; you need to answer to me."[17]

The Roberts Republicans' Pollyannaish perspective on political spending is belied by the income bias, by the opinion of retired Justice O'Connor, and by the billions of dollars invested in public officials by S&P 500 firm CEOs, the Waltons, the Kochs, and others of the *fittest fifty*.

Further, there is a forty-year skein of scholarly studies providing evidence that donations and third-party independent expenditures sway legislators. The effectiveness of such vote buying has been documented for a wide variety of economic public policy issues, including derailing minimum wage increases (researchers Jonathan Silverman and Garey Durden, 1976), trucking deregulation (John Frendreis and Richard Waterman, 1985),[18] and telecom industry deregulation (Rui de Figueiredo and Geoff Edwards, 2005).[19] The digitization of statistical databases has added considerable heft and breadth to this body of work in recent years, with analyses definitively documenting causal linkages between political spending and changes in voting behavior by lawmakers and judges. Examples include:

- A 2015 analysis in the *Journal of the American Accounting Association* by Jennifer Brown, Katharine Drake, and Laura Wellman concluded that targeted corporate donations to Congressional lawmakers sitting on tax law committees (Senate Finance and House Ways and Means Committee members) during the 2000s lowered firm-specific future expected tax rates an average 1.66 percent— for an average enterprise tax savings of $33 million.[20] That is an astronomical investment return for a slew of 4-digit personal and PAC donations.
- Finance professors Ran Duchin and Denis Sosyura parsed the link between corporate donations prior to 2008 and the allocation of the $205 billion in Troubled Asset Relief Program (TARP) bank bailout subsidies that year: "We find that banks' political ties played a significant role in TARP fund distribution . . . The TARP investment amounts are positively related to banks' political contributions and lobbying expenditures . . . The estimated magnitudes of political influence are substantial . . . [A] bank's connection to a House member on key finance committees is associated with an 18.2 percent increase [in TARP funds], controlling for other factors."[21]
- Journalist Steven Brill, founder of *American Lawyer* magazine, examined the consequence of $15 million in donations from hedge funds and other money managers intended to dilute the Obama administration's Dodd-Frank reregulation legislation. His July

2010 analysis found that the largesse induced members of Congress to insert a number of loopholes in Dodd-Frank, saving the industry an estimated $10 billion in taxes annually. That translates to an astronomical return he calculated of 660 percent.[22]

- US multinationals in the mid-2000s were refusing to repatriate billions of dollars in profits held in foreign banks in order to avoid paying the US 35 percent corporate income tax rate. Corporate contributions induced Congress and the George W. Bush administration to open a temporary tax loophole in 2005, momentarily cutting rates for such repatriations to 5.25 percent.[23] Corporations took quick advantage of the loophole to repatriate $312 billion in profits, saving over $90 billion in taxes. Economists at the University of Kansas concluded the loophole returned $220 for every lobbying dollar spent.[24] A replay of this lush scenario is a likely element in Trump administration tax changes.

Vote buying is also bipartisan. In a study for the National Bureau of Economic Research in April 2017, Jeffrey Brown and Jiekun Huang found that meetings by senior corporate officials with key White House Obama administration policymakers from 2009 through 2015 were associated with more government contracts, regulatory relief, and "abnormal stock returns." They also found, following the 2016 election of Donald Trump, "that firms with access to the Obama administration experience significantly lower stock returns" than otherwise similar firms.[25]

Stratmann: Donations Buy Congressional Votes on Agriculture Commodity Subsidies

Economist Thomas Stratmann conducted an expansive statistical analysis in 1990 that documented the purchase of votes in the House of Representatives regarding agricultural commodity price supports (subsidies). This is an unusually powerful data set because there are affluent donors on both sides of such votes, such as sugar growers opposed by confectionary and other industries favoring lower sweetener prices. Moreover, examining the impact of donations utilizing commodity subsidy votes is a particularly revealing analysis because most House members have few if any constituents directly connected with commodity price supports.

They are essentially nonpartisan free votes for most lawmakers, making the influence of donors relatively transparent.

Stratmann began with a database of individual members' historic Congressional voting behaviors. He then evaluated their reaction to donations by PACs representing growers. Compared to historic vote patterns, such donations switched an average 23.8 votes to yes (aye) on each of the ten agriculture price support subsidy bills he examined. On three of the bills, political donations swayed sufficient votes to determine the final outcome (chart 7.1). For instance, a vote to continue dairy subsidies (favored by farmers) passed the House by a count of 245–167 in 1990. Had the dairy industry not made campaign contributions in the several years prior to the vote—or had their contributions been neutralized by contributions from opponents—past individual voting histories predicted that the outcome would have been a vote of 204–208, killing dairy price supports. Similarly, Stratmann found that a vote to continue sugar subsidies, enacted by a margin of 267–146, would have failed by a projected vote of 194–219 in the absence of political spending by sugar beet and cane growers; donations switched the votes of seventy-three members of

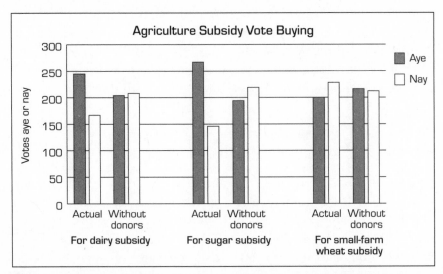

Chart 7.1 Farm commodity subsidies are determined by contributors.

Thomas Stratmann, "What Do Campaign Contributions Buy? Deciphering Causal Effects of Money and Votes," *Southern Economic Journal* 57:3 (January 1991), table IV, www.jstor.org/table/1059776

Congress on that one. Stratmann also discovered that lawmaker votes are sold pretty darn cheaply: "A $3,000 sugar PAC contribution maps into a yes vote with almost certainty."[26]

Buying Courtroom Verdicts

The vast majority of judicial verdicts in America are rendered in state and local courts, and nearly 90 percent of the judges in those courts are elected. This pervasive reliance on elections to select state and local jurists stands in sharp contrast with the practice of other wealthy democracies where judges are appointed on merit and are nonpartisan. Indeed, judges abroad are on a much more demanding, professionalized career track. Retired Supreme Court Justice O'Connor explains why other nations reject American-style judicial elections: "No other nation in the world does that because they realize they're not going to get fair and impartial judges that way."[27]

Traditionally, US judicial elections have been modest affairs. But like state and local legislative elections, that has changed in recent years. Supreme Court justices in Florida, for instance, raised a total of just $7,500 between 2000 and 2010 for their elections and most races were uncontested. In 2014 alone, however, the three judges seeking reelection raised $1.5 million in donations.[28] More than $2.6 million was spent on electioneering to fill an open Supreme Court seat in Wisconsin in April 2016.[29] And judges in Ohio now routinely raise millions of dollars for their election.[30]

Contributions and independent expenditures by favor seekers involving judicial races have soared for two reasons. First, Republican politicians since 2010 in some states have run afoul of state courts that have opposed GOP budget cuts, especially for public education. In Kansas, for instance, tax-cutting Republicans in control of the state government reduced inflation-adjusted per-student spending statewide by 16.5 percent between 2008 and 2014.[31] Concerned parents sued, and the state Supreme Court judged that the size and distribution of the cuts (with wealthy suburbs protected) violated the state constitution. The governor and legislators refused court orders to ameliorate the cuts. Frustrated with their recalcitrance, the state Supreme Court threatened to close all public schools until lawmakers enacted remedies. That put GOP Governor

Sam Brownback and the legislature in the awkward position of having to raise taxes and education spending, offending the Kochs, their neighboring donors headquartered in Wichita. They chose instead to mimic the Turkish autocrat Recep Erdoğan and the extreme right Polish Law and Justice political party by seeking removal of the disfavored judges. Kansas GOP lawmakers opposed the reelection of Supreme Court justices in 2016 and also voted to strip the court of power to rule on the constitutionality of education spending.[32] Kansans are pretty conservative, but even they were disappointed with the GOP lawmakers, voting fourteen of them out of office in the August 2016 primaries; previously, only three GOP incumbents had been ousted in sixteen years. In November 2016, voters reelected all the proeducation state Supreme Court justices, and replaced thirteen Republican state lawmakers with Democrats.[33] Chastened lawmakers joined with Democrats to reverse most of the income tax cuts at the root of the problem in June 2017. Even so, Kansas income taxes retained their Republican flavor: the poorest will be paying more than twice the share of their income in taxes (11.8 percent) as the richest 1 percent of Kansans pay 4.8 percent.

Second, interest groups, including corporations, have come to appreciate the windfalls on offer from buying favorable court rulings. Judicial vote buying has paid off spectacularly in some instances. West Virginia Supreme Court Justice Brent Benjamin cast the deciding vote absolving the Massey Coal Company of negligence for miner deaths after receiving its $3 million campaign donation. That instance of vote buying was subsequently held to be constitutional by the Roberts Republicans.[34] Voters took a dimmer view of the corruption than the Roberts Republicans, however, defeating Benjamin's bid for reelection in 2016. Another example is Illinois Supreme Court Judge Lloyd Karmeier. He cast the deciding vote to overturn a $1.18 billion appellate court verdict (*Avery v. State Farm*) against the State Farm insurance firm after receiving that firm's $1.35 million donation.[35]

Such incidents have become sufficiently commonplace for the American Bar Association to contend that there is "a pervasive public perception that campaign contributions influence judicial decision-making."[36] And surveys support that contention. Polling by the Brennan Center for Justice in October 2013, for instance, found that 87 percent of Americans believe contributions and independent political/issue advertising involving judicial candidates has some or a great deal of influence on court rulings.[37] Indeed, surveyed separately and anonymously, nearly one-half of the polled judges themselves agreed that rulings are sold at auction.

These contentions and perceptions are supported by facts. A variety of scholarly analyses have documented extensive vote buying by litigants before state courts, including:

- In 2013, law professor Joanna Shepherd examined 175,000 donations to state supreme court judges nationwide and found that elected judges chronically favor donors. As the share of contributions to judges from business interests rose from 1 percent to 50 percent of all donations received, for instance, the likelihood of the typical judge rendering probusiness rulings rose by 42 percentage points. Any firm—and especially those whose business model skirts regulations or the law—would be foolish indeed not to invest in a clutch of judges.[38] It is also revealing that judges on the verge of retirement abandon their donors. In a separate study, Shepherd and coauthor Michael Kang discovered: "In the last term before mandatory retirement, the favoritism toward business litigants by judges facing partisan and non-partisan elections essentially disappears."[39]

- The Center for American Progress examined the impact of pay-to-play on judicial rulings in states electing judges in the wake of *Citizens United*. It concluded, "In the span of a few short years, big business succeeded in transforming courts such as the Texas and Ohio Supreme Courts into forums where individuals face steep hurdles to holding corporations accountable."[40]

- In an analysis of the Ohio Supreme Court published in 2006 covering about 1,500 contested cases, a *New York Times* investigation documented that donors bought judicial rulings: "Its justices routinely sat on cases after receiving campaign contributions from the parties involved or from groups that filed supporting briefs. On average, they voted in favor of contributors 70 percent of the time." One justice voted in favor 91 percent of the time.[41] "The justices almost never disqualified themselves from hearing their contributors' cases."[42]

Palmer and Levendis: Donations Buy Judicial Rulings

Over a fourteen-year period (1992–2006), Tulane law professor Vernon Valentine Palmer and Loyola University professor John Levendis reviewed donor records and ensuing judicial decisions involving the seven Louisiana State Supreme Court justices. The scholars began with a statistical baseline revealing the justices' history of favoring plaintiffs or defendants in cases not involving contributors. About one-half of all cases did not involve contributors, and the justices tended to favor defendants in slightly more than one-half (53 percent) of those rulings, as reproduced in chart 7.2.

The remainder were cases where at least one litigant (or their litigator) was a donor but justices did not recuse (they almost never recused). The presence of donors as party to suits significantly changed voting behavior. When a preponderance of contributions had been received from the defendants' side, judges favored defendants in 67 percent of their rulings. But, when plaintiffs were the dominant donors, the judges supported defendants only 39 percent of the time. Overall, Palmer and Levendis

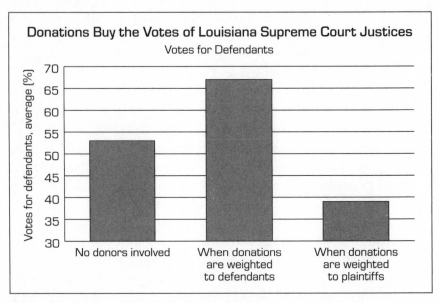

Chart 7.2 1992–2006 Donors buy court justice.

Vernon Valentine Palmer and John Levendis, "The Louisiana Supreme Court in Question: An Empirical and Statistical Study of the Effects of Campaign Money on the Judicial Function," *Tulane Law Review* 82 (2008), www.law.tulane.edu/uploaded-Files/Tulane_Journal_Sites/Tulane_Law_Review/docs/824palmer27.pdf

determined that buying judicial rulings was a sound investment. Political spending increased the bribers' odds of favorable court rulings by 26 percent: "The data indicate that judicial voting favors plaintiffs' or defendants' positions not on the basis of judicial leaning or philosophical orientation but on the basis of the size and timing of a political donation."[43]

Palast: Judges Acknowledge a Pay-to-Play Judicial System

On behalf of the reform group Justice at Stake, attorney Geri Palast compiled results from a 2002 survey by the Greenberg, Quinlan, Rosner Research firm. The survey included 2,428 judges serving on state supreme courts, appellate courts, and lower courts, nearly all subject to election. The survey was anonymous.

The responses revealed that a huge share of judges anonymously believed pay-to-play has created a two-tier American judicial system at the state level: 81 percent were concerned that America has one judicial system for the wealthy and powerful and another for everyone else.[44] As reproduced in chart 7.3, 46 percent of the justices candidly acknowledged that judicial votes are influenced by donors. Some 57 percent admitted to anxiety about obtaining sufficient donations in election years. And 84 percent acknowledged that special interest groups, corporations, and individuals use donations to influence judges and shape public policy. Some 56 percent of the judges agreed anonymously that "judges should be prohibited from presiding over and ruling in cases where one of the sides has given money to their campaign."[45]

Recusal Is Not a Remedy

The pervasiveness of vote buying means that recusal is not a feasible remedy to judicial bribery. Requiring recusal is popularly viewed as the solution to judicial pay-to-play. A Marist poll, for example, found that 87 percent of New Yorkers favored judicial recusal in instances involving donors that were litigants in a suit.[46] And the survey noted earlier conducted for the Brennan Center during October 2013 found an even larger 92 percent of respondents believed "when one party in a court case has either donated directly to a judge's campaign or spent significantly on election materials

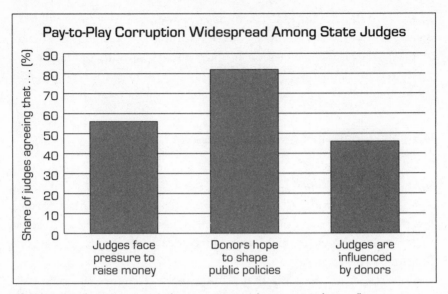

Chart 7.3 "When guaranteed anonymity, judges assert that . . ."

Geri Palast, "Justice at Stake," *American Viewpoint*, January 2002, www.justiceatstake.org/media/cms/JASJudgesSurveyResults_EA8838C0504A5.pdf

designed to help elect the judge, the judge should step aside:"[47] Finally, in the analysis of the Ohio Supreme Court noted earlier covering about 1,500 contested cases, the authors concluded: "In the 12 years that were studied, the justices almost never disqualified themselves from hearing their contributors' cases. In the 215 cases with the most direct potential conflicts of interest, for example, justices recused themselves just 9 times."[48]

Unfortunately, the prevalence of lax ethical standards has caused vote buying to become so embedded in state-level jurisprudence that recusal is now impractical. The Ohio Supreme Court justices participating in the 2006 study explained that requiring recusal in suits involving donor-litigants would be "a recipe for havoc," leaving far too few judges left to man courtrooms. The only feasible remedy is to bring a halt to the election of judges.

As we see next, the broad pattern of widespread vote buying that involves lawmakers and judges has sown deep cynicism about American democracy.

CHAPTER 8

The *Buckley* Era: Cynicism and Diminished Faith in Democracy

The appearance of influence or access . . . will not cause the electorate to lose faith in our democracy.[1]

> —Justice Anthony Kennedy, *Citizens United* majority opinion, 2010

Sixty-three percent of voters also still think most members of Congress are willing to sell their vote for either cash or a campaign contribution.[2]

> —Rasmussen survey, August 2014

It [harsh antigovernment rhetoric] did produce a deep cynicism that is an existential threat to democracy.[3]

—Eric O'Keefe, multimillionaire Republican party donor, March 2012

AMERICANS HAVE LOST FAITH in their democracy. In 1964, 77 percent of respondents to a Pew Research Center survey trusted the government in Washington "to do what is right just about always or most of the time." By 2015, only 19 percent believed that, a record low. The only less-trusted entities are big business (18 percent) and Congress (9 percent). It is the pay-to-play culture that most respondents view as responsible for the cynicism responsible for this plunge in confidence in American governance.[4] Indeed, 74 percent of Pew respondents agreed that "most elected officials put their own interests ahead of the country's interest."[5] Americans' high degree of distrust in politics reveals as sophistry the *Citizens United* majority opinion written by Justice Kennedy: "We now conclude that independent expenditures, including those made by corporations, do not give rise to corruption or the appearance of corruption . . . The appearance of influence or access . . . will not cause the electorate to lose faith in our democracy."[6]

The cynicism revealed by this Pew data suggests many Americans would view Kennedy as a fool. That attitude is both widespread and is a bipartisan phenomenon. Reproduced in chart 8.1, for instance, a *New York Times*/CBS News survey released in June 2015 found that supermajorities of Democrats, Republicans, and Independents alike believe that "money has too much influence" in politics. Moreover, a solid majority of the respondents were pessimistic that lawmakers would ever reform pay-to-play.[7]

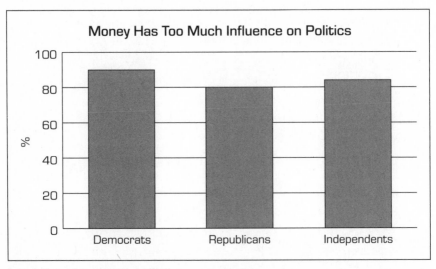

Chart 8.1 Share of respondents agreeing that . . .

Nicholas Confessore and Megan Thee-Brenan, "Poll Shows Americans Favor an Overhaul of Campaign Financing," *New York Times*, June 3, 2015; and "Americans' Views on Money in Politics," *New York Times*/CBS News poll, June 2, 2015.

Deep cynicism is even evident among American youth. Surveys by Professor Jennifer Lawless of American University and law professor Richard Fox of Loyola University found that pay-to-play politics "has turned off an entire generation." They polled 4,200 high school and college students during the 2012 election cycle. Some 85 percent did not think elected officials want to help people, with 60 percent convinced they are actually dishonest. In considering careers, "they'd rather do almost anything else" than run for political office.[8] As the former British Labor Party leader Ed Miliband noted, corrupted politics diminishes the spirit of community so vital to a generous, caring society because it "sends the message that anything goes, that right and wrong don't matter, that we can all be in it for ourselves as long as we can get away with it. What is a young person just starting out in life, trying to do the right thing, supposed to think when he sees a politician fiddling the expenses system, a banker raking off millions without deserving it, or a press baron abusing the trust of ordinary people?"[9]

Even the business community is dismayed by American democracy. A survey of hundreds of corporate leaders jointly by the business-supported Conference Board and the Committee for Economic Development in mid-2013 found extremely high levels of cynicism about American governance. Indeed, only 5 percent of respondents disagreed with the term "pay-to-play" to describe American democracy in the *Buckley* era. Virtually all (94 percent) agreed that pay-to-play causes "politicians to cast votes to please special interests rather than voters." Some 71 percent agreed that major donors have "too much influence on politicians," 79 percent agreed that the *Buckley* genre drives "politicians and political parties to be more extreme," and 83 percent believed pay-to-play is "contributing to Congressional inability to solve big problems the country is facing." Some 74 percent agreed that it is "harming our democracy."[10]

The growth of corporate political donations following the *Citizens United* ruling in 2010 exacerbated this cynicism. Surveys by the Rasmussen polling firm found that the share of Americans believing their elected representatives sell access and policy outcomes to donors rose from an already elevated 59 percent in 2006 to 79 percent in 2013.[11] One of the most detailed assessments of public attitudes toward corporate donations in the wake of that ruling is the October 2012 survey by the Corporate Reform

Coalition (CRC) noted in chapter 5. The survey found supermajorities of respondents believing that corporate donations and independent political expenditures make politics more negative and exacerbate corruption in state and federal government.[12] Reproduced in chart 8.2, 75 percent or more of CRC respondents believed donations induce Congress to reject laws protecting consumers, that corporate donations make politics more negative, and that they worsen Congressional corruption. Some 84 percent of respondents believed that corporate donations drown out the voices of ordinary voters. As with other surveys, this cynicism is bipartisan. At least 72 percent of every major political cohort—conservatives, liberals, independents, Democrats, and Republicans—believed that corporate political spending in any form is corrupting.

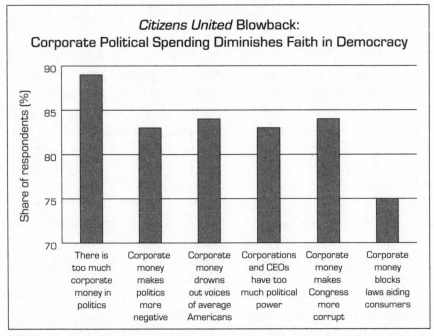

Chart 8.2 The business community recognizes the dangers posed by *Citizen United*.

Liz Kennedy, "Citizens Actually United: The Bi-partisan Opposition to Corporate Political Spending and Support for Common Sense Reform," *Demos*, October 25, 2012, www.demos.org/publication/citizens-actually-united-bi-partisan-opposition -corporate-political-spending-and-support

Perceived Congressional Corruption Creates Cynicism

Surveys and scholarly research have found that dismay with vote buying is centered on its impact on Congress. An expansive survey by political scientists at the University of Texas, for example, found that 82 percent of respondents agreed corruption in Congress was "very serious or somewhat serious" (chart 8.3). Two-thirds believed that members of Congress are dishonest. And two-thirds also believed that donations and independent political spending do ingratiate, belying Justice Kennedy's opinion.

Similar levels of cynicism are revealed by a number of Rasmussen surveys, including one conducted by telephone in February 2016, reproduced in chart 8.4 (next page). Supermajorities of respondents believe that wealthy individuals and American corporations "have too much influence over elections." And the level of cynicism is such that majorities are convinced their own representatives in Congress routinely sell votes for cash or campaign contributions regardless of constituent preferences.

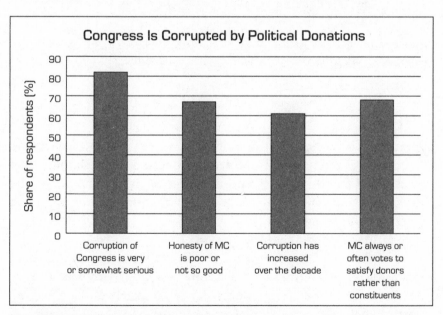

Chart 8.3 MC is Member of Congress (2009).

Money in Politics National Survey, November 3, 2009, reported by Ross Ramsey, "Americans Worry About Sources of Political Cash," *The Texas Tribune*, November 16, 2009, www.texastribune.org/2009/11/16/americans-worry-about-sources-of -political-cash/

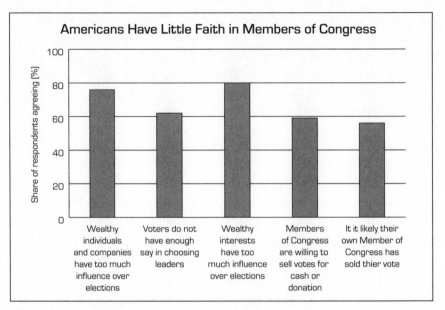

Chart 8.4 Their own member of Congress sells votes.

"Voters Say Money, Media Have Too Much Political Clout," *Rasmussen Reports*, February16, 2016, www.rasmussenreports.com/public_content/politics/general _politics/february_2016/voters_say_money_media_have_too_much_political_clout

International Comparisons

Supermajorities believe the American Congress and state courts are routinely suborned by donors. Moreover, Americans' perception of that corruption is the most severe self-assessment by citizens in any wealthy democracy—and on a par with government corruption as perceived domestically in countries such as Azerbaijan, Belize, India, Indonesia, Pakistan, Turkey, and Venezuela.

Berlin-based Transparency International (TI) is a world leader in monitoring, documenting, and advocating against government corruption. A global resource, TI produces an annual matrix of the perceived extent of public sector corruption in a number of nations, drawing on surveys of local citizens in each country. It measures "the degree to which corruption is perceived to exist among a country's public officials and politicians."

In 2015, the cynicism of Americans caused the United States to be ranked only sixteenth, worse than New Zealand, Singapore, Iceland, Canada, and a number of northern European nations. Since pay-to-play ballooned in the 1990s, America has never ranked better than fourteenth (in 2000). Indeed, in recent years, these domestic assessments have variously rated the US government as more corrupt than governments in Barbados or Hong Kong, just as corrupt as Uruguay, and only slightly less corrupt than governments in the Bahamas, Chile, and Qatar.[13]

The TI findings are affirmed by other global surveys, including the periodic Gallup World Polls. Among peer nations—those with a free press (earning the authoritative Freedom House *Media Freedom* status)—domestic surveys put the extent of corruption in American governance at a poor twenty-fifth in the Gallup 2015 evaluation.[14] The extent of what US respondents termed "widespread" corruption in American governance was more severe than the level perceived by respondents about their own governments in Belize, Estonia, Latvia, Malta, or Slovakia, and was tied with Mauritius.

TI also surveys domestic opinion in the hundred most developed nations regarding the extent of corruption specifically in national legislatures. The US Congress receives quite poor marks, reproduced in chart 8.5. The share of Americans asserting that Congress is either "corrupt or extremely corrupt" was twice that of respondents in northern European nations and on a par with local assessments of parliaments in India, Pakistan, and Venezuela.

The cynicism of Americans regarding their judiciary is just as severe as their rather dismal assessment of Congress. Chart 8.6 (page 121) is reproduced from the TI 2010/2011 Global Corruption Barometer survey asking locals to judge the degree of corruption exhibited by their domestic judiciaries. The share of Americans believing the US judiciary is corrupt or extremely corrupt—from the Supreme Court down to local courts—is 45 percent; that is on a par with the level of cynicism expressed by respondents in Azerbaijan or Indonesia. This share of cynical Americans is by far the highest of any wealthy democracy and higher than local opinion even in authoritarian Turkey (41 percent) or India (41 percent) where judicial bribery is also commonplace.

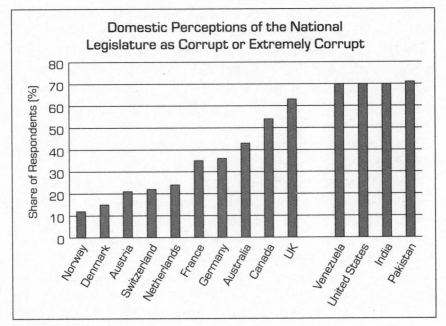

Chart 8.5 Congress viewed as corrupt as the Indian Parliament.

"Perception of Corruption," Domestic Share of Respondents Viewing Their National Legislature as "Corrupt" or "Extremely Corrupt," table 1b, Global Corruption Barometer 2010/2011, Transparency International, www.gcb.transparency.org/gcb201011/in_detail/

These sentiments are crystallized in the authoritative Freedom House assessment of the quality of national representative governance across the globe. Primarily for its weak electoral system and pay-to-play, the United States was stripped of its place in the first rank of democracies by Freedom House in 2016. The quality of its governance placed a woeful thirty-second behind nations such as Kiribati and Palau, its ranking on a par with Cape Verde and Costa Rica.[15]

Cynicism Caused by *Buckley* Empowers American Authoritarianism

Cynicism about the honesty of its lawmakers and jurists has caused Americans to question the values of democracy itself. A rather startling World Value Survey (WVS) reported by lead investigator Roberto Foa and

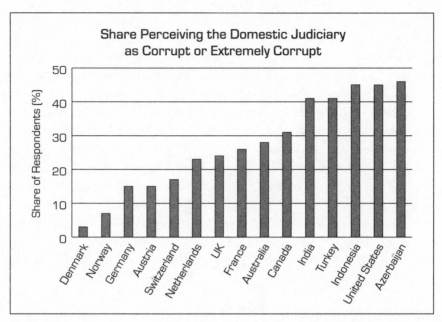

Chart 8.6 American courts viewed as corrupt as those in India and Turkey.

"Perception of Corruption," table 1b, Global Corruption Barometer 2010/2011, Transparency International, www.gcb.transparency.org/gcb201011/in_detail/

Yascha Mounk of Harvard found rising support between 1995 and 2011 among Americans for authoritarian government (chart 8.7). This increase certainly reflects a high level of dismay and frustration with pay-to-play in Congress and the courts. But it also likely reflects dismay with the betrayal by political elites of economic expectations of average Americans: profits rise briskly as wages stagnate, high value jobs are offshored, economic mobility dwindles, and income disparities worsen. Even so, it is stunning that fewer than half (46.5 percent) of American respondents in the WVS agreed it is "absolutely important" to even live in a democracy.[16] That is the lowest share among citizens of any wealthy democracy. Even more dismaying, it is a lower share than in nearly *any* other democracy, including quite imperfect ones such as Armenia, Cyprus, Qatar, Romania, South Africa, Tunisia, Uruguay, and Uzbekistan.[17]

At 32 percent, the share of Americans in July 2016 who supported a strong leader dispensing with elections and Congress was not a fringe group. This support is considerably more pronounced among Republicans, who also came to increasingly admire Russian President Vladimir Putin during the course of the 2016 election. Only 12 percent of Republicans polled by Gallup viewed the murderous Putin favorably in 2015. But Russian meddling in the 2016 election, candidate Trump's embrace of that meddling, and his surprising win may well be responsible for normalizing Putin with GOP supporters. Putin's favorability rating tripled to 37 percent among Republican respondents in a YouGov/*Economist* survey in December 2016 (also chart 8.7).

Recall that during the campaign, Donald Trump urged the Russian government to release hacked information casting Hillary Clinton in an unfavorable light. Earlier, his oldest son, son-in-law, and campaign manager met with four Russians promising confidential Kremlin information embarrassing to Clinton as "part of Russia and its government's support for Mr. Trump."[18] This interference reflected the Kremlin's tactic (in France,

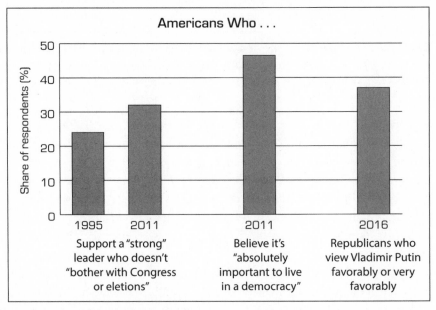

Chart 8.7 Share of respondents (%) . . .

Live in Democracy: World Value Survey, Wave 6 (question 140). Strong leader: Roberto S. Foa and Yascha Mounk, "The Danger of Deconsolidation," *Journal of Democracy*, 27:3 (July 2016), 13. Putin: Mary Pascaline, "Putin's Popularity Among Republicans Soars: Poll," *International Business Times*, December 15, 2016, www .yahoo.com/news/putin-popularity-among-republicans-soars-094921610.html

Germany, the Netherlands, and elsewhere as well as the United States) to aggressively bombard voters with misinformation during elections.

American intelligence agencies have concluded that the Russians intervened in the 2016 election for two reasons. First, Putin sought to enhance electoral gain for candidate Trump (as reviewed in chapter 14) by demonizing Hillary Clinton.[19] His second objective more broadly was to deploy fake news to spin corruption and conspiracy theories that besmirched the democratic process itself. Psychology professor Karen Douglas at the University of Kent in Britain explained Putin's logic: "Therefore rather than empowering people to stand up and act on perceived injustices, conspiracy theories appear to make them disengage and instead do nothing. They seem to erode trust in politicians and institutions and lead to apathy rather than action. Why would people want to vote for a political system that they think is constantly committing crimes and hiding information from the public?"[20]

While the impact of Putin's strategy on the 2016 election will never be known, it is certainly evident that Americans are relatively cynical regarding the values of democracy. Overall, the share of Americans who reject democracy is more than double the share in the wealthy democracies of Europe.[21] That sentiment includes right-wing fringe groups such as white supremacists empowered by President Trump in the wake of the Charlottesville riot. More problematic, it includes too many American youths. Those who consider a democratic system to be a "bad" or "very bad" way to run a nation are only a fringe among youths aged 12 to 24 in peer nations, but reflect the opinions of nearly 25 percent of American youths.[22]

The greater support for democracy in northern Europe reflects their historical experience with fascism and communism. But it also reflects in some measure the more robust economic outcomes yielded by these higher quality democracies. Their citizens have a lifetime of experience with the practices of home-grown firms. These include prioritizing the creation of high-value domestic jobs and steadily rising real wages—practices demanded by lawmakers in Germany and elsewhere responding to the preferences of voters.

The lower quality of American democracy enables US firms to eschew such practices. And foreign investment by American multinationals in recent decades has enabled Canadians and northern Europeans to experience firsthand the consequential behaviors and antics of US enterprises. Those antics had soured them on the America variant of capitalism even before the 2016 election outcome.

CHAPTER 9

International Dismay with the Variant of Capitalism Produced by Low-Quality American Democracy

[England is] being shown a thing or two by its German rivals about fostering young talent, learning from mistakes and planning for the long term . . . The ascent, on and off the pitch, has not been lost on UK observers, with policymakers across the political spectrum looking to Germany for economic inspiration.[1]

—Chris Bryant, Brian Groom, Michael Steen, and James Wilson, *Financial Times*, May 2013

[T]he United States, by many of the standard indicators of inequality, is now the most unequal long-standing democracy in a developed country in the world.[2]

—Alfred Stepan and Juan Linz, *Perspective on Politics*, December 2011

AMAZON IS AN EXEMPLAR of American-style capitalism, seizing market share in America and Europe in numerous business lines. Its profits are built on process and product innovation but also on vigorous wage suppression. The lack of voter sovereignty in American permits it to pursue practices that are forbidden to competitors in higher quality democracies. At home, it exploits loopholes in labor laws first opened by the Reagan administration to commoditize its work force—combining weak wages, paltry benefits, and low job security with manifest hostility to labor unions and collective bargaining. An investigation by the *New York Times* in 2015 highlighted Amazon's bruising worksite culture, centered on generating workplace stress—with supervisors encouraging conflict and peer criticism between workers to spur more innovation.

Amazon lugs this same culture overseas wherever it can. The sharp contrast of its practices with those of firms in higher quality democracies engenders resentment abroad from even surprising quarters. For instance, Amazon is a large employer in the former coal mining town of Rugeley in Staffordshire, England. It was a dying town that initially heartily welcomed the new mail-order jobs. The District Council's economic development manager, Glenn Watson, has since become dismayed by Amazon's culture: "They're not seen as a good employer . . . Our definition of a good employer is someone who takes on people and provides them with sustainable employment week in week out, not somebody who takes on workers one week and gets rid of them the next . . . We had no idea Amazon was going to be as indifferent to these issues as they have been. It's come as a shock to us how intransigent they are."[3]

The treatment of employees by Amazon in Germany is similar. Amazon provides its German employees with scant benefits and a pay scale that's 25 percent below prevailing employer–employee agreements for similar mail-order work. And to keep it that way, Amazon relentlessly fights German unions seeking to organize its employees. That stonewalling also enables it to install US-style gig-employment practices, including reliance on low-paid, insecure, temp jobs as in Rugeley; the temporary employee share of Amazon's German workforce is double that at competitors such as Otto or Hermes Fulfillment.[4]

Nor is Amazon an exception. Other nameplate firms like Apple and Honeywell also pursue the same strategy of suppressing wages and resisting collective bargaining. In Australia in 2016, for example, Coca-Cola incited a nationwide boycott with plans to cut wages for its fifty-six higher-wage employees at its Abbotsford facility. The plans were withdrawn, but Coca-Cola did not learn a lesson. In 2017, Coca-Cola promised a hefty immediate retirement bonus if senior workers at its Richlands, Australia, bottling facility agreed to weaker rules and double-digit wage cuts for junior colleagues—a tactic one labor leader termed "a real mate against mate scenario . . . They're trying to get rid of an existing workforce (as at Abbotsford) and hire people to do the same job at a hell of a lot less pay . . . They're going to cop a huge decrease in earnings over their lifetime."[5]

American multinationals like Amazon and Coca-Cola despise the high-wage and collaborative stakeholder capitalism in the higher quality democracies of Australia, Canada, and much of Europe. Yet, in order to gain access to the richest consumer markets on earth, they have been forced to reach some accommodation with the European middle-class economic model. Across the EU, for example, there are more than 1,050 domestic and foreign firms with works councils covering 19 million employees. (Recall that works councils are labor/management committees that substitute for what would be midmanagement in US firms.) Some 171 of these firms are US multinationals, because any non-European firm with more than 150 employees in two or more EU nations must establish works councils. It has been a positive experience, with many American managers proving able to operate profitably in the EU high-wage environment where collaboration between workers and management is the norm. Works councils cannot dictate pay or avoid job layoffs, but as a former UK Minister for Europe explains, "they are an important mechanism for workers employed by the same firm to keep in touch and for the senior managers to hear about and try and resolve problems before they turn conflictual."[6]

US firms have proven far more hostile to the concept of codetermination, commonplace among all large firms in nineteen nations of the EU. By law, corporate boards of directors at larger firms in these nations must include employee representatives.[7] One-half of the directors at every German firm you can name, for instance, are elected by employees while the other half are elected by shareholders. This collaboration by employees and employers is more than fifty years old. It has a stabilizing influence and accounts for the longer term business horizon and superior investment performance of European firms compared to their US competitors. It explains why job offshoring is rare in Europe, as noted earlier, and why rising real wages, sound benefits, employee up-skilling, and secure retirements are common.[8] Employees in nations like Denmark, France, and Germany earn more per hour, with wages broadly set through collective bargaining. That's why they have enjoyed real wage gains since 1981 that vastly exceed the gains made by 95 percent of US employees. And recall that more of them work than in America.

High Wages, No Employee Subsidies

The higher wages, greater economic mobility, and superior living stan-dards compared to the United States reflect the higher quality of democ-racy in northern Europe. European voters demand that firms pay well enough to avoid taxpayers having to subsidize their employees. In contrast, the US Congress pays little heed to middle-class concerns or raising wages, more focused on the agenda of the *fittest fifty*. They enhance profits by permitting firms to pay unduly low wages, insisting that taxpayers make up the difference by funding food stamps, Medicaid, and the like used by their poorly paid employees. The consequence is that wages at the largest US employers such as fast food firms or Walmart are so low that hun-dreds of thousands of their employees routinely rely on public assistance. Economists have concluded that taxpayers provide nearly $7 billion in food stamps, Medicaid, Children's Health Insurance, and other income supplements for fast food employees.[9] Data on Walmart is rare, but equally revealing: some 15,246 Walmart employees in Ohio, for example, during 2009 relied on Medicaid and 12,731 utilized food stamps.[10] And Walmart employees in Wisconsin receive more than $5,800 apiece annually in tax-payer funded Medicaid benefits, according to *Business Week*.[11] Overall, Americans for Tax Fairness found that Walmart employees receive as much as $6.2 billion in taxpayer funds annually for food, health, and other low-income supports.[12]

Too many of the *fittest fifty* believe that too much is never enough, exemplified by the four major Walton heirs. Their fortunes rose by $20.9 billion between March 2014 and March 2015. For one-half that amount, each Walmart employee could have received a $5-per-hour raise, ending all taxpayer subsidies.[13]

Foreign Distrust of American Enterprises

Informed by the practices of home-grown firms, exposure to the practices commonplace with American multinationals have caused Canadians and Europeans to grow wary, viewing them with nearly the same trepidation they reserve for Chinese firms. The reputation of American firms abroad reflects the antics of firms such as Amazon but also lingering memories of practices at US firms like Walmart before it abandoned the German market a decade or so ago. Walmart departed in disgrace for encouraging employees at its eighty-five stores to eavesdrop on one another, their policy reminiscent of Soviet and fascist regimes from recent history. In combination with Walmart's attempts to undercut the German wage structure, such antics proved simply too much for continental consumers.[14] They shopped at competitors they considered better corporate citizens.

The poor reputation of American-style capitalism in Europe also reflects behavior like that of the US auto firm Molex. It closed its factory in Villemur-sur-Tarn, Haute-Garonne, in October 2009, leaving unpaid about €4 million ($4.4 million) in wages to its nearly three hundred French employees. Not only did it embarrassingly haul away valuable equipment in the middle of the night, Molex subsequently reported record profits, including paying out a 14 percent dividend.[15]

Bitterness and recriminations have also followed the takeover of local enterprises abroad by US firms. Eager to acquire cutting edge railway locomotion technology, for example, Caterpillar purchased Electro-Motive Canada from General Motors in 2010. GM had paid Canadian-scale wages in line with European wages at Electro-Motive that were well above US wages. Caterpillar's takeover calculations included reaping savings with large wage cutbacks to US levels. Despite record profits in 2011, Caterpillar demanded significant wage concessions from its new Canadian employees soon after the purchase. In the common American style, its demands featured a threat to close Electro-Motive and transfer its technology to a plant in a lower-wage country—Muncie, Indiana, in this instance. Canadian employees resisted and Caterpillar promptly closed the plant. Also in the usual American style, Caterpillar demanded that fired Canadian employees first train their foreign (American) low-wage replacements. Rachel Mendleson of *Huffington Post Canada* explained Caterpillar's tactics this way: "Contract talks broke down after union leaders refused a deal that would have cut benefits and slashed wages by more than half, from $35 to $16.50 per hour, giving rise to rumors that the company was planning to shift operations to a newly opened plant in Muncie, Ind., where workers are paid between $12 and $18 an hour."[16]

Many US multinationals are innovative, some remarkably so. But virtually all behave like the blue-chip firms Amazon, Caterpillar, and Coca-Cola. They dodge regulations, provide extravagant executive compensation too often delinked from performance, are serial practitioners of the independent contractor and gig-employment scams to lower wages, buy votes in Congress and the courts with donations, are serial tax dodgers utilizing foreign tax havens, are chronic exporters of high-value jobs, and strongly resist collective bargaining to suppress wages and spike profits.

Foreign observers have tumbled to these pathologies and logically have come to distrust American firms. Evidence comes from an expansive database compiled by the Edelman public relations firm. As an occasional element of its annual surveys, it garners opinion toward American firms by informed citizens in northern Europe, Canada, and elsewhere; respondents are described by the *Financial Times* as "well-educated, highly paid and engaged 25–64 year olds."[17] The surveys reveal that "US Companies Have a Trust Deficit in Europe." In a detailed 2006 Edelman survey, for example, reproduced as chart 9.1, about 70 percent of elite Germans trusted the management and boards of German or Canadian firms "to do the right thing," by sharing their prosperity with employees and customers; only 41 percent had the same trust in leadership of American firms. Indeed, the behavior of American management is viewed with only slightly more favor than that anticipated from the owners of Chinese firms. American firms were consistently ranked as markedly less trustworthy than either Canadian firms or indigenous firms by elites in Canada, France, Germany, and the United Kingdom.[18]

The trust deficit documented in chart 9.1 also applied to specific iconic American firms. The 2006 Edelman survey found that its European respondents had a significant trust deficit with major US corporations such as Coca-Cola, General Electric, Johnson & Johnson, McDonald's, and Starbucks. That distrust means foreign observers view these firms considerably less favorably than do Americans themselves. Some 65 percent of American participants in the survey viewed Coca-Cola as trustworthy, for example, while only 41 percent of European respondents did so (chart 9.2).[19] The marks for McDonald's were particularly low. As professor Tony Royle at the National University of Ireland explains, its outlets in Europe have become notorious for resisting collective bargaining, violating wage standards, manipulating low-wage programs intended solely for trainees, and ignoring labor regulations. Like Amazon or Walmart, that firm is determined to exploit loopholes to pay American-style wages rather than higher European ones.[20]

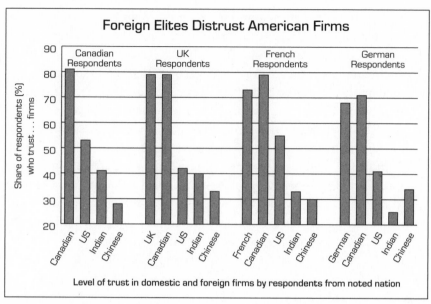

Chart 9.1 Responses to "How Much Do You Trust Global Companies Headquartered in the Following Countries to Do What Is Right?"

2006 Annual Edelman Trust Barometer, "Trust in Companies Headquartered in Other Countries," www.edelman.edelman1.netdna-cdn.com/assets/uploads/2014/01/2006 -Trust-Barometer-Global-Results.pdf

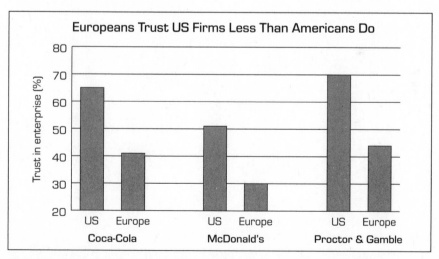

Chart 9.2 Responses to "Do You Trust [firm] to Do the Right Thing?"

2006 Annual Edelman Trust Barometer, "Trust in Companies Headquartered in Other Countries."

Jaundiced sentiment about American business practices based on unfavorable comparisons with domestic firms is pervasive in other wealthy democracies, including Canada. The prospect of a takeover of local firms by American ones is thus viewed with alarm. The 2006 Edelman survey included questions on the extent of unease should American, European, Chinese, South Korean, or Indian firms seek to acquire local firms. The degree of dismay at the prospect of US takeovers was dramatically worse than for firms from any other wealthy democracy, including Japanese firms. Only potential takeovers by Chinese firms were viewed with more concern (chart 9.3). Indeed, respondents in Canada, Germany, the United Kingdom, and France viewed American takeovers with *more* mistrust than they did takeovers by firms from India; they prefer local firms being taken over by Indian corporations than by American corporations. Overall, among Germans, the intensity of dismay should US firms buy out German firms was a stunning twenty-two times greater than for Japanese

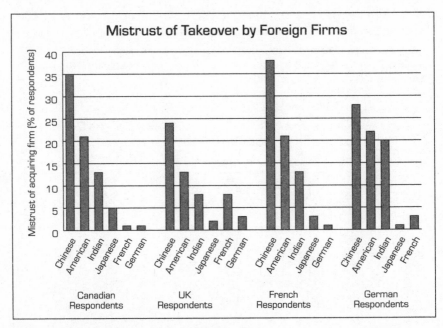

Chart 9.3 Mistrust of takeover by foreign firms.

2006 Annual Edelman Trust Barometer, page 13, "Mistrust in Foreign Companies Acquiring National Companies," www.yooyahcloud.com/MOSSCOMMUNICATIONS/ftFsP/Edelman_Trust_Barometer.pdf

takeovers, and five to seven times greater than for takeovers by firms from their historic adversaries in France or Britain.

Europeans are decidedly unimpressed with the wages, job security, and other labor practices of US firms chiseled by Ronald Reagan and Ayn Rand onto tablets atop Mont Pelerin. When asked if "Europe's economy should be more like that of the United States," in a *Financial Times*/Harris poll in September 2007, 78 percent of Germans and 73 percent of French respondents replied no.

SECTION 3

Achieving Political Equality

CITIZENS IN HIGHER QUALITY democracies benefit economically from legislative decisions ensuring that the gains from growth are widely broadcast. They see an America superficially much like their own countries, but burdened with a system of decriminalized political bribery that permits powerful economic interests to readily prey on most citizens. Political equality is poor, with one political party even aggressively disenfranchising voters. Voter sovereignty is weak. This profile of America highlights the tenuous nature of high-quality democracy, Piketty's endless inegalitarian spiral always lurking.[1]

Ending Piketty's spiral by improving wages, job security, and the like hinges on raising the quality of American democracy. Political practices responsible for a higher quality of democracy abroad start with the criminalization of vote buying. While necessary, that step alone is insufficient. Higher quality democracies also feature electoral characteristics that empower political equality, particularly multiple-member legislative districts, runoff voting for national leaders, mandatory voting as in Australia, and proportional representation in legislatures (what political scientists term "single vote transferable electoral vote systems").

The various electoral policies and practices utilized abroad to corral economic elites and sustain political equality begin this section.

CHAPTER 10

Other Wealthy Democracies
Corral Oligarchs

Britain's Parties Should be Funded [entirely] by the State.[1]

— *Financial Times* editorial, February 2015

Our politicians hire American electoral advisers as though
Washington and Westminster were comparable polities. When
they arrive, they see they cannot buy television advertising, or raise
serious sums of money, or treat the election as a two-party race, and
they quietly recede.[2]

— Janan Ganesh, *Financial Times,* April 2015

In comparison to the US, the UK has what appears to be a tough set
of controls on campaign spending.[3]

— Jacob Rowbottom, *The New Republic,* 2011

A S WE HAVE SEEN in earlier chapters, the American election system is
a stark outlier among wealthy democracies. Nearly all other wealthy
democracies tightly proscribe campaign contributions and independent
political spending to prevent political inequality, the distortion of public
opinion, and corrupted lawmakers. Another goal is to prevent American-
style polarization caused by negative advertising. The particulars vary,
but nearly all mimic Germany and the United Kingdom in preventing

pay-to-play by sharply capping electioneering campaign spending. With far less scope for electioneering spending than in America, candidates and political parties have far less legitimate need for donations. Moreover, peer nations also subsidize candidates and small donors to further free political parties and candidates from reliance on large donors.

These higher quality democracies also restrict political TV and radio advertising opportunities, with those limited opportunities usually provided free or inexpensively. Campaigns are limited to a few months in duration as well. In addition, corporations and entities that are independent of candidates and political parties (similar to Warren Buffett or the Koch brothers' Americans for Prosperity) are prohibited or strictly circumscribed from contributing to, or purchasing political speech during elections on behalf of politicians or policies. Thus, American-style negative advertising on TV and elsewhere is absent, with the glaring exception everywhere of social media.

Taken together, this policy array in higher quality democracies affords candidates abundant communication resources while maximizing political equality and individual free speech rights. Any person can speak freely for as long as they choose on any street corner or soapbox on nearly any subject.

The Fittest in Other Wealthy Democracies Cannot Outshout Neighbors

There are tight limits on electioneering spending by parties or candidates in higher quality democracies. For instance, the nationwide campaign spending by German chancellor Angela Merkel in 2013 was $27 million.[4] It was even lower in France in 2012 and 2017. Other tight limits apply to citizen donations and independent spending. Voters in other wealthy democracies are comfortable with such tight caps. They would be shocked if opaque, powerful groups could spend unlimited amounts of money for years to mold public opinion and influence election outcomes—or if individuals such as Sheldon Adelson or Paul Singer were allowed to speak with the voice of tens of millions.

Pay-to-play is rejected because peer nations strive mightily to guarantee political equality and voter sovereignty while nurturing a consensus--driven political middle by supporting electoral and representational integrity. They covet these *desiderata* as pillars of a prosperous democracy rather than as the niceties or novelties they are to the American eye. Indeed, peer nations are so determined to avoid vote buying that even the *Financial Times*—Britain's equivalent of the *Wall Street Journal*—rather remarkably demanded in a 2015 editorial that private contributions be entirely abolished, with British politics funded solely by taxpayers: "If the political class at Westminster is to have any chance of winning back public trust, it needs to end the suspicion that the culture of political donations is corruptible. The only way to do this is a system of taxpayer funding . . ."[5]

It's ironic that Britain—the abhorred example of political corruption for colonial Americans—has come to hew far more closely than America to both the political equality proclaimed by the Declaration of Independence and the original intent of the founding fathers and the framers to excise all political corruption, defined most broadly.

The success of Britain and other wealthy nations in corralling Aristotle's oligarchs and crafting high-quality democracies is a consequence of two centuries of revolution, debate, and contemplation. It has taken almost that long to devise their refined political systems which maximize and equilibrate individual political freedom, rendering voters sovereign. Precluding vote buying by strictly limiting the need for donations has emerged as the time-tested technique to ensure that citizens are equally heard and equally heeded by lawmakers. Some go further and actually impose de jure limits on the amount of donations by individuals and independent entities, while others such as Britain don't bother. It makes no practical difference because the operational key preventing pay-to-play is national caps on electioneering spending. Candidates or their parties cannot legally spend many tens of millions of dollars American-style to win political office.

Australia is the only wealthy democracy other than the United States to allow unlimited political donations and independent third-party political spending, including by corporations. The similarities end there, however, because Australian pay-to-play is on a tiny scale. The ten biggest donor corporations, for instance, contributed a total of US$3 million during the 2016 general election there—a rounding error in American pay-to-play.[6] The other Anglo-Saxon nations (Canada, New Zealand, and Britain) follow the high-quality democracies of Europe in severely limiting overall electioneering spending—de facto or de jure tightly capping

campaign donations and independent spending while prohibiting corporate donations.

(Genuine) Free Speech

We saw earlier that Roberts Republicans conflate the First Amendment
guarantee of speech *content* with speech *volume* or amount. They do so by
treating money as having the same validity as speech, thereby enabling the
fittest to insist that limits on their political contributions and independent
spending amount to censorship of constitutionally protected free speech.
Their self-serving claims would be jeered at in nearly all other democracies. Limits on the donor class in wealthy democracies such as Canada
are not considered censorship because the caps serve to maximize speech
equality and thus maximize individual speech rights. In other wealthy
democracies, the right of individual citizens to say their piece as often as
possible is a political foundation. The German versions of Charles Koch
can opine endlessly on street corners and elsewhere, but they cannot rent
a sound-truck or purchase TV spots to drown out their neighbors' opinions. As of this writing, however, the *fittest fifty* can purchase unlimited
exposure on social media, a deficiency discussed later.

How well does this formulation abroad maximize individual speech
rights? Well, the conservative Freedom House's iconic "Freedom in the
World" index grants these peers the same perfect scores awarded the
United States under all three of its free speech categories—"Freedom,"
"Political Rights," and "Civil Liberties."[7]

Political Systems in Other Wealthy Democracies

As noted, limits on electioneering spending in nearly all peer nations are
set sufficiently low to obviate the need for large donations. Tobias Döring
and Christof Kerkmann writing in the Düsseldorf-based *Handelsblatt*
described the feverish final weeks in the 2013 German elections this way:
"The election campaign is in the final sprint. Billboards, online advertising and a lot of pens."[8]

More than seventy nations further reduce the need for private campaign donations by providing candidates with public funding to defray
electioneering costs. The goal is to avail citizens of a factual, full airing

of genuine policy differences between candidates and between political parties. The outcome is robust and highly competitive elections where the weight of ideas and policy prescriptions are determinant rather than weight of wallet.

European nations provide candidates and their political parties an average of about $5 per voter in public funding with the greatest level at $15 in Norway.[9] Such subsidies represent about 40 percent of spending by candidates and political parties over an election cycle. In France, for instance, public subsidies equal 47.5 percent of permitted electioneering spending.[10] The balance of campaign funding is derived from small donations, typically incentivized by tax credit as in Canada, France, and Germany. Political parties in Germany garnering 0.5 percent of votes for Bundestag (federal) candidates receive €1 ($1.10) for each of their first 4 million votes and 83 cents per vote received thereafter, with an upper cap on tax credits granted for individual and total donations.[11]

Combining a limited need for campaign donations with public funding has successfully freed lawmakers from reliance on wealthy contributors. The proof is voter sovereignty: Policy outcomes of other wealthy democracies do not reflect an American-style income bias. Cynics argue that political bribery is so profitable that money inevitably leeches into politics regardless of rules. But that assertion is belied by evidence in peer nations of the efficacy of their comprehensive monitoring and their aggressive enforcement of spending rules. Indeed, exposés of dubious campaign finance practices routinely cause electoral blowback: Voters in these nations harshly punish parties or candidates who appear implicated in vote buying. For instance, disgusted Germans voted out the entire Free Democratic Party's (FDP) parliamentary delegation following a donation exposé in 2013. The FDP had opened a tax loophole after receiving a €1 million contribution from August von Finck, the billionaire owner of the Mövenpick hotel empire.[12]

Here are specifics from the UK, Canada, and Northern European electoral systems.

United Kingdom

Total electioneering spending per campaign in the United Kingdom is capped by law at about $150 million. That includes spending by parliamentary candidates, which is capped at £39,400 (about $50,000) apiece plus a 9 pence (11 cents) per-voter bonus. A separate nationwide cap of £19.5 million ($24 million) exists for each major political party over the year concluding on Election Day.[13] Quite remarkably, these caps have remained in that neighborhood (in inflation-adjusted terms) for 135 years since political spending was first limited by the 1883 reforms to end vote buying. You read that date correctly. Electioneering spending since then has been capped at about one-half the cost of the 1880 campaign, with no evident deterioration in British democracy.[14] These limits, of course, are a tiny fraction of US spending. The amount spent in the last English national campaign roughly equals the political spending during the 2014 midterm election in the state of Georgia.[15] And more was spent by candidates Obama and Romney *raising* money in 2012 than was spent in *total* by the two major British political parties.[16]

In further dramatic contrast with the United States, where candidates rush to reserve popular TV times and digital access, candidates in England rush to reserve, well, scarce billboards. Political advertising is restricted to leaflets, canvassing, billboards, and social media, supplemented with free but limited TV time and one free mass mailing to every residence. Like nearly every other wealthy democracy, political spending by independent entities, including donations, advertising, or issue advocacy, is limited. The specific UK cap on such independent spending per entity nationwide (such as Warren Buffett or Charles Koch) is £988,000 ($1,200,000) during the entire one-year period concluding with Election Day.[17] *New York Times* journalist Steven Castle explains the impact of this system:

> In a country where television election spots are banned, billboards are booked long before voting day, and other strict laws constrain election spending, that task proved so hard that the [UKIP] party says it is unlikely to use all the money before Britons go to the polls . . . Campaigning in Britain remains local, with candidates pounding the streets, knocking on doors, issuing leaflets and sending mail. Even these expenditures have to be recorded in minute detail and submitted to the election authorities. Spending limits also apply to organizations like charities or unions that want to campaign ahead of elections.[18]

Like Canada and its richer European neighbors, Britain finances elections with a blend of state subsidies allocated on a per capita basis, supplemented with private donations that are tightly capped by law at small amounts.[19] This array of regulations devised since 1883 prevent the British *fittest* from influencing elections—with the exception of press barons like Rupert Murdoch, as noted later.

Even so, the United Kingdom's electoral system shares two features with America that reduce the quality of its democracy. Parliamentarians represent single-member districts—giving rise to both millions of wasted votes and gerrymandering. Single-member districts mean all voters for the loser are unrepresented in the legislature, unlike outcomes in proportional representation systems, discussed later, that are common in higher quality democracies. Proportional systems also prevent gerrymandering.

Canada

Like Britain, Canada caps donations for national elections, including parliamentary contests. A few provinces such as British Columbia do permit large donations to candidates seeking provincial or local offices. In contrast, donation limits for such contests in other provinces (Alberta, Manitoba, Nova Scotia, Ontario, and Quebec) are much tighter than national limits.[20]

Electioneering spending is also limited in Canada to reduce the need for private campaign donations.[21] For candidates in the general election in October 2015, for instance, the caps on electioneering spending varied by population in each Riding (electoral district), but averaged slightly over C$200,000 ($150,000) for individual federal parliamentary candidates. The cap was C$55 million ($43 million) for each of the leading political parties or in the neighborhood of C$250 million combined for all parties. The entirety of political advertising on television is limited to about ten hours during the two to three months of campaigning, with some airtime provided free.[22] Political TV ads purchased by independent third parties are permitted but severely limited in number. Consequently, Canadians are subject to a fraction of the number of 30-second political spots that Americans see. Their *nationwide* total is equivalent to what viewers in some US media markets experience over a *weekend* in election season.[23] Such caps are prevalent across continental Europe as well. In Germany for instance, Chancellor Merkel's campaign sponsored a total of 140 TV ads in 2013, compared to 100,000 by President Obama in 2012 just in Ohio.[24]

Note that these electioneering spending caps are ceilings. Actual Canadian outlays traditionally are lower because amounts hinge on the good graces of small donors. That means amounts spent by individual candidates and parties in elections vary a great deal depending on their popularity, although major party candidates tend to achieve a rough spending parity. Like other higher quality democracies, Canada provides public funding to ensure that all candidates who qualify for the ballot have adequate communications opportunity. The subsidies can total as much as one-half of all permitted spending by political parties and up to 60 percent of permitted spending by candidates themselves.[25]

Individual campaign contributions are limited to no more than C$4,575 (US$3,400) per annum (indexed for inflation), including C$1,525 in total permitted to be donated to political parties, up to another C$1,525 to candidate(s), and another C$1,525 to candidates should an intraparty leadership contest occur.[26] Donors of more than C$200 must be identified by name. Donors of more than C$200 to independent outside entities must also appear on all ensuing political advertising. Wealthy candidates are limited to just C$5,000 in contributions to their own campaigns.[27]

Independent political spending by outside entities is also strictly limited. If George Soros and the Koch brothers were Canadians, they would have been limited to donations or spending in 2015 of slightly more than C$208,200 (US$155,000).[28] Note that these caps apply for the usual thirty-seven day campaign; they were adjusted upward proportionately in 2015 because the general election ran seventy-eight days.[29] Perhaps Canada's largest remaining loophole is that huge donations are still permitted to foundations or universities favored by politicians.[30] Such donations can obviously curry favor.

Donors to independent entities must be publicly identified. Moreover, the definition of political spending and donations subject to these rules utilized by Elections Canada (the federal election supervisor) is encompassing. It covers any political spending involving the "transmission to the public by any means during any election period of an advertising message that promotes or opposes a registered party or the election of a candidate, including one that takes a position on an issue with which a registered party or candidate is associated."[31]

Elections Canada is vigilant for attempts by wealthy political activists to use independent entities to bypass spending limits: "A third party shall not circumvent, or attempt to circumvent, a limit set out in section 350 in any manner, including by splitting itself into two or more third parties for the purpose of circumventing the limit or acting in collusion with another third party so that their combined election advertising expenses exceed the limit" (section 351, Canadian Elections Act).[32] Conservatives have pleaded with the Canadian Supreme Court to nullify these limits on independent political spending in hopes of enabling American-style PACs to flourish. Very much unlike America, however, Canadian electoral jurisprudence is nonpartisan, mirroring that of nearly all other higher quality democracies, and has consistently affirmed support of independent spending limits. The Court's logic is explained in the landmark ruling *Harper v. Canada* (2004):

> Unlimited third party advertising can undermine election fairness in several ways. First, it can lead to dominance of political discourse by the wealthy . . . Second it may allow political parties and candidates to circumvent their own spending limits through the creation of third parties. Third, unlimited third party spending can have an unfair effect on the outcome of an election. Fourth, the absence of limits on third party advertising expenses can erode the confidence of the Canadian electorate who perceive the electoral process as being dominated by the wealthy.[33]

Western Europe

As in Canada and the UK, electioneering spending limits are commonplace in the wealthy democracies of Europe. Total spending by all Swiss political parties in the run-up to the 2011 general election was SF44 million ($50 million), for instance.[34] In France, each political party in the 2017 presidential campaign was capped at €16.8 million ($18 million) and another €22.5 million ($24 million) for the binary runoff.[35] Political party spending is limited in Italy by law to €96 million ($105 million), funded with a blend of private donations and public subsidies (tied per capita to votes and donations received).[36] In Germany as noted, caps held the reelection campaign spending of German chancellor Angela Merkel in 2013 to $27 million. German spending by legislative candidates is also capped. For example, total nationwide electioneering spending by Merkel's entire Christian Democratic Union slate four years earlier involving campaigns for 598 parliament races, six state legislatures, and numerous regional and municipal elections was $112 million.[37] That is not much more than the $93 million that Sheldon Adelson alone spent in 2012 and less than one-sixth of the $750 million spent over the 2016 election cycle by the Koch political behemoth.

Caps on independent spending mean that American-style purchased speech is either nonexistent or quite limited in Europe, Canada, and Britain. Candidates inform voters utilizing free or inexpensive TV advertising, supplemented by print, social media, canvassing, leaflets, and billboards. Campaign lengths are limited, reaching sixty days in France, up to seventy-eight days in Canada, up to thirty-five days in Australia, and six weeks in Germany. And elections are typically conducted on Sundays to make voting convenient for workers. Voter registration is automated.

The election processes in superior democracies offer lessons for improving the quality of American democracy. The first step is an end to pay-to-play. And that step depends on the Supreme Court. As American politics unfolded after 2016 with the appointment of Judge Gorsuch, the *Buckley* era seems likely to persist for some years. In the future, recriminalizing vote buying hinges on a reconstituted Supreme Court willing to reassert *originalism*, hewing to the framers' intent to prevent corruption. That reassertion must rest on a clear understanding of the various rationales justifying an end to the *Buckley* era, examined in the next chapter.

CHAPTER 11

Recriminalizing Vote Buying

Nor shall any person holding any office of profit or trust under the United States, or any of them, accept any present, emolument, office or title of any kind.[1]

—Articles of Confederation, 1777

If access to political power in a democracy becomes purchasable, governments turn into bazaars made up not of elected officials who govern according to law, but of entrepreneurs who sell their wares to the highest bidder.[2]

—David Crossland, *Berliner Zeitung,* February 2010

I T IS THE MOST famous presidential speech in American history. Lincoln's Gettysburg address is lionized by historians. It eloquently consecrated the sacrifice of the thousands of American sons, brothers, and husbands who fell on the battlefield. But Lincoln's 272 words were not only a moving tribute to the fallen. He also sought to resurrect the foundation of the nation set forth in the Declaration of Independence by the Second Continental Congress. Indeed, the Republican Party emerged in 1854, built on Abraham Lincoln's intention. Garry Wills, Pulitzer Prize winning historian, explains that Lincoln rejected the discriminatory, selective liberty embodied in the Constitution in favor of individual equality as the seminal inspiration and principle for American democracy.[3] On that November afternoon in 1863, Lincoln spoke of lifting from the nation the dead hand of a constitution empowering a slaveocracy and political inequality.

Lincoln invoked the better angels in all Americans. But his call—like the 1776 vision of Jefferson, Benjamin Franklin, John Jay, the abolitionists, advocates of women's rights, and others—would fail. The Jim Crow era, empowered by embarrassing supreme courts, would soon follow. Indeed, Lincoln's hope remains unfulfilled as you read this. Political equality has been repeatedly rejected by *Buckley* era supreme courts in mimicry of the nineteenth-century Chase, Waite, and Fuller courts. American democracy is low quality because representatives neither fairly hear nor heed citizens. The *Buckley* genre sustains a criminalized political system that disrupts both the electoral integrity and representational equality that are central features of higher quality democracies. Yes, there are additional factors contributing to America's poor quality of democracy including the Electoral College and the severely malapportioned Senate. But ending the *Buckley* era is the crucial step—an epochal reform that hinges solely on recomposition of the Supreme Court. That is a prerequisite for Lincoln's hope of individual equality to be realized.

The Roberts Republicans may hope that their rulings have firmly placed the income bias at the center of American democracy—that the *Buckley* genre has definitively tipped the scales against original intent and two centuries of judicial precedent and jurisprudence. The late Justice Scalia asserted in *Williams-Yulee v. Florida Bar* (2015), for instance, that pay-to-play is a "settled First Amendment principle . . ."[4] Their hopes are certain to be thwarted at some point by judicial review.

Episodes of abandonment of original intent like the *Buckley* era are not unusual in the history of the Supreme Court, whose dynamics are routinely influenced by personal preferences, events, better information, or turnover. In fact, the foremost conservative American jurist, Judge Posner, argues that the evolution in Supreme Court rulings regarding vote buying (especially after 2006 when Justice Samuel Alito replaced the retiring Justice Sandra Day O'Connor) "underscores the question of the personal and political elements in judging and thus of the sense in which the nation is ruled by judges rather than by law."[5]

It is ironic that the practice of judicial review utilized since 1976 to decriminalize vote buying is also the pathway for its remediation. The constitutional shield for corruption erected by the Burger, Rehnquist, and Roberts courts rests on quicksand, not original intent. The lottery of appointment and lifespan will assuredly produce at some future date a progressive Supreme Court majority willing to hew to original intent. That court can seek comfort by looking to rulings beginning in 1937, which began to balance the economics of labor and capital and bring life finally to the New Deal agenda.[6] That and subsequent courts lifted the dead hand of economic Darwinism from Americans for nearly half a century, temporarily creating the grandest middle class in history. And a future one will have the rare opportunity, as historian James MacGregor Burns wrote of the Earl Warren Court, "to forge a luminous exception to the Court's historic role as the bulwark of anti-democratic, anti-egalitarian conservatism . . ."[7]

Indeed, Supreme Court turnover in the past has produced seismic new directions in national policy. Courts embracing Jim Crow and apartheid, beginning with the 1873 *Slaughterhouse* ruling, eventually gave way generations later to the Warren Court and its 1954 ruling in *Brown v. Board of Education,* reasserting the meaning and intent of the Fourteenth Amendment. And a new court configuration will eventually install political equality and voter sovereignty by ending vote buying as the foundational principle of American democracy.

The *fittest fifty* and small-government conservatives have benefited disproportionately from the *Buckley* genre. But some conservatives are keenly aware that the *Buckley* era is on shaky ground, resting entirely on a court of dynamic composition. It was instructive that soon after the passing of Justice Scalia, the Koch behemoth began spending $42 million in attack ads against six Democratic senate candidates such as Ted Strickland to (successfully) ensure continued GOP control of the Senate in 2016.[8]

The Kochs have reason to fear recomposition of the Supreme Court. Limits on campaign donations (including by foreigners and some military personnel) have been constitutional since 1867. Limits on political speech itself are commonplace in America, including fastidious rules for local government meetings, polling stations, state and federal legislative hearings, courtrooms, and the like. Moreover, supreme courts in the past have issued rulings explicitly to improve political equality, including *Reynolds v. Sims* (1964) requiring one person one vote.

And then there is original intent. The founding fathers and the framers sought to prohibit vote buying, determined to avoid the judgment of public officials being distorted by "interested men" bearing gifts or campaign donations. Acknowledging this original intent by recriminalizing vote buying to minimize corruption is *the* most compelling rationale within the American constitutional framework for ending pay-to-play. But there are other justifications, including maximizing political equality, enhancing electoral integrity, strengthening First Amendment individual speech rights, and removing the advantages afforded incumbency by pay-to-play to render voters sovereign by reducing the income bias. Each is a vital national interest.

Minimizing Corruption

The founders' and the framers' concern with vote buying was a culmination of the anticorruption themes in the writings of Plato, Edmund Burke, and Montesquieu as well as the 1651 Dutch law forbidding even trivial "gifts" to public officials. The founders' intent was a sine qua non for states as they began writing their own charters and constitutions, and creating legislatures in the wake of the Second Continental Congress in 1776. In instructing the members of Congress scattering back to their states (while dodging Redcoats) to lead these truly remarkable events, John Adam admonished: "Great care should be taken to effect this, and to prevent unfair, partial, and corrupt elections."[9] Moreover, as noted in the introduction, unabashed opposition to corruption in any guise was written into the Articles of Confederation the founding fathers soon crafted: "Nor shall any person holding any office of profit or trust under the United States, or any of them, accept any present, emolument, office or title of any kind."[10]

The founding fathers could not have more forcefully provided future generations with clarity of their intent. A decade later, in 1787, the framers were equally adamant, exemplified by the concerns of James Madison and George Mason, noted in chapter 3. That is why they included more than twenty anticorruption provisions in the Constitution—more than any other topic. As in the Articles, their definition of corruption was all encompassing. Constitution scholars like Robert Post have emphasized that the framers had an obsessive focus on indirect as well as quid pro quo corruption. Their definition of vote buying was perceived in the broadest possible terms—exemplified by their concern over King George III's suborning of parliamentarians. Royal grants were considered corrupting regardless of whether any quid pro quo occurred. Indeed, even royal grants and emoluments to loyal Tory parliamentarians were viewed as corruption. Emphasizing this original intent, Justice Sandra Day O'Connor echoed the founding fathers' broad definition of corruption in her opinion in *McConnell v. FEC* (2003), quoted in chapter 7.[11] Professor Zephyr Teachout explains their broadest possible definition this way: "[Delegates] started their experiment in self-government committed to expanding the scope of the actions that were called corrupt to encompass activities treated as noncorrupt in British and French cultures . . . [*Buckley*] is incompatible with the traditional American theory of corruption."[12]

The founding fathers and the constitutional framers' criminalization of political bribery in any form and forum was soon reflected in state statutes. Public officials of the day were generally considered guilty of corruption when accepting support even when their votes or behavior went unchanged.[13] An 1816 statute in Georgia and similar laws that followed in Kentucky, Michigan, North Carolina, Minnesota, and other states went well beyond quid pro quo exchanges to quite broadly criminalize political donations of any kind. Teachout explains: "For example, in Michigan, the briber was guilty if he gave something of value 'with intent to influence his [public official's] act, vote, decision or judgment on any matter'."[14] Federal law later (*Acts to Prevent Frauds on the Treasury*) similarly criminalized political donations intended to influence a public official's "vote or decision on any question . . . before him in his official capacity, or in his place of trust or profit."[15]

Colonial era anticorruption statutes expanded to keep pace with the ingenuity of favor seekers, especially following the 1896 McKinley presidential campaign, which rather famously featured voluminous fund-raising from corporate donors by Senator Mark Hanna. Within a decade, the Tillman Act (1907) had criminalized such corporate political donations and independent spending as well. UCLA law professor Adam Winkler writes "in the early 1900s, Congress and the majority of state legislatures adopted laws completely barring corporations from contributing money to candidates for public office."[16] Included was Montana's Corrupt Practices Act of 1912, barring corporate political donations and spending by "Copper Kings" and other bribers. Enacted by citizens' initiative, this law stood for a century until struck down by the Roberts Republicans in June 2012.

Maximizing Political Equality

A second justification for ending pay-to-play is to place political equality at the center of American democracy, a concept viewed with hostility by Roberts Republicans. The opportunity for citizens to speak freely and for as long and forcibly as any other citizen should not be infringed by the *fittest fifty*'s ability to purchase television time or sound trucks to speak louder than their neighbors. As Justice Louis Brandeis concluded in 1920, protecting every citizen's speech rights enables and thus promotes direct involvement in government.[17] Many American political scientists and some jurists nowadays place political equality at the center of their arguments that justify limits on political spending.[18] For example, retired Justice John Paul Stevens believes it is the most compelling argument, because with pay-to-play, "The voter is less important than the man who provides money to the candidate."[19] And Teachout joins legal theorists such as Cass Sunstein, Richard Hasen, David Strauss, and Kathleen Sullivan in arguing that the *Buckley* genre is designed to strip concerns of equality or inequality from campaign financing laws.[20]

Every other wealthy democracy has centered its governance model on political equality, marking it the global gold standard. Like the United States, free speech in Canada for instance is a constitutional guarantee. It exalts protections on speech content. But unlike the Roberts Republicans, Canada's Supreme Court has found that political equality is a foundational value to a high-quality democracy that justifies limits on speech volume. Over strident opposition from then-conservative Prime Minister Stephen Harper, the Canadian Supreme Court held in the landmark ruling, *Harper v. Canada* (2004), that such strict limits on donations and independent political spending will "create a level playing field for those who wish to engage in the election discourse. This, in turn, enables voters to be better informed; no one voice is overwhelmed by another . . . Individuals should have an equal opportunity to participate in the electoral process . . . that requires the wealthy to be prevented from controlling the electoral process to the detriment of others with less economic power."[21]

Judge Guido Calabresi of the Second Circuit Court agreed, writing in 2012:

> If an external factor, such as wealth, allows some individuals to communicate their political views too powerfully, then persons who lack wealth may, for all intents and purposes, be excluded from the democratic dialogue... Contribution limits, like noise ordinances, still allow those who have the capacity a full opportunity to make their speech widely heard... but such limits make sure that this is done only in ways that leave room for everyone else to do the same.[22]

Calabresi makes a second point, that purchasable political speech lends itself to misjudgments in the *intensity* of feelings held by voters:

> To return to the example of the megaphone in the public square, the problem with its loudness is not just that it drowns out the voices of others, but also that it *misrepresents,* to an outside observer, the relative intensity of the speaker's views... The one speaker's relative loudness— along with the other speakers' relative softness—obscures the depth of each speaker's views, thereby degrading the communicative value of everyone's message . . . The ability to express one's feelings with all the intensity that one has—and to be heard—is a central element of the right to speak freely... Today, the amount of an individual's campaign contribution reflects the strength of that individual's preferences far less than it does the size of his wallet.[23]

Maximizing Electoral Integrity

Robert Post posits that "electoral integrity" is a more precise justification for limiting vote buying than political equality. The outcome is the same: in the absence of political bribery, public confidence in the democratic process is maximized because representatives can thereby best hear and heed each citizen. In his book *Citizens Divided,* Post emphasized that it is paramount for each vote to be equally valued by representatives "because political decisions are characteristically imposed on all."[24]

Maximizing Individual First Amendment Rights

A high-quality democracy features elected representatives who hear citizens' voices equally, or what Post and Justice Stephen Breyer term a sturdy political "chain of communication." By providing a constitutional shield for unequal political voices, the *Buckley* genre diminishes the quality, vicissitude, and variety of speech being heard. That diminishes First Amendment rights, as Justice Breyer explained in his dissent to *McCutcheon v. FEC* (2014), quoted here at length:

> The First Amendment advances not only the individual's right to engage in political speech, but also the public's interest in preserving a democratic order in which collective speech matters. What has this to do with corruption? It has everything to do with corruption. Corruption breaks the constitutionally necessary "chain of communication" between the people and their representatives. It derails the essential speech-to-government-action tie. Where enough money calls the tune, the general public will not be heard. Insofar as corruption cuts the link between political thought and political action, a free marketplace of political ideas loses its point. That is one reason why the Court has stressed the constitutional importance of Congress' concern that a few large donations not drown out the voices of the many.[25]

The majority opinion in *Buckley* argues that limits on the volume of political speech will disrupt the constitutional goal of promoting "the unfettered interchange of ideas," diminishing free speech rights. By this illogic, it would seem that a sound truck enhances the exchange of ideas while its absence inhibits such exchanges. In actuality, political equality, electoral integrity, and the chain of communication are enhanced by limits that preserve the free speech rights of each and every citizen—thereby strengthening an individual's First Amendment rights, as argued by Judge Calabresi:

> [Unfettered political spending] garbles the political debate, trumpeting voices that would otherwise be muted and muting voices that would otherwise be trumpeted . . . the only way to ensure a truly "unfettered interchange of ideas"—an interchange, that is, where each voice is heard in reasonable proportion to the intensity of the beliefs it expresses—is

to give the government some freedom to mitigate the fettering impact of these inequalities.[26]

Maximizing Electoral Competition for Incumbents

Justice Kennedy argues that limits on contributions and independent political spending is an "incumbency protection plan."[27] His contention is that such limits suppress well-funded challengers. Columnists such as George Will agree, writing that limits rather cunningly "will be set by incumbent legislators . . . [to] serve incumbent interests." George Will is correct; the limit favored by incumbents is infinity. And Justice Scalia argued that, "If incumbents and challengers are limited to the same quantity of electioneering, incumbents are favored. In other words, any restrictions upon a type of campaign speech . . . tend to favor incumbents."[28]

These contentions by Kennedy, Will, and Scalia assume a fanciful vision of every challenger as a multimillionaire of pure heart willing to bury larcenous incumbents with dollars. That stylized and vanishingly rare scenario is belied by facts. A domain of unlimited donations enhances the electoral prospects of incumbents. In virtually all elections, incumbents easily outraise and outspend opponents. They spend their careers pandering to donors, as the income bias documents, making them nearly invulnerable at the ballot box (read on). The *Buckley* genre is the real incumbency protection plan.

Evidence shows that making incumbents vulnerable requires corralling their monetary advantage by limiting electioneering spending, capping contributions, and capping independent political spending, while nurturing challengers with public funding. When limits are imposed in a fashion that equalizes electioneering resources, political competition is enhanced. Political scientists Kenneth Mayer, Timothy Werner, and Amanda Williams concluded in a Brookings Paper, for instance, that "The fear that spending limits would put challengers in an impossible strategic situation and make incumbents even more unbeatable has simply not been realized."[29] Other scholarly analyses reached the same conclusion; Harvard-Enching Institute scholar Kihong Eom and political scientist Donald Gross determined that donation caps reduce the advantage of incumbency: "If anything, contribution limits can work to reduce the bias that traditionally works in favor of incumbents."[30]

A February 2013 analysis by George Washington University political science professor John Sides and Public Policy Institute of California research fellow Eric McGhee examined the 2012 election cycle and concluded that incumbency provides about a five percentage points electoral edge.[31] That advantage includes name recognition and at least a two-year head start in raising donations, which is why *Buckley* has resulted in the typical Congressional incumbent outspending opponents by almost four to one. Consequently, more than 90 percent of Congress members are routinely reelected, including 97 percent of those seeking reelection in 2016.[32] Elections are even less competitive at the state level where 93 percent of incumbents typically win reelection. In a sentiment uniformly expressed by political scientists, University of Illinois professor Michael Miller notes that, "A career as an American legislator comes with a great deal of job security . . . Incumbents are practically unassailable . . . Most of the time, incumbents are able to bury challengers in campaign cash."[33]

The necessary factors to reduce this incumbency advantage are to limit contributions and independent political spending and equalize electioneering resources to all candidates. These are common practices in higher quality democracies to ensure competitive elections by roughly equalizing resources to all candidates, as we learned in the previous chapter. Yet equalizing resources to ensure competitive elections are vigorously rejected by the Roberts Republicans. During oral argument on *Arizona Free Enterprise Club PAC v. Bennett* (2011), for instance, Chief Justice Roberts asserted: "Well, I checked the Citizens' Clean Election commission website this morning and it says that this act was passed to, quote, 'level the playing field' when it comes to running for office. Why isn't that clear evidence that it's unconstitutional?"[34]

Evidence that political spending limits reduce the edge associated with incumbency comes from Arizona and Maine, states with the most seasoned public campaign funding programs in the United States. An analysis of these programs by political science professors Seth Masket and Michael Miller in 2014 concluded that limits combined with public funding "appear to 'manufacture' quality candidates who might otherwise lack the attributes or experience to run viable campaigns."[35]

Documentation is also provided in a subsequent analysis by Miller in his book *Subsidizing Democracy*. Miller drew on more than twenty years of data and surveys from more than one thousand candidates in states that limit electioneering spending while providing public funding to challengers. That combination creates more robust competition. In Arizona, for instance, the share of incumbents forced to confront major party challengers rose from 68 percent before public funding to 85 percent afterward. It improved the quality of that competition as well. Nearly 60 percent of candidates in public funding campaigns believed they were consequently more competitive; Miller writes they "cited public funding as vaulting them to a level of competitiveness that they would not have been able to achieve otherwise." The improvement in competitiveness is also suggested by a decline in electoral winning margins.[36]

The most expansive database bearing on the question of incumbency protection, political spending, and competition is from Albuquerque. Strict limits on donations and on electioneering spending existed there for several decades in municipal races—from 1974 until terminated by lawsuits based on *Buckley* in the mid-1990s. Its system also utilized public funding to equalize electioneering resources for candidates during these decades, providing a data-rich base. The first lawsuit challenging the Albuquerque donation limits induced a comprehensive assessment that has since been parsed by Richard Hasen. He noted that "The court made a number of factual findings suggesting robust campaigning and widespread satisfaction with the system of candidate spending limits." That satisfaction certainly did not include incumbent mayors. The city's combination of public funding with caps on both donations and electioneering spending proved to be an existential threat to them—*none* was able to win reelection in these two decades. Hasen explained:

> In contrast to the nationwide incumbency rate of 88 percent for mayors, Albuquerque had a zero percent incumbency rate in city mayoral elections held under spending limits. Many candidates spent less than the spending limits, and the 1997 winner spent less than $44,000 on his campaign . . . Candidate campaigns were vigorous and contested; incumbents did not benefit and perhaps may have been hurt by spending

limits; voter turnout was higher than in other cities; and the public approved of the programs.[37]

The analysis also concluded that spending limits did not constitute censorship, with Hasen noting, "the trial court's findings do not show significant government suppression of speech."

Public surveys became another element of the Albuquerque record when provided in a separate federal district court lawsuit filing. The share of local respondents who believed that *federal* elections featuring unlimited political spending favored "special interest money" was well more than double the share believing that *Albuquerque* elections featuring limits favored such interests. The federal district court in *Homans v. City of Albuquerque* (2001) concluded that: "57 percent of surveyed Albuquerque voters think that federal elections are overly influenced by special interest money. In contrast, only 23 percent think that Albuquerque elections are overly influenced by special interest money."[38]

You have just read how best to begin restoring the faith of Americans in their democracy.

Most Americans Support Recriminalizing Vote Buying

A Pew Research Center survey in 2015 found that 76 percent of Americans believe "government is run by big interests" with only 19 percent believing that it is run for the benefit of everyone.[39] A Bloomberg survey in September 2015 found 87 percent of respondents agreed that the campaign finance "system should be reformed so that a rich person does not have more influence than a person without money."[40] Results are similar in the joint *New York Times*/CBS News survey released in June 2015, noted in chapter 2. Some 84 percent of respondents—including 80 percent of self-described Republicans, 84 percent of independents, and 90 percent of Democrats—believe "money has too much influence in American politics."[41] Respondents were critical of the Roberts Supreme Court, more than half rejecting any constitutional basis for the *Buckley* genre. Nearly 80 percent of them agreed that contributions and independent political spending should be capped (chart 11.1). Overall, a remarkable 85 percent of respondents believed the pay-to-play US political system requires

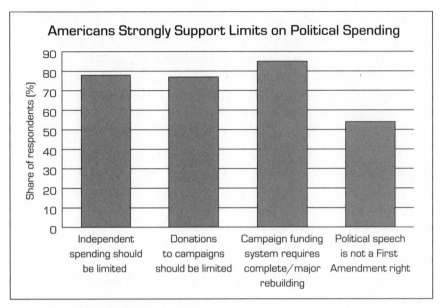

Chart 11.1 Americans believe that . . .

New York Times/CBS News poll, May 28–31, 2015, www.scribd.com/doc/267409090
/cbs-news-new-york-times-money-and-politics-poll; www.nytimes.com/interactive
/2015/06/01/us/politics/document-poll-may-28-31.html

"fundamental changes," including 46 percent who agreed that it should
be abandoned entirely: "the system for funding political campaigns has
so much wrong with it that we must completely rebuild it."[42]

Americans' preference to extinguish pay-to-play extends to corporate
contributions and their political/issue advertising as well. Supermajorities
of Americans today would agree with President Theodore Roosevelt, writing in 1907, that "All contributions by corporations . . . for any political
purpose should be forbidden by law; directors should not be permitted
to use shareholders' money for such purposes . . ."[43] Even business sector
respondents agree. The polling in *Demos* reported by Liz Kennedy noted in
chapter 8 concluded that some 70 percent of business-sector respondents to
the 2012 Corporate Reform Coalition survey "[b]elieve a ban on corporate
funded political ads would improve politics. And a majority was in favor of
a constitutional amendment to ban all corporate contributions and politi-
cal/issue advertising." Those majorities include 57 percent of self-described

"moderates" and also 57 percent of "independents."[44] If *Citizens United* cannot be overturned, respondents favored requiring full transparency, with corporate donor names released immediately. And corporate and CEO donor names should be prominently displayed in all advertising.

The widespread dismay with *Citizens United* is bipartisan, indicated by citizens in relatively conservative Montana and the swing state of Colorado. Montanans in 2012 approved Initiative 166, which requires its Congressional delegation to sponsor a constitutional amendment to prohibit corporate donations or spending in state elections. And some 74 percent of voters in Colorado in 2012 also supported a referendum calling for a US constitutional amendment to reverse *Citizens United*. The referendum won in every Colorado County.[45]

Americans largely reject vote buying. Their knowledge that it remains widespread is certainly one of the primary factors responsible for their sense of political impotence and loss of faith in the nation's governance. The next chapter shows how this angst can be remediated by a national will to adopt the practices and electoral systems of higher quality democracies.

CHAPTER 12

Rehabilitating America's Flawed Democracy: A Framework for Ending Vote Buying

[A] flawed democracy . . . Popular trust in government, elected representatives and political parties has fallen to extremely low levels in the US . . . The US now keeps company with countries that include Italy, Botswana, Sri Lanka, and Mexico.[1]

—Economist Intelligence Unit, Jan. 2017

[Electioneering spending limits] serve an important complement to corruption-reducing contribution limits . . . When campaign costs are so high that only the rich have the reach to throw their hats into the ring, we fail "to protect the political process from undue influence of large aggregations of capital and to promote individual responsibility for democratic government."[2]

—Justice John Paul Stevens, *Randall v. Sorrell*, 2006
(including quote from the Supreme Court ruling in
Automobile Workers, 352, US at 590)

[Reforms can] draw on the experience of Canada and Great Britain, both of which impose strict limits on money in campaigns, yet have robust elections in which there is no appreciable censorship.[3]

—Richard Hasen

THE INCOME BIAS IS compelling evidence that American democracy is of low quality. Voters are neither equal nor sovereign. The remedy is to recriminalize vote buying with limits on both donations and independent political spending. Following the example of other wealthy democracies, limits are also warranted on issue advocacy during election periods. Caps or bans in other wealthy democracies strengthen political competition, political equality, and voter sovereignty while eliminating most negative appeals. Their candidates, as exemplified by German chancellor Angela Merkel, are eager to co-opt popular policy positions from any source—thereby edging politics to the center. *Washington Post* columnist Ruth Marcus explains: "In Merkel's Germany, it has resulted in a race to the middle—not just in forming a coalition government but in the campaign itself."[4]

The most compelling lawyerly rationale in America for recriminalizing campaign donations and independent political spending is to honor original intent, as discussed in the previous chapter. Definitional precision is paramount, and when a future Supreme Court seeks to end the *Buckley* era, it should recall what Justice Sandra Day O'Connor concluded in *McConnell v. FEC* (2003). Defining and identifying corruption is so fraught, she wrote, that "[t]he best means of prevention is to identify and to remove the temptation."[5]

The O'Connor maxim—a sweeping, encompassing definition "to remove the temptation"—translates to an electoral system that permits only de minimis campaign donations and does not permit expansive political/issue advertising or donations by nominal or genuinely independent entities. Any weaker standard invites inventive evasion. Drawing on experience in Denmark, France, Latvia, and Lithuania, for instance, the UK Committee on Standards in Public Life noted in 2011 that vote buyers stridently endeavor to bypass limits using loans, by divvying-up donations among family members and trusted colleagues, by funneling gifts through nominally independent entities, and by creating new political parties.[6]

The O'Connor maxim would provide a clarity that's common in other wealthy nations as noted by Professor Andrea Römmele of Berlin's Hertie School of Government: "In Germany, giving money in politics is always seen as trying to buy access."[7]

Within an overarching commitment to recriminalize vote buying, America can raise the quality of its democracy with the following agenda of rules, procedures, and practices drawn from superior democracies.

Limit Electioneering Spending

Electioneering spending caps are imposed abroad to preclude a significant role for private capital in any guise in political campaigns. In Canada, as noted earlier, electioneering outlays by major parties at the federal level were capped in 2015 at about $43 million apiece in a nation of 26 million registered voters. There and elsewhere, limits are typically imposed on a per registered voter basis, and vary with the scope of office sought. A common companion component is prohibitions or limits on broadcast advertising, with the bulk of electioneering spending devoted to inexpensive marketing options like billboards, get-out-the-vote, and more recently social media messaging.

Limits on electioneering spending are closely monitored, audited, and rigorously enforced. For instance, the senior French court, the Constitutional Council, concluded in July 2013 that the party of presidential candidate Nicolas Sarkozy had overspent during his 2012 election contest. His overspending totaled a modest €460,000 ($500,000), but the penalty was huge—a fine of €10 million ($11 million). The penalty was more than one-third of the legally allowed overall party spending (including a binary runoff) in 2012, reported *Financial Times* journalist Hugh Carnegy.[8] The French paper *Le Figaro* speculated that the penalty would be "financially asphyxiating" for Sarkozy's center-right UMP party for several years to come.[9] Exactly.

Ensuring that all qualified candidates have adequate electioneering resources to challenge incumbents is a key means of ensuring competitive elections. As in the US, debates in other wealthy democracies are vibrant. The pool of candidates is quite diverse, representing a broad range of domestic opinion. Elections are vigorously challenged, with new issues and new candidates readily emerging. Limits on spending do not quell candidate communications or voter choice. Quite the contrary, limits require a focus of scarce political communications opportunities on building candidate and party brand, while clarifying policy differences.

Higher quality democracies typically provide some level of public subsidy for candidates in order to maximize political competition. Public funding accompanied by a cap on electioneering outlays ensures a high degree of citizen confidence in the outcome, a characteristic of what Robert Post termed electoral integrity. That does not mean equality of electioneering resources to each candidate, by the way. Instead, other wealthy democracies like Canada typically adopt systems that de facto or de jure link the actual amount of electioneering spending beneath the official ceiling to the robustness of public support as measured by the number of small donations garnered.

Limits on electioneering spending eliminate negative political advertising. Comprehensive transparency and content attribution rules in other wealthy democracies mean negative political messaging cannot be conducted anonymously. Candidates and parties risk voter blowback from attack ads. By contrast, negative advertising is common in the United States in good part because sponsorship can be veiled, absolving political parties of accountability, especially on social media.

Americans have their own considerable, satisfactory experience with limits on electioneering spending. They are a central element of public campaign funding programs in a number of localities, such as Maine and New York City. The spending caps in New York City's Campaign Finance Act (CFA) enacted in 1988 are $168,000 for city council candidates and $6,426,000 for mayoral aspirants. Similar caps exist for primary elections as well. As in every other public campaign funding program in America, participation by candidates must be voluntary under prevailing *Buckley* era court rulings.

Tight electioneering spending limits would be popular with Americans. Some 77 percent of respondents in a Pew Research Center survey in late 2015 believed there "should be limits on the amount of money individuals and organizations can spend on political campaigns and issues." Only 20 percent believed that organizations or individuals should be able to donate or spend without limit. And the sentiment was bipartisan, with 72 percent of Republicans and 84 percent of Democrats agreeing on limits.[10]

Limit Donations to Candidates and Parties

Many higher quality democracies that limit electioneering spending such as Belgium, Canada, France, and Japan also choose to cap donations at modest levels. American communities that adopt public campaign funding programs have followed suit. Individual donations to New York City politicians participating in its CFA program, for instance, are capped at $2,750 for city council contests and $4,950 for mayoral races.[11]

In New York as well as in peer nations, capping contributions to encourage numerous small-dollar donations serves two purposes. First, in the formative stages of an election cycle, the robustness of small donations is utilized to gauge community support for candidates, and thus eligibility to receive public subsidies. Requiring a show of small donor support is a practical market-test of aspirants while winnowing marginal, ideologically extreme, or novelty candidates. To appear on ballots, aspirants typically must raise a threshold, modest amount from a predetermined number of donors. City Council aspirants under the CFA program, for instance, must garner contributions totaling at least $5,000 from at least seventy-five donors to qualify for the ballot.[12] And gubernatorial candidates participating in Maine's public campaign financing system must receive threshold donations from at least 3,200 voters.[13]

Second, an emphasis on small donations appears to incentivize engagement in civic affairs and politics. When large donors were sidelined by Albuquerque's innovative program of limited donations in the 1970s, citizen participation in civic affairs rose. Analyses of the CFA by the Brennan Center and by political scientists Michael Malbin, Peter Brusoe, and Brendan Glavin in 2012 found similar results. They concluded that permitting only small donations forces candidates to solicit an entirely novel and vastly more representative set of donors.[14]

Most other wealthy democracies consider small donations so important to competitive elections that they subsidize them with tax credits and by offering matching funds. In Canada, contributors receive a 75 percent tax credit for the first C$400 of a political donation, the credit diminishing at higher amounts. And under CFA, any donation up to $175 is matched 6:1 from public coffers, making a small donation of that amount actually worth $1,225 to the recipient candidate.[15]

There have been campaign spending reform proposals introduced in Congress that feature such incentives as well. The Fair Elections Now Act, for instance, first introduced in 2009, caps political contributions but encourages small donations with a 5:1 match for the first $100 of donations."[16] More recently, the Government by the People Act sponsored by Congressman John Sarbanes provides both a tax credit ($25) and a 6:1 match to encourage small donations.[17]

Limit Independent Political Spending

In 2012, California public health advocates placed a referendum on ballots in El Monte and Richmond to impose a tax on sugary drinks in an effort to reduce consumption, a proven technique to reduce demand. As is sometimes the case in referendums like this, voters were subjected to a barrage of issue advocacy advertising by affected enterprises. Opponents commanded far more resources: the $114,000 mustered by health advocates was swamped by $4 million spent on broadcast and cable TV ads, canvassing teams, phone banks, billboards, public rallies, and the like by the sugar industry. Each antitax vote actually cast on Election Day cost the sugar advocates $115, but it was money well spent. The tax was defeated.[18] Indeed, American commercial interests of every stripe in recent decades have refined a sophisticated expertise to sway voters on policy issues with lavish independent expenditures.

To reduce the risk of such manipulation, higher quality democracies limit or ban donations and political issue advocacy by independent interests for some months preceding elections. Many utilize a definition of such spending similar to that adopted by Elections Canada, as noted in chapter 10.[19] And if adopted in the United States, that definition should also feature the quaint standard proposed by Senator Barry Goldwater in *The Conscience of a Conservative* in 1960.[20] Advocates sponsoring political appeals must be able to breathe.

Recall that in Canada, nationwide political advertising and issue advocacy by independent entities during the federal election period is capped at $155,000 (proportionately higher for campaigns longer than thirty-seven days). Donors must be identified in all advertising. In Britain, the limits are also modest, as noted by journalist Jacob Rowbottom writing in the *New Republic*: "Independent organizations can spend no more than £988,000

($1,250,000) in support of a political party in the UK in the 12 months before a general election and no more than £500 ($625) in support of an individual candidate in the month before an election. As it happens, in the 2010 UK election, very few independent organizations came close to spending anything near the national limit."[21]

The UK approach is a good model for America. Independent political spending and issue advocacy are limited during the year preceding elections. Yet public debate is vibrant, as judged by international speech advocates such as Freedom House. Accepting Goldwater's proposal, independent spending should only be permitted by human beings. As in Canada, any cash from individuals choosing to support independent efforts should be deducted from an overall national individual donation and spending cap.

In such an election structure, there would be no scope for social-welfare 501(c)(3), 501(c)(4) advocacy organizations, PACs, or super PACs, including groups such as Americans for Prosperity. Nor would there be room for special purpose slush funds created by politicians for non-election purposes, such as the entities created to deflect accountability for the Flint water contamination from Governor Rick Snyder.[22] The logic for limits on independent entities was explained by the Canadian Supreme Court, as noted earlier. And here is an explanation by Simon Fraser University political scientist Andrew Heard: "There are two main justifications for the third-party limits. The first is to protect the spending limits on political parties and candidates; otherwise, parallel campaigns could be conducted by groups allied to particular parties. The other is to protect individual candidates from being targeted by expensive ad campaigns to which they could not respond because of both their own limited funds or the spending limits imposed on candidates."[23]

Adopting the UK structure would still leave considerable leeway for organizations to opine, particularly outside the year-long election window. Entities could continue traditional branding advertising. Moreover, lobbying activities would continue. Finally, many corporate leaders are viewed as generators of wealth and employment, guaranteeing that their voices would be heard and heeded by lawmakers and their constituents. Indeed, scholars have documented that their influence can sway public opinion even in the absence of pay-to-play. Duke business professor Aaron Chatterji and Harvard professor Michael Toffel in 2016 assessed the ability of CEOs to influence public opinion. They chose a controversial social issue for their project—whether Indiana state law should permit discrimination against homosexuals. As a precursor to their experiment, about half of their 3,400 respondents were told that Apple CEO Timothy Cook, the CEO of Indiana-based Angie's List, William Oesterle, and the mayor of Indianapolis opposed any law that permitted discrimination: "We found that public support for the law declined sharply, and roughly equally, if respondents were informed that Mr. Cook, Mr. Oesterle, or the mayor of Indianapolis were concerned about it . . . Prominent chief executives . . . can shape public opinion about controversial social issues."[24]

Voter equality is maximized by election systems abroad because of effective and timely monitoring of donors and of electioneering spending, which facilitates the prosecution of political corruption. Independent third parties are also closely monitored abroad and must register immediately upon establishment. A revamped, expanded, independent Federal Election Commission or any successor in the United States ideally should be able to track outlays and to obtain the names and amounts of individual donations and of spending on a real-time basis. Both Elections Canada and the California's Fair Political Practices Commission provide useful models. Regulators in the latter were responsible for peeling away four layers of obfuscating 501(c)4 cutouts in 2012, for instance, to discover that the Koch brothers, Sheldon Adelson, and Charles Schwab were behind an $11 million campaign of attack ads to kill Proposition 30 in that state. The proposition—raising state income taxes on higher incomes to fund a $6 billion increase in education spending—was approved by voters nonetheless.[25] A useful reform was instituted in reaction to this exposé: California in 2014 enacted a law requiring groups with political spending of $50,000 or more in one year (or $100,000 within four years) to reveal every donor of more than $1,000.[26]

An additional monitoring tactic is the use of undercover investigations by authorities to ferret out corrupt public officials. Such stings have been utilized to snare corrupt American and European parliamentarians.[27] For instance, over one hundred (of 480) Romanian legislators responded to a fake bribe attempt by sham firms in the United Arab Emirates in a sting engineered by the daily *Romania Libera*.[28]

Finally, monitoring systems need to be dynamic in order to keep pace with advances in voter-influencing technology. The *fittest fifty* mostly fund traditional political techniques—advertising, grass roots mobilization, and the like—that should be subject to reports and auditing. But pioneers such as billionaire Robert Mercer are marrying big data from social media to target voters utilizing psychological warfare techniques derived from the military. It's called psychometrics and targets individual voters in gargantuan numbers more effectively than traditional media.[29] Mercer has spent at least $15 million refining such tools using social data analytics to pinpoint individual swing or "persuadable" voters.[30] A test run in early 2016 targeted 600,000 identified persuadables in Britain who were soon deluged with pro-Brexit information. Similar influencer programs were likely conducted by the Koch data mining firm i360 and the Trump campaign (in collaboration with Mercer's Cambridge Analytica) using ad buy on Twitter and Facebook during 2016. Such psychographic practices manipulate rather than persuade voters. Their use for political purposes should be prohibited, whether conducted by Russians or Americans.

Limit Length of Campaigns

Other wealthy democracies limit the period for campaigns and so should the United States. Campaign seasons are set by law or in some instances as in Canada by common practice. The longest are nearly five months (139 days) in the United Kingdom and Mexico (147 days), but are shorter elsewhere.[31] Compare that to the 2016 US election cycle, which began well before the first primaries on February 1, 2016. A relatively short campaign season would be welcomed by Americans. In most if not all other wealthy democracies, electioneering spending by candidates and political parties are prohibited except during the campaign season. Limits on third-party political spending and issue advocacy are imposed for even longer periods preceding Election Day, including the noted UK caps on independent political spending and political issue advocacy applicable for the year concluding on Election Day.[32]

Limit Political and Issue Advertising in Broadcast and Other Media

Peer nations have concluded that limits on broadcast advertising are an important element to controlling electioneering spending and ensuring

that a factual, informative political discourse occurs between candidates, parties, and voters. Paid political advertisements on TV (but not
on social media) are banned in Belgium, Britain, Brazil, France, Ireland,
Japan, and others, although some airtime is variously provided free.[33] In
France, for instance, six hours of air time is provided gratis, split among
all presidential candidates equally. In Canada, some 214 minutes of political air time is provided free on public television split between parties.
And private broadcasters must make available for sale at relatively low
rates an additional 6.5 hours split between parties.[34] (Political parties
can purchase this additional airtime as long as they remain beneath
their overall nationwide electioneering spending cap.) Advertising on
American TV stations is prohibited.[35] Political parties in Germany are
given modest airtime on public networks and can purchase a bit more on
private networks. But as noted earlier, spending limits nonetheless held
the number of times political ads by Chancellor Merkel were aired in
2013 to 140 in total. In addition, TV advertising by independent entities
or associations, if permitted at all, is capped at quite low levels during
the campaign season everywhere.[36]

American political advertising should be limited, with airtime ideally provided gratis and in equal portions on public television and by
broadcasters enjoying use of the public airways. Such spending caps
would doubtless be welcomed by viewers. The Wesleyan Media Project
determined that 1.35 million ads were aired during the 2014 midterm
elections in the United States.[37] If each was thirty seconds in duration,
that translates to 11,000 hours of political advertising—vastly more than
permitted in peer nations.

A major benefit of capping broadcast airtime abroad is a flight to
positive campaigning by candidates and parties. That characteristic is
magnified further if anonymity is stripped away, with actual donors
identified in all independent political spending. And regulations abroad
are sufficiently robust that public monitors reject outright fabrications,
analogous to the US Swift Boat ads regarding John Kerry in 2004, or ads
during the 2012 Republican primary in South Carolina alleging that Mitt
Romney was a serial killer.[38] Political speech on social media is discussed
in Chapter 15.

Mandate Public Funding of Elections

In crafting a replacement for pay-to-play in financing elections, American courts or lawmakers can draw on the rich and successful domestic history of publicly funded elections, time-tested at every level of US politics. The concept was first introduced by Theodore Roosevelt in the wake of the 1907 financial panic to weaken the political influence of the *fittest fifty* of his day. But implementation was fitful until the Watergate scandal in 1974. The first nationwide American public funding mechanism was adopted as one element of the new campaign finance reforms enacted then by Congress. The law *mandated* that presidential candidates utilize only public funding for campaigns; that mandate was removed two years later in the *Buckley* ruling, leaving participation voluntary ever since. Even so, public funding comprised the bulk of presidential campaign spending until 1996, when surpassed by independent expenditures and PAC spending.[39] All major party presidential candidates utilized public funding until 2008 when President Obama opted to fund his campaign entirely with private donations.

Albuquerque adopted public funding in 1974, with other adventuresome states and localities following, supported by advocates from both political parties. The political benefits have also been bipartisan. For example, the election of grassroots conservatives in Arizona who later emerged as the foundation of the Tea Party was enabled by that state's public financing program. And earlier, Ronald Reagan became president thanks to public campaign financing. Challenging President Gerald Ford for the GOP nomination in 1976, Reagan ran out of money during the primaries.[40] Accepting taxpayer funds from the newly established presidential public financing program enabled him to campaign expansively in primary states in 1976. His charisma and impressive political skills emerged and were powerful elements in his success four years later.

Despite this history, contemporary conservatives seem unhappily surprised by the popularity of public campaign funding, with *Washington Post* neoconservative David Ignatius writing, "the public funding idea isn't as unpopular as you might think."[41] In fact, grassroots staunch conservatives find it attractive as one step toward shrinking the influence of political elites. The public funding program in Tallahassee installed by 67 percent of referendum voters in 2014, for instance, was a joint effort of the local Tea Party and progressive grassroots.[42]

Surveys confirm the broad base of support for public campaign financing. For example, some 74 percent of respondents to the Corporate Reform Coalition survey in 2012 noted in chapter 5 favor a campaign finance system featuring small-dollar private donations supplemented with public funding. Some 72 percent believed that "politics would improve with public funding of Congressional campaigns instead of special interest spending."[43] Support for public funding also emerged in a detailed survey of reform ideas in 2009, conducted by political scientists at the University of Texas. On a scale of 1 (no support) to 10 (strongly support), support was strongest for reforms that provided free and equal TV airtime to candidates (mean score 7.23), that strengthened the Federal Election Commission (6.69), that shortened campaigns to four weeks (6.00), and that replaced all private political contributions with public funding (5.83).[44]

Mandate Public Funding of Judicial Elections

Hefty majorities of Americans also prefer eliminating contributions and independent political/issue advertising in judicial elections. And judges themselves have long agreed. Surveys by the nonpartisan National Center for State Courts beginning in 2001 found public funding of such elections were favored by 53 percent of judges surveyed in California (2001), 56 percent in Florida (2001), 69 percent in Illinois (2001), 74 percent in New York (2001), 60 percent (of voters) in Idaho (2002), and 65 percent (of voters) in Wisconsin (2008).[45] The legal profession also supports public funding, exemplified by this declaration by an American Bar Association commission in 2002: "The Commission unanimously recommends that states that elect judges in contested elections finance judicial elections with public funds . . . The Commission concludes that public financing of judicial elections will address the perceived impropriety associated with judicial candidates accepting private contributions from individuals and organizations interested in the outcomes of cases those candidates may later decide as judges."[46]

In addition, recall that Geri Palast evaluated survey data garnered anonymously from 2,428 judges serving on state supreme courts, appellate courts, and lower courts on behalf of Justice at Stake. Most respondents were subject to election, and thus had firsthand experience with the range of pathologies in state courts induced by pay-to-play. The survey revealed considerable angst regarding the influence of money, with 71 percent of the judges believing that campaign donations to judicial candidates should be limited. Some 61 percent supported a publicly financed campaign system for judicial elections. In the interim, until such reforms occur, a majority of respondents (56 percent) agreed that judges should recuse from cases involving campaign contributors; as noted earlier, that is an impractical solution.[47]

American Experience with Public Funding

The broad appeal of programs for public funding of political or judicial campaigns is responsible for their spread in various forms to some twenty-five states since the 1970s, including thirteen statewide programs in various formulations.[48] Aside from New York City (established in 1988), the most expansive are elaborate statewide programs in Maine (1996), Arizona (1998), and Connecticut (2005). These are "clean election" programs where full funding for campaigns is provided once a candidate qualifies by raising numerous small donations. Ten other states provide campaign funding to match small donations. A few states like Maryland provide public funding just to gubernatorial and judicial candidates. Public funding programs have also been adopted in various forms by a host of localities beyond Albuquerque and New York City, including Chapel Hill, North Carolina, Long Beach, Los Angeles, Santa Fe, San Francisco, Seattle, and most recently in Chicago, Howard and Montgomery Counties in Maryland, and Tallahassee. California in 2016 lifted its twenty-nine-year-old ban that will enable public financing to be broadly adopted beyond the few current city programs. In contrast, programs have been pared back or dropped in recent years in Wisconsin and North Carolina (the repeal by North Carolina Republicans included terminating the public funding of judicial elections also). Public funding is popular with Americans. When the decision is left to voters rather than politicians, public funding generally is approved. For instance, voters in Maine in 2015 rejected GOP efforts to end the state program, instead voting to considerably expand funding.

Under *Buckley* era rulings, participation by aspirants in these programs must be voluntary; candidates are given the option to participate by accepting some public funding or to opt out and rely instead on private contributions. All programs require participating candidates (but not those opting out) to accept electioneering spending limits. It is also common for candidates to be required to qualify for public support by raising a sizable number of small donations, as already noted. Participants are usually required to engage in debates with rivals; in Seattle, for instance, the minimum is three debates. Program revenues are typically derived from civil and other fines such as speeding tickets or from general revenue. Seattle voters in November 2015 approved an innovative and user-friendly public campaign financing program that began in 2017. Financed by a token increase in local real estate taxes (i.e., $9), each registered voter receives four $25 "democracy vouchers" during each election cycle to donate to as many as four candidates in city elections.[49] Expanding that program statewide, however, was rejected by voters in 2016.

Public funding programs succeed in drawing participation from well more than one-half of all candidates. Some 74 percent of winning Maine state senate candidates in 2016 were clean election candidates, for instance; overall, 64 percent of winning state legislators in 2016 were clean election candidates, up from 58 percent in the previous legislature.[50] In Connecticut in 2014, both gubernatorial candidates participated, as did all six winning candidates for statewide office and 83.4 percent of winning state legislators.[51] And some 196 candidates of both parties participated in 2016, receiving a total of $8 million. To receive $95,710, senate candidates had to qualify by raising $15,000 from at least 300 constituents. House candidates received $28,150 upon raising $5,000 from at least 150 district residents.[52] The outcome has been a more diverse group of competitive candidates and legislators, including more women and members of minority groups. For instance, 89 percent (51 out of 57) of the women elected in Connecticut in 2014 were public funding candidates.[53]

As University of Illinois professor Michael Miller noted in a detailed 2014 analysis, when publicly funded candidates are freed of most fundraising chores, they spend more time interacting with voters and refining electoral skills than do traditionally funded candidates.[54] Consequently, incumbents face more and higher quality competitors.[55] Recall that no mayoral incumbents were reelected during the two decades of public campaign funding in Albuquerque. A study by Kenneth R. Mayer, Timothy

Werner, and Amanda Williams summarized the academic perspective on such programs this way:

> Public funding programs increase the pool of candidates willing and able to run for state legislative office. This effect is most pronounced for challengers, who were far more likely than incumbents to accept public funding. Public funding increases the likelihood that an incumbent will have a competitive race . . . public funding has *not* made incumbents safer. Fears that public funding would amount to an incumbency protection act are unfounded . . . In the end, we conclude that public funding programs—particularly the full "clean elections" systems in Arizona and Maine—increase the competitiveness of state legislative elections.[56]

Public funding also focuses candidates on middle-class concerns as explained by George Leventhal, a local elected official in Montgomery County, Maryland: "When you are looking for campaign support in chunks of $1,000 or more, you spend a lot of time with millionaires. What I'm finding now is that to get to $500 [donor threshold], I've spent most of my time with ordinary working people."[57]

Public campaign funding programs in this country and others have successfully relied on small donors to provide adequate resources for more competitive elections. They have also proven that small donors combined with some public funding can replace large donors in sufficiently financing electoral systems. The most comprehensive analysis of small donors is by Public Campaign, an advocacy group supporting public funding of campaigns. It found that small donors of $200 or less gave a total of $1 billion during the 2014 election cycle.[58] Real-world experience in Canada, Britain, and numerous American localities such as Albuquerque, Connecticut, and Maine are evidence that public campaign finance systems and spending caps ensure informative, robust, and competitive elections—and make incumbents nervous.

A Partisan Divide Created by the *Fittest Fifty*

Participation by candidates has been robust and bipartisan since the inception of public campaign funding, and remains so today: Some 78 percent of winning Republicans in Connecticut in 2014, for instance, utilized public funding.[59] Indeed, Tea Party activists and state/local GOP officials were cochairs of the successful ballot referendum in 2016 that established the South Dakota campaign finance voucher program featuring an independent ethics board and a $100 limit on lobbyists' gifts. Opponents included the Koch brothers who funded 95 percent of spending on the losing side. The Kochs don't take defeats easily, however. More anxious to please the Kochs by preserving pay-to-play than their constituents, Republican state legislators and the governor in South Dakota defiantly repealed the reforms on February 2, 2017. Such defiance is rare. The other recent episode was when GOP lawmakers in 2017 gutted implementation of an anti-gerrymandering constitutional amendment supported by 63 percent of Florida voters.[60]

The reaction of these South Dakota politicians dramatizes the opposition among Republican officials (but not grassroots) to public campaign financing programs. Recall that such programs have recently been terminated by GOP state officials in North Carolina and Wisconsin. In Congress, the GOP majority on the Administration Committee in the House of Representatives in early 2015 voted to entirely extinguish the presidential public financing program. And the Trump administration may support its demise. Even so, political scientists such as Michael Miller have found empirically that public funding does not disadvantage conservatives or Republicans.[61]

Republican distaste for public funding appears rooted in three factors: their small-government ideology, their (possible) superior ability to garner private donations, and their allegiance to the *fittest fifty*, who naturally have an extreme antipathy toward contribution limits and public funding. Thus, GOP candidates make somewhat less use of public funding opportunities than Democrats. For instance, the share of Republican candidates for state house seats in Arizona, Connecticut (2008 only), and Maine utilizing public funding ranged between 40 percent and 66 percent from 2002 to 2008. The share of Democrats in those states varied between 70 percent and 85 percent.[62]

Public campaign funding advocates have also had to overcome opposition rooted in the jurisprudence of Roberts Republicans, whose rulings have notably diminished the lure of such programs. In *Randall v. Sorrell* (2006), for example, they rejected mandatory electioneering spending caps and donations limits imposed on participating candidates in state and local public campaign funding programs. And in 2011 (*Arizona Free Enterprise v. Bennett* and *McComish v. Bennett*), they rejected provisions allowing participating candidates to receive a large infusion of taxpayer funds to match lavish electioneering spending by a nonparticipating (privately funded) rival. Such a provision had enabled Janet Napolitano to defeat a well-funded Congressman in 2006 in Arizona, becoming the first governor elected with public funding.

These rulings reduced participation in some public funding programs. In Maine, for instance, candidate participation in 2016 fell below its peak of 81 percent in 2008. In Arizona, the share of general election candidates participating fell by more than half (66 percent to 28 percent) between 2008 and 2014. Indeed, in the Arizona election of 2012, eighteen legislators who had previously been elected using public funding switched to relying solely on private donations.[63]

These steps to roll back public funding programs by Republicans have met resistance. Unhappy voters in Maine reacted to the *Arizona Free Enterprise* ruling by approving a referendum in November 2015 increasing the amount of money available to publicly funded candidates. The referendum mandated other improvements as well and requires disclosure on political advertisements of the top three donors to each candidate not participating in public funding. The events in Maine are indicative of persistently broad support for public campaign funding programs despite the hostility of Roberts Republicans. Connecticut's statewide program and the CFA program in New York City are especially thriving. In 2013, New York City's program saw a 92 percent participation rate by candidates during the primary and 72 percent during the general election. The next year, participation in Connecticut was a record 84 percent of winning candidates.[64]

This enthusiasm is also reflected in successful 2016 referenda designed to improve the quality of American democracy. They included:

- South Dakota voters established a program to encourage small donations, providing each voter $100 in vouchers to donate to eligible candidates in future elections.[65] (This is the aforementioned program subsequently killed by GOP legislators and governor in February 2017.)

- Missouri voters reestablished campaign donation limits that had been removed in 2008 by state legislators. In the future, individual donations to candidates are capped at $2,600 and at $25,000 to political parties.
- Programs to provide a public match for small donations were approved in Berkeley, California, and Howard County, Maryland.
- Voters in California, Washington, and Wisconsin approved resolutions to overturn the Roberts Republicans' *Citizens United* ruling.

Rehabilitate the Electoral System

The *Buckley* genre's embrace of pay-to-play is responsible for the income bias identified by Giles, Page, and other scholars. This chapter has outlined the specific steps that higher quality democracies utilize to remediate that bias. They do more by also utilizing superior electoral systems to enhance voter equality and sovereignty. These systems provide a model for America to upgrade its own system—a system judged to be of dismal quality by international experts. The most compelling and sustentative international analysis of the quality of electoral systems is produced by the Election Integrity Project (EIP), a joint effort of 2,000 political scientists and other independent observers across the globe under the auspices of the Australian Research Council, the University of Sydney, and Harvard University. Its most recent survey analyzed 213 elections conducted by 153 nations between 2012 and 2016.[66] Experts evaluated practices in each nation against a global standard of 49 components measuring the quality of elections—assessing how well individual political rights and voter preferences were safeguarded and reflected in electoral outcomes.

The EIP experts found American elections to be of poor and deteriorating quality judged using impartial global criteria. In two of the last five presidential elections, for instance, also-ran aspirants were jumped over the winning candidates—once (in 2000) by court decree: "American elections are risky enterprises where outcomes may be determined by the legal wisdom of the courts rather than a count of the votes cast in the ballot box . . . The evidence shows that recent US elections display the worst performance among two-dozen Western democracies . . . The evidence does not suggest that the quality of American elections has improved over these successive contests; if anything, problems are perceived to have worsened."[67]

The nonpartisan EIP experts were particularly critical of the role played by wealthy donors and of the extraordinary ability of partisans in Congress and state legislatures to establish and police self-serving electoral rules governing their own career prospects: "Matters of electoral governance should not be determined through laws enacted by self-interested partisan representatives in state houses—the equivalent to putting the fox in charge of the chicken coop."

EIP found the quality of American elections to be so low that it ranked only fifty-second in electoral integrity among the 153 nations, well behind other wealthy democracies, and also below the caliber of elections in a large number of middle-income nations such as Croatia, Tunisia, and Brazil. Indeed, the poor quality of American elections was determined to be no better than those conducted by a group of other underperforming democracies including Rwanda, Barbados, Panama, and South Africa (chart 12.1). You read that correctly.

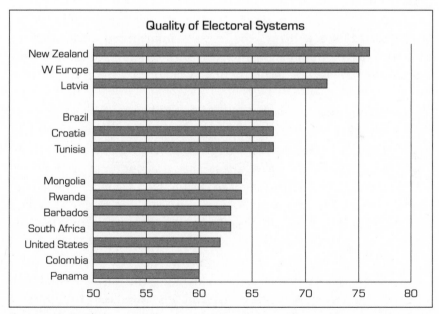

Chart 12.1 Mean assessment values ranged from 0 (poor) to 100 (excellent).

Election Integrity Project, Pippa Norris, "Why American Elections Are Flawed (And How to Fix Them)," Faculty Research Working Paper Series 16-038, September 30, 2016, www.research.hks.harvard.edu/publications/getFile.aspx?Id=1431

A separate study released in January 2017 by the *Economist*, summarized in an epigraph to this chapter, reached similar findings, the magazine's editors concluding that the United States is a "flawed democracy." "Popular trust in government, elected representatives and political parties has fallen to extremely low levels in the US . . . The US now keeps company with countries that include Italy, Botswana, Sri Lanka, and Mexico."[68]

Other foreign experts concur. American elections are characterized by partisan voter suppression, tens of millions of wasted votes, maladministration, and a host of ensuing second-order malpractices. As noted by Australian professor Pippa Norris, US elections are "[e]xemplified by inaccurate voter registers, partisan gerrymandering, maladministration of polling, vote-buying, clientalistic politics . . . erroneous counts, campaigns awash with money, and excessively high legal barriers to elected office. 'Second-order' malpractices can happen anywhere . . . as exemplified by the notorious hanging chads in Florida in 2000."[69]

The EIP assessment lamented the "massive influence of wealthy private donors on electoral campaigns and programs."[70] It fingered the following specific practices as responsible for the low quality of American elections:

- Winner-take-all electoral systems and single member districts that misrepresent voter preferences and produce tens of millions of wasted votes (cast for losing candidates)—a phenomenon rare in wealthy democracies. The remedy is adoption of proportional representation (PR) systems to ensure that each voter's preference is reflected in composition of legislatures. Conceived in Denmark during the 1850s, PR's leading proponents included Alexis de Tocqueville in France and John Stuart Mill in England. Utilized in over twenty higher quality democracies in Europe such as Germany, PR eliminates gerrymandering and wasted votes. But in the United States, political party officials have successfully resisted efforts to install PR and have eliminated those established by voter referendum in cities such as Cincinnati. Today, it attracts little attention aside from advocates such as Democratic Congressman Don Beyer and the nonpartisan advocacy organization FairVote.[71]

(A different, narrower definition of "wasted votes" is utilized by American political scientists; it is a measure of the degree to which partisan lawmakers create gerrymandered legislative districts that are lopsided in favor of one political party.)[72]

- Gerrymandering of legislative districts to favor the ruling party. The success of US political parties in cornering state governments and Congressional seats regardless of popular vote outcomes is a consequence of gerrymandering. The dark corners of American democracy are gerrymandered, single-party legislative districts fostering lawmakers on the political fringe. Gerrymandering is only possible in the rare winner-take-all, single member legislative district structures like the United States, not in the PR electoral systems nearly universal in higher quality democracies. Until PR is adopted, an interim reform is to rely on entities independent of politicians to draw legislative district lines. Of the forty-three states with more than one seat in Congress, eight, including California, no longer permit lawmakers themselves to design their legislative districts. Instead, they rely on independent commissions, most installed by citizen referenda. And one state, Democratic-leaning Maryland, has proposed that five other mid-Atlantic states (New York, New Jersey, Pennsylvania, Virginia, and North Carolina) join it in establishing such nonpartisan commissions; the imaginative proposal was vetoed by the Republican governor in 2017. Importantly, the Supreme Court in *Arizona State Legislature v. Arizona Independent Redistricting Commission* (2015) ruled such independent entities constitutional. Winner-take-all elections and single member districts cause electoral outcomes in the most gerrymandered American state (North Carolina) to reflect popular choices and voter opinion no better than do elections in notoriously faux democracies such as Cuba, Indonesia, or Sierra Leone.

- Extremely low turnout for Congressional and other down-ballot offices. Negative political advertising, indifference by legislators to popular sentiment, and the oppressive influence of wealthy donors has discouraged participation. Moreover, with major elections held on Tuesdays, many Americans must leave work to vote. Low turnout is exacerbated by partisan steps limiting early voting opportunities and reducing the availability of ballot stations in states controlled by the Republican Party, such as Ohio.

- Partisan disenfranchisement through targeted voter registration restrictions. The EIP analysts noted that the burdensome American "voter registration system *de facto* discriminates against lower classes and African-Americans in particular." Partisans should not be involved in voter registration or balloting mechanisms. The success of American Republican officials in restricting registration opportunities reflects the absence of a federalized, automated national voter registration system. Restrictive practices include needless voter ID requirements, limited Election Day registration opportunities, the curtailing of registration campaigns by non-partisan groups such as the League of Women Voters, and the unwarranted purge of voter registration rolls (e.g., in Florida, North Carolina, Ohio, and Wisconsin) particularly targeting minorities. (In higher quality democracies, voter systems register citizens at age eighteen and autonomously update them during their lives.) These practices have been justified by members of the Republican Party with bogus assertions, including Trump advisor Stephen Miller who has mendaciously asserted that "14 percent of noncitizens," including Latino immigrants, are registered to vote.[73]
- The Electoral College and absence of a binary runoff mechanism allows electoral losers to ascend to the presidency. America stands alone among wealthy democracies in thwarting the majoritarian will of voters in selecting national leaders. Other nations select national leaders by absolute majority vote (France) or by parliamentary vote (Germany). As Swiss researcher Nils-Christian Bormann and Penn State political science professor Matt Golder explain, "The [concept of an] electoral college is currently used only in the United States, after Argentina and Finland abandoned it in the 1980s."[74]

Reforms Threatened by Institutionalized Voter Suppression

The institutionalized disenfranchisement and suppression of political opponents pinpointed by the EIP is rooted in two judicial rulings by the Roberts Republicans. As noted in chapter 5, *Crawford* empowered voter ID laws while *Shelby* declared section 5 of the Voting Rights Act unconstitutional. *Shelby* restored the Jim Crow era doctrine of undue state sovereignty on voter eligibility—federal authority subservient—belying the Fifteenth Amendment. In the wake of that ruling, numerous Republican state governments enacted voter suppression laws aimed at Democratic-leaning voters. Some 600,000 mostly poor or elderly whites and minorities in Texas alone who lacked required IDs were stripped of eligibility. The types of suppression highlighted by the EIP report include burdensome new voter ID rules, elimination of hundreds of polling stations in Democratic precincts, elimination of voter registration drives in high schools and on college campuses, purges of eligible voters from registration rolls, reduction in early voting opportunities, and ending Election Day registration. For instance, GOP election officials since 2008 in Indiana have manipulated the early voting process to expand Republican voting opportunities while shrinking Democratic ones. They tripled the number of locations in Republican-leaning counties like Hamilton to facilitate voters with transportation or schedule challenges while restricting Democratic-heavy Indianapolis (Marion County) to just one site. Consequently, each early voting site serves roughly 100,000 registered voters in Hamilton but more than 700,000 in Marion. The strategy was quite effective: Compared to 2008, early voting rose by 21,000 (63 percent) in Hamilton in 2016 while actually shrinking by 24,000 (26 percent) in Marion. The share of all ballots cast early rose from 25 percent to 34 percent in Hamilton County, while declining to 19 percent from 24 percent in Marion County.[75]

Abolishing the ability of citizens to register on Election Day is a particularly effective vote suppression tactic. The fifteen states permitting such registration consistently have the nation's highest electoral turnout rates, including the top state of Minnesota where 75 percent of eligible (registered and unregistered) citizens cast ballots in 2016—25 percent greater than the national average of 60 percent in presidential election cycles.[76]

With the share of nonwhite eligible voters rising briskly nationally, institutionalized suppression has emerged as an imperative for the Republican Party, fully supported by the Trump administration. Its Justice Department in January 2017, for instance, reversed long-standing practice by ceasing all investigations of alleged violations by state and local GOP officials of the Voting Rights Act. A few months later, it conjured a "Presidential Advisory Commission on Electoral Integrity" stacked with GOP officials experienced in stripping Democratic-leaning citizens from state voter rolls. In-person voter fraud in America is essentially nonexistent—a sham. Yet the goal of the Commission is to sow doubts about that fact in order to justify the widespread disenfranchisement of voters who bend Democratic. The commission is chaired by Kansas Secretary of State Kris Kobach, whose "Crosscheck" initiative in the past has widely disseminated bogus registration information used to purge voters in states like Idaho and Iowa.[77] For instance, it fingered 240,000 Iowans in 2012 and 2014 as purge targets because they shared with out-of-state voters common birthdates and (first and last) names like Maria Rodriguez.[78] Yet researchers at Stanford, Harvard, the University of Pennsylvania, and Microsoft determined that only a minuscule *six* of them had cast double ballots.[79]

The Trump administration has also refused to intervene in Ohio where GOP Governor John Kasich has purged 2 million mostly young, poor, and nonwhite occasional voters since 2011. The purges have affected Democratic-leaning neighborhoods at roughly twice the rate of Republican-leaning neighborhoods, according to an independent analysis by Reuters.[80]

Looking ahead, the Trump administration, Roberts Republicans, and the GOP Congress may prohibit online voter registration, which significantly eases the chore of registration. Some thirty-one states allowed online registration in 2016, a dramatic increase since 2010 when only six did.[81] There are three other electoral reforms expanding voting that may also be targeted. The first could be repeal of the National Voter Registration Act, also known as Motor Voter. This law facilitates voter registration for citizens interacting with state agencies. Indeed, some ten states and the District of Columbia have or are installing automatic registration mechanisms for such citizens, including Oregon. Under its first-in-the-nation law, citizens interacting with that state's Division of Motor Vehicles are automatically registered to vote. Some 272,000 were registered in its first year. Easing the burden of registration paid off in November 2016 when participation by these new voters caused the increase in turnout in Oregon to lead the nation.[82]

A second target could be reforms that ensure binary runoffs occur, like the Louisiana electoral system. A variation that prevents a second election when no candidate wins a majority initially is called ranked-choice, in use in a few localities such as Takoma Park, Maryland. Residents cast votes for candidates in hierarchical order, ensuring that only candidates favored by a majority of voters can be elected.[83]

Third could be a ban on nonpartisan or open primaries. All aspirants for a political office in California, Washington state, and Louisiana are required to first compete in a single primary—the so-called "jungle" primary—regardless of political party affiliation. The two aspirants receiving the most votes subsequently compete in a binary runoff in the November general election. This system has quite dramatically moderated the voting behavior of Congressional Republicans in California.[84] They have been forced since 2012 out of the dark corners of American democracy to compete in primaries not dominated by staunchly conservative party grassroots. (Importantly, California also eliminated gerrymandered legislative districts at the same time.) In 2013, for instance, the median left-right Congressional voting record of California Republicans shifted from the quite conservative eighty-fifth percentile among all Members of Congress to the sixtieth percentile.[85]

Ending pay-to-play would ease the path for legislators to then pursue the reforms explored in this chapter. It would enable members of Congress so inclined to meet the preferences of middle-class voters rather than donors, raising the quality of American democracy, diminishing the income bias, and affirming original intent. Another important pillar of democracy identified by the framers was the quality of information available to voters. This original intent, derailed by the fake news phenomenon during the 2016 presidential election, is examined in the following chapters.

Original Intent to Prevent Fake News

T HE FRAMERS DRAMATICALLY SPREAD the franchise but realized that the poorly informed voters of their day needed to be provided with facts and knowledge in order to bring informed opinions into the voting booth. They were concerned with the dangers posed by an electorate misled by "artful misrepresentations by interested men," or "pretend patriots."

Their concerns have resurfaced of late with one of the two major political parties concluding that partisan success can be found by diminishing the quality of factual information available to voters. That is a harsh conclusion, but the Republican Party today seeks to prosper by providing voters with fake news supporting afactual narratives for partisan advantage. Their Orwellian news strategy includes delegitimizing factual journalism with persistent attacks on the mainstream media. Both practices would leave the framers apoplectic.

By institutionalizing fake news as a seminal party principle, the GOP strategy is to inveigle voters with a compelling alternative to truth. Americans have become more divided than at any time since the Vietnam War and perhaps since the antebellum era. Compromise has become toxic. Convinced that they are disdained by big government elites who are indifferent to wage stagnation, and threatened by immigrants and minorities, a sizable cohort of mostly conservative white voters has grown suspicious of collaboration and cooperation with Democrats. This Republican tactic centered on misinformation has reduced the political middle, diminishing the moderation and respect for opponents that are essential for a high-quality democracy. It has promoted a polarized society where neighbors no longer share the same facts and view each other as fools or worse, significantly exacerbating the divide explored by Mann and Ornstein in 2012. For example, in the wake of 9/11 in 2001, Gallup surveys found that 74 percent of respondents believed the nation was united. In 2004, that sentiment stood at 45 percent. But, the 2016 election drove that figure down to a bare 21 percent.[1] Michigan State political science professor Corwin Smidt has documented a dramatic decline in the share of floating or swing voters in the American electorate. They comprise only 5 percent of voters now—one-half their share in the early 1990s and down from a high of 15 percent in the late 1960s.[2]

Eliminating pay-to-play is central to raising the quality of American democracy. Integral to that goal is realizing the framers' hope by expunging fake news from American politics to elevate the factual foundation of voter decisions and rebuild a moderate center.

CHAPTER 13

Original Intent: A Fact-Based Media

The First Amendment goal of producing an informed public . . . It is the right of viewers and listeners, not the right of the broadcasters, which is paramount.[1]

> —*Red Lion Broadcasting v. FCC*, Majority Opinion, 1969,
> The Warren Supreme Court

Behind the Scenes, Billionaires' Growing Control of News [headline][2]

> —Jim Rutenberg, *New York Times*, May 28, 2016

FOCUSING SOLELY ON THE founding fathers' and the framers' intent to avoid corruption by ending pay-to-play will leave unaddressed their equally grave concern with the quality of information available to voters.

The unique contributions of the nation's founders were the Bill of Rights and their expansion of the franchise, which they achieved by sharply reducing the high property standards for male voters in contemporary republics of the day. At the extreme, leaders in 1777 of what became Vermont entirely delinked the franchise from financial circumstances.[3]

The framers realized that a greatly expanded franchise renders a democracy vulnerable if it is not complemented by voters armed with facts. As this chapter's epigraph notes, one goal A key objective of their First Amendment was an "informed public," free of temptation by fabulists.

They wrote and spoke repeatedly of the dangers posed to the new nation by charlatans or demagogues seeking partisan gain or profit by inflaming and misleading voters with what we today call fake news. As noted in the Introduction, Elbridge Gerry worried about voters being duped by "pretend patriots. In Massachusetts it had been fully confirmed by experience, that they are daily misled into the most baneful measures and opinions, by the false reports circulated by designing men, and which no one on the spot can refute."[4] And Madison in *Federalist 63* coveted fact-based voters resistant to "artful misrepresentations by interested men."[5] He later explained the urgency of an electorate armed with fact-based information as noted earlier: "A popular government, without popular information, or the means of acquiring it, is but a prologue to a farce or a tragedy; or perhaps both. Knowledge will forever govern ignorance; and a people who mean to be their own governors must arm themselves with the power which knowledge gives."[6]

Constitutional Framers: The Vital Role of a Free Press

The framers envisaged a key role for a free press in providing a fact-based forum. One of their remedies for fake news was to build a central role for the media of the day—newspapers and broadsheets—into the nation's architecture. They created the concept of a free press in hopes that the media would serve as a fact-based narrator, investigator, reporter, truth-teller, and commentator on politics and policy free of government or other influence. Their naïve hopes were quickly dashed. Too many media owners since colonial times have exercised their independence to misinform and mislead the public, molding public opinion to mirror their own biases. Thomas Jefferson in 1800 attributed the disingenuous and malicious coverage of politics in the new nation in "great degree" to the ninety colonial era newspaper proprietors disseminating fake news: "I deplore . . . the putrid state into which our newspapers have passed and the malignity, the vulgarity, and mendacious spirit of those who write for them."[7]

The Revolutionary War and the War of 1812 were replete with fake news intended to enhance American fervor using bogus reports of massacres by Indians allied with the British.[8] Indeed, the colonial era and the antebellum era that followed featured harshly partisan local broadsheets. By the 1920s, economies of scale had enabled some media firms to grow sufficiently large to reshape public opinion and preferences nationwide. Fictitious claims were still commonly disseminated.[9] As Sigmund Freud's

American nephew, Edward Bernays, explained, "our minds are molded, our tastes formed, our ideas suggested, largely by men we have never heard of."[10] Indeed, American media proprietors of the day were continuing a practice reaching back thousands of years in history, including weaponized fake news deployed during the Roman civil war circa 35 BC between Mark Antony and Octavian.[11]

The threat of fake news to democracy feared by the framers reached new heights with the marriage of state-directed propaganda and radio in the 1930s. Authoritarians in Russia, Germany, Italy, and elsewhere utilized slick audio versions of fake news to cement dictatorships. In politics, that period was the most prominent precedent for the dramatic surge in weaponized fake news by Russians and partisan Americans seeking to sway voters in 2016.

The Fairness Doctrine: The Rights of Viewers Trump the Rights of Broadcasters

In reaction to the biased news foisted on the public by foreign authoritarians and news barons of the 1930s and 1940s, Congress successfully upgraded the quality of information to voters. Like the framers, Congress hoped to elevate the media to an unbiased and nonpartisan source of news. Government investment played a key role in the R&D that produced broadcast technology, so Congress centered its reforms on media outlets that exploited government-funded R&D. Public radio and television were supported. And after considerable contemplation and debate, a policy known as the Fairness Doctrine was devised for private broadcasters. Not originally reliant on government R&D, print media were excluded. Enacted by the Federal Communications Commission (FCC) under President Truman in 1949, the Fairness Doctrine was extremely successful in meeting original intent. It reined in partisanship and extremism in broadcast reporting. The process featured self-regulation with proprietors filtering content to achieve factual and nonpartisan objectivity in the discussion of policy and politics.

The doctrine's central principle was an obligation for broadcasters to give factual coverage to all sides of issues and to all candidates. It also included equal time for a prompt response by those victimized by on-air attacks. Importantly, proprietor filtration proved remarkably effective—producing fact-based, unbiased, and judicious presentations. The logic of the Fairness Doctrine was explained by Princeton politics professor Jan-Werner Müller in January 2016: "An election, after all, can be undemocratic even if the ruling party refrains from stuffing ballot boxes. If opposition parties have been hindered in making their case to the electorate . . . the ballot boxes have already been stuffed."[12]

Proprietors of broadcast properties argued that the doctrine's obligations amounted to content censorship, violating their First Amendment rights. The Warren Supreme Court disagreed, pointing to the media's central role envisaged by the framers in a democracy. In *Red Lion Broadcasting Co. v. FCC* (1969), they found the doctrine constitutional, concluding that it furthered "the right of the public to receive suitable access to social, political, esthetic, moral and other ideas and experiences . . . [and] the First Amendment goal of producing an informed public capable of conducting its own affairs . . ."[13]

Media proprietors were galled that the FCC regulation compelled them to provide exposure to opinions expressed by those unable to purchase airtime. The Warren Supreme Court highlighted this concern in *Red Lion*; Judge Guido Calabresi of the US Court of Appeals for the Second District explained their thinking in his December 2011 concurring opinion in *Ognibene et al. v. Parkes et al.*:

> For an articulation of this concern—i.e., that, without regulation, the wealthy would be able to use their wealth to overwhelm the voices of the poor—one need look no further than the Supreme Court's decision in *Red Lion Broadcasting Co. v. FCC* (1969) where, in upholding the FCC's "fairness doctrine," the High Court long ago explained that, without the rule in place, "station owners and a few networks would have unfettered power to make time available only to the highest bidders" and thereby broadcast only those bidders' political views; (again quoting *Red Lion Broadcasting Co. v. FCC*). "Just as the Government may limit the use of sound-amplifying equipment potentially so noisy that it drowns out civilized private speech, so may the Government limit the use of broadcast equipment. The right of free speech of a broadcaster, the user of a sound truck, or any other individual does not embrace a right to snuff out the free speech of others."[14]

Broadcast proprietors were further galled that the FCC regulation mandated coverage of opinions they disfavored. Indeed, gaining the autonomy to torpedo original intent by unilaterally skewing information to voters was the goal uppermost in broadcasters' minds as events unfolded in 1987 during the Reagan administration: Edward O. Fritts, president of the National Association of Broadcasters, described the doctrine as "an intrusion into broadcasters' journalistic judgment."[15] The Warren Court had already rejected that concern, holding that it was unconstitutional for proprietors to foist only their opinions and ideologies on voters. The *Red Lion Broadcasting* ruling insisted that "it is the right of viewers and listeners, not the right of the broadcasters, which is paramount."[16]

Collapse of the Fairness Doctrine: Talk Radio, Fox News, and Sinclair Broadcasting Group

By 1987 President Reagan was in a position to respond to the ardent parochial desires of broadcasters. He had appointed industry straw men to the FCC as openings occurred, and finally had the votes to kill the Fairness Doctrine. An alarmed Congress reacted, with large bipartisan majorities voting to codify the doctrine into law in order to shield it from Reagan. The Senate passed such legislation in April by a vote of 59–31 and the House followed suit on June 3, 1987, by a vote of 302–102.[17] But Reagan vetoed the legislation, and his appointees to the FCC soon thereafter killed the doctrine. Its abandonment has meant the only constraints that broadcasters confront in pressing their personal ideologies on voters are the de minimus "equal time" and "reasonable access" rules promulgated by the FCC more than eighty years ago (1934). And those rules serve only to prevent gross injustices such as refusal to sell comparable airtime for campaign ads to all (financially able) candidates at comparable ad rates.[18] The new environment it ushered in was aptly described by A.J. Liebling: "Freedom of the press is guaranteed only to those who own one.[19]

In the years since Ronald Reagan mocked original intent, broadcasters have abandoned objectivity in favor of an afactual, partisan din. Fables foisted as reality have become commonplace, buttressed by demonizing and discrediting fact-based investigative reporting. The ensuing polarization of voters has caused the moderate center of US politics to dwindle, with Americans now often selecting only their own ideologically compatible information regardless of factual content.[20]

Data indicate these trends are especially evident on the right, with some 40 percent of voters who supported candidate Trump in 2016, for instance, citing conservative Fox News rather than fact-based mainstream media as their "main source" of information. In contrast, the main news sources for Clinton voters were scattered among CNN (18 percent), MSNBC (9 percent), local TV (8 percent), National Public Radio, and ABC (each at 7 percent).[21] That is significant because Fox News is an especially active purveyor of fake, afactual news, evidenced in a survey by Fairleigh Dickinson political scientist Dan Cassino. Some 52 percent of Fox News viewers still believed as late as 2015 the bogus claim that weapons of mass destruction had been found following the invasion of Iraq. Only 14 percent of MSNBC viewers were still fooled.[22]

Recall it was Frank Rich who contended that Fox was instrumental, in cooperation with the Koch brothers, in empowering the Tea Party movement. Its owner, Rupert Murdoch, is a charter member (with the Scaifes, Coors, Ricketts, and Kochs) in what Jane Mayer describes as "a small, rarefied group of hugely wealthy, archconservative families that for decades poured money, often with little public exposure, into influencing how the Americans thought and voted."[23]

The Democrats certainly bend in some measure to the will of their own donor class. But the *fittest fifty* enjoy far greater sway on the right, their agenda morphing into that of the Republican Party, aggressively propagated by conservative media outlets. The most impactful exemplar is the Sinclair Broadcasting conglomerate (read on). Less important if far better known is the Fox cable news channel. Fox News under Roger Ailes emerged as the most faithful and effective inheritor of Reagan, peddling the animus of the *fittest fifty* toward higher wages, public education, collective bargaining, and government programs that expand scientific knowledge and opportunity. A Pew survey in October 2014 found that few moderates or liberals watch Fox because of its slanted reporting. In contrast, 47 percent of those self-identifying as "consistently conservative" named Fox as their "main source for government and political news"; some 84 percent obtained political news from Fox in the previous week.[24] Fox News cable viewership is sizable enough that the Pew Research Center in December 2016 found more Americans believed Fox News than National Public Radio.[25]

Fox has cornered a portion of the market for conservative TV viewership dollars in the same fashion that Donald Trump won the 2016 GOP presidential nomination, by being the most extreme, hyperbolic, and often fact-free critic of government and all things progressive. This strategy is facilitated by its on-air model, blending opinion with partisan, slanted, and too often afactual reporting. The network disseminates misleading or fake news with fanfare, only rarely and belatedly offering muted retractions or corrections. During the 2008 election, Fox News disseminated numerous bogus claims to demonize candidate Obama. Indeed, some 30 percent of Fox News viewers in 2015 still believed the birtherism canard that he was not a citizen (another 9 percent remained uncertain); only 7 percent of MSNBC viewers remained snookered.[26] And during the 2016 political campaign, Fox News was a global sound truck for sensational partisan fabrications, some sourced by Russian cyber hackers. They readily aired fantasies (terrorist attack in Sweden!) and repeatedly hosted poseurs of fictitious provenance such as Nils Bildt.[27] Today, it is by far the most favored outlet for interviews by President Donald Trump.

Fox News presenters and articulate alternative-reality radio hosts such as Glenn Beck and Rush Limbaugh have infused the conservative movement with such a sense of camaraderie, excitement, and purpose that 84 percent of self-identified Tea Partiers by 2010 believed that their "movement generally reflects the views of most Americans." In reality, that same poll found that only 25 percent of respondents nationally believed that Tea Partiers reflect the views of most Americans.[28]

The nation's largest TV conglomerate, Sinclair Broadcasting Group of beautiful Hunt Valley, Maryland, is a less conspicuous but more powerful advocate of the GOP and the *fittest fifty* agenda. With deregulation, it had grown from three stations in 1996 to 173 by 2016. And under Trump, the Federal Communications Commission relaxed legal limits in 2017, allowing Sinclair to expand to 215 stations. Its sweep enables it to wield more influence than Fox in shaping public attitudes. For example, once he secured the GOP nomination, candidate Trump restricted TV interviews mostly to alternative-reality media platforms such as Fox News and Sinclair, eschewing news conferences entirely. First revealed by *Politico,* based on a speech to donors by Trump son-in-law Jared Kushner, the arrangement with Sinclair was described this way by Paul Farhi of the *Washington Post.* "The Trump campaign struck a deal with Sinclair to provide access and coverage . . . Sinclair's stations, particularly in swing states such as Ohio and Florida, reached a far greater audience in their local areas than a national network . . . A review of Sinclair's reporting and internal documents show a strong tilt toward Trump . . . while often casting Clinton in an unfavorable light."[29]

The Sinclair conglomerate aired thirty-one exclusive interviews, for instance, after July 2016 with Trump, his running mate Mike Pence, or campaign surrogates such as Ben Carson compared to seven with the Clinton campaign. Some were as long as eighteen minutes and most were distributed to stations as "must-run" stories. Moreover, Sinclair's on-air commentators, such as executive Mark Hyman, routinely traffic in fake news, arguing breathlessly on October 27, 2016, for instance, that "Most Americans know very little about the leaked Clinton emails. Major news organizations buried the most damaging. So we're sharing them with you." Factual news that cast GOP candidates in a poor light went unreported, including Trump's failure to release medical or tax records or to document the justification for his Vietnam War era draft deferments. Sinclair had previously aired fake news in 2004, impugning Democratic candidate John Kerry's service in Vietnam. In 2016, its TV stations in Pittsburgh persisted in airing attack ads against Democratic senate candidate Joe Sestak despite knowing they contained falsehoods.[30]

The conservative media have had considerable success in sowing distrust of government programs and elevating tribalism. For example, Pew Research Center polling in 2015 found that three-quarters of conservative respondents believed government benefits enable the impoverished to "have it easy." Only one in seven acknowledged the reality that the poor "have it hard."[31] Be mindful that we are talking about the 22 percent of Americans who work two jobs to make ends meet.[32] Or the 42 percent of Americans living in or near poverty, earning less than $15 per hour, and the 46 percent of Americans unable to scrape together $400 in cash to meet an emergency.[33] They live paycheck to paycheck in a downtrodden lifestyle described by Barbara Ehrenreich in *Nickled and Dimed*, and by Kathryn Edin and H. Luke Shaefer in *$2 a Day: Living on Almost Nothing in America*. How strapped are they for cash? Look to Virginia where one-sixth of motorists (more than 900,000) lost their licenses in 2015 because of their inability to pay modest court fines and fees.[34]

In contrast, absent from the conservative media are reports of malfeasance by the *fittest* or the business sector's suppression of wages, job offshoring in favor of profits, and routine use of corporate tax havens. Indeed, Fox News has good reason to downplay the latter, since its highly profitable Australian parent 21st Century Fox (Rupert Murdoch's original News Corporation) pays less than a 1 percent tax rate.[35] It is viewed by the Australian Taxation Office as the most egregious tax dodger in that nation.[36]

The conservative media deflect middle-class attention from wage stagnation, facilitating the GOP pursuit of the *fittest* agenda by stoking race and class resentment. Former *Washington Post* columnist Harold Meyerson explained that it "tapped into and built a right-wing populism that focuses the white working class's blame for its woes downward—at the racial other—rather than up."[37] It is Jim Crow era class incitement updated to include Latinos and city dwellers.

The Democratic Party certainly has partisan advocates in the media such as the *Huffington Post*, but audience data confirm they are outgunned by Sinclair and Fox. As we see in the next chapter, the 2016 election cycle saw America's energetic and entrepreneurial conservatives expand beyond broadcast media to be eager innovators in the explosion of partisan and fake news on social media platforms.

CHAPTER 14

Fake News Exacerbates Political Polarization, Tribalism, and the Income Bias

We assess Russian President Vladimir Putin ordered an influence campaign in 2016 aimed at the US presidential election . . . Putin and the Russian government aspired to help President-elect Trump's election chances when possible by discrediting Secretary Clinton and publicly contrasting her unfavorably to him.[1]

—US intelligence agencies' investigation of Russian cyber espionage, January 2017

Over the years, we've effectively brainwashed the core of our audience to distrust anything that they disagree with.[2]

—John Ziegler, conservative radio host, December 2016

THE FRAMERS REALIZED THAT afactual information is corrosive to democracy. It fractures the centrality of collaborative governance: wisdom derived from a body of commonly accepted facts that form the basis for informed decision making by citizens, facilitating tolerance and moderation in public affairs. Fake news dilutes that wisdom, thereby posing an existential danger to high-quality democracy. That danger was dramatized in 2016, when fake news surged, allowing a spread of misinformation by partisans akin to Elbridge Gerry's "pretend patriots." Political analyst Richard Heydarian described the consequence of that election: "Voices that were lurking in the shadows are now at the center of the public discourse."[3]

This surge occurred on outlets such as Fox News that cater to conservatives. But it was also powerfully disseminated in an unprecedented fashion on social media platforms or POPS—privately owned public spaces—including Facebook, Google (including YouTube), and Twitter. Inexpensive, unfiltered, and hyperaccessible social media communications have supplanted much of the traditional informational functions of broadcast and print media for Americans under the age of fifty. Some 57 percent of Americans in a July 2016 Pew survey cited television among their news sources while online sources overall were cited second at 38 percent. But that disguises a huge generational gap. The internet was cited as the most frequent news source by Americans under the age of fifty; for those under age thirty, it was cited first by a 2:1 margin over TV.[4] This seismic shift in news sources is documented by the reaction of marketers, who have rationally shifted ad placements online. Digital advertising now rivals the $70 billion spent on TV.[5]

This transformation poses a considerable challenge to prospects for an informed electorate. Potentially malicious or mendacious corner soapbox rants accessible to a handful within hearing distance just a few years ago are abruptly now accessible to billions. The surge of fake news during the 2016 election marks a sea change, casting yet another shadow over the quality of American democracy. Jonathan Taplin, Director Emeritus of the Annenberg Innovation Lab at the University of Southern California explains: "The original mission of the internet was hijacked by a small group of right-wing radicals to whom the ideas of democracy and decentralization were anathema."[6] Even Twitter founder Evan Williams is dismayed by the extremism and toxicity abounding as entrepreneurs and partisans glamorize or monetize the outlandish and far worse on social media: "And it's a lot more obvious to a lot of people that it's broken . . . I thought once everybody could speak freely and exchange information and ideas, the world is automatically going to be a better place. I was wrong about that."[7] Indeed, the level of toxicity is stunning: The Pew Research Center has found that four in ten internet users have been harassed online—and these are adult users, not adolescents or youths.[8] And according to the

Washington Post, 4 percent of internet users, including Marine Corps personnel, are victims of explicit images.[9]

This trend will persist because, while voters tend to be skeptics about general news sources, a sizable minority of Americans seemingly have yet to develop skepticism for information gleaned from cyberspace. That especially includes younger Americans, the most internet-reliant cohort. For example, researchers at the Stanford Graduate School of Education in 2016 tested student acumen in evaluating the *sourcing* of internet information, a key variable determining viewer trust. Their analysis of some 7,800 students nationwide found they "predominantly relied on social media for news." No surprise there. Yet, the students proved to be quite inept at assessing the veracity of information because they failed to discriminate between news sources: a remarkable 93 percent were unable to winnow fact from fake news. The researchers found that test subjects accepted at face value self-serving claims and misleading graphics made by special interest groups including financial information proffered by a bank advertisement, information from the National Rifle Association, or commentary by employers opposed to minimum wages. The analysts found "a dismaying inability by students to reason about information they see on the internet. Students, for example, had a hard time distinguishing advertisements from news articles or identifying where information came from . . . Many people assume that because young people are fluent in social media they are equally perceptive about what they find there. Our work shows the opposite to be true . . ."[10]

Fake News Is Circulated More Widely Than Factual News

The Stanford analysis reveals a generalized weakness among Americans of all ages in identifying fake news, evidenced by the willingness of many internet users to circulate bogus postings as readily as they circulate factual news stories. Twitter provides the data. Professor Philip Howard and colleagues at Oxford University's Internet Institute evaluated all 138,686 tweets of a political nature sent by residents of Michigan during ten days ending on November 11, 2016, surrounding the election. The sharing of links on social media like Twitter is a persuasive signal that users consider the information important and credible. Slightly more than 24,000 of these political tweets included links and thus were subsequently evaluated. Some 23 percent of those links (5,615) proved to be to fake news stories. This volume nearly equaled the number of links tweeted to stories originating with fact-based media (5,668).[11] However, when links to Russian-origin news stories and to unverified WikiLeaks news reports were added, the volume of searches involving political fake news sources surpassed professional news sources.[12]

In a separate analysis, the news website BuzzFeed also concluded that fake news was shared among Facebook users more than real news.[13]

Fake News Is Widely Believed

When a large pool of Americans with underdeveloped skills in evaluating news sources enter into an ecosystem of factual and fake news on POPS platforms, many millions are certain to be misled. That outcome was quantified by New York University professor Hunt Allcott and Stanford professor Matthew Gentzkow in the wake of the 2016 election. Survey data of voters they evaluated found that only about 15 percent (14.1 percent and 15.3 percent in two waves) of respondents recalled seeing fake news on social media during the election, such as the Pope endorsing candidate Trump. That's the good news. The bad news is that over half of those viewers (59 percent and 52 percent in the two waves) believed the fables.[14] That suggests about 11 million American voters were misled in 2016, an enormous cohort who both saw and believed fake news.

Political scientists have not yet measured the impact of fake news on the 2016 balloting. If these 11 million snookered voters disproportionately selected President Trump, the outcome may have been influenced. A definitive answer is elusive, however, because any misled Trump (or Clinton) voter may have already been committed; viewing the fake news merely served to reinforce a preexisting bias. Political scientists call that syndrome "confirmation bias," where viewers seek out or best retain information that fuels preexisting opinion. What seems certain is that millions of American voters were influenced in some measure by fake news. After all, BuzzFeed concluded that the fake news story about Pope Francis endorsing Donald Trump was the single most visited item of news on Facebook in the three months before the US election.[15]

Conservatives Have Proven Disproportionately Susceptible to Fake News

Research surrounding the 2016 election has produced other notable findings. Perhaps most importantly, political scientists have concluded that conservative voters are unduly inclined to believe fake news. The machinations involving fake news during the 2016 presidential election led to the discovery that conservatives are considerably more suggestible than other Americans. This conclusion is based on real-world data and the experience of entrepreneurs in the media marketplace.

Fake news websites proffering political information in 2016 were divided between for-profit ventures and ideological, partisan ventures on behalf of candidates. Beginning in the spring of 2016, for-profit sites carrying political news proliferated at the hands of hundreds of entrepreneurs, including folks such as John Egan of Vancouver, Beqa Latsabidze of Tbilisi, Georgia, and a number of Macedonian computer experts from the town of Veles.[16] The business model was to entice viewers on Facebook and other social media platforms to click over to (linked) for-profit websites festooned with ads. Initially agnostic about US politics, these international entrepreneurs tried generating clicks for websites with hyperbolic postings using pro-Clinton themes, football themes, food themes, and anti-Clinton/pro-Trump themes. This cottage industry soon discovered through trial and error that Trump supporters were far more prone to respond to their fallacious posts, many merely responding to hoax headlines alone. They were readily gulled and thus held the greatest promise of profit. These entrepreneurs quickly honed in with pro-Trump/anti-Clinton fake news posting on POPS platforms in order to drive traffic to mendacious websites with names like TrumpVision365.com, USConservativeToday.com, and DonaldTrumpNews.com. According to the *Guardian*, the Veles contingent of cyber profiteers alone ended up creating 150 sites bashing Clinton, some allegedly receiving 1 million visits monthly.[17] (Mr. Latsabidze's hoax that Mexico would close its border with the US should Trump be elected was the third-most-trafficked story on Facebook between May and July 2016 according to Buzzfeed.)[18]

American web entrepreneurs made the same discovery and also quickly pivoted to profit from gullible Trump supporters. The star is

Brandon Vallorani, whose Liberty Alliance grossed $11 million in 2016. His forty employees produced/copied incendiary content that pandered to the right and far-right, using 176 Facebook identities during the election to drive tens of millions of followers to his websites.[19] (You read that figure correctly.) San Francisco computer experts and former waiters Paris Wade and Ben Goldman similarly used Facebook to drive traffic to their anti-Clinton site *Liberty Writers News*. Daily dashing off flamboyant 400-word fake stories, they earned tens of thousands of dollars monthly from clicks on their website. Another prominent practitioner of fake news for profit, Paul Horner, admitted in late 2016 that customizing bogus claims for undiscerning conservatives was highly profitable: "Honestly, people . . . just keep passing stuff around. Nobody fact-checks anything anymore—I mean, that's how Trump got elected. He just said whatever he wanted, and people believed everything, and when the things he said turned out not to be true, people didn't care because they'd already accepted it. It's real scary. I've never seen anything like it."[20]

This massive pivot to hoodwink conservatives by entrepreneurs across the globe has been documented. For example, BuzzFeed found that seventeen of the twenty most popular fake news sites on Facebook in the last three months of the 2016 election cycle were either pro-Trump or anti-Clinton.[21] Political scientists researching Tea Party loyalists earlier had identified the same characteristic vulnerability, as noted by Skocpol and Williamson: "At times to be sure, national rightwing advocates and media stars are handling out a load of bull to grassroots Tea Party people, who accept outlandish claims a bit too readily. In meetings and interviews, we found that misinformation was prevalent among Tea Party supporters . . . Tea partiers seem to be trusting to the point of gullibility."[22]

Important in a broader context, as Cornell economist Nancy Folbre explains, their gullibility and brand loyalty in the face of counterfactuals also means that party grassroots are unaware how quickly the Republican lawmakers they elect, like Andy Barr, switch loyalties. Lawmakers soon ignore constituent concerns to pander to the *fittest fifty* agenda of raising profits at the expense of wages, with constituents left in the dark: "Many Tea party members may be unaware of the extent to which wealthy political conservatives like the Koch brothers have controlled their efforts and shaped legislative priorities."[23]

Fake News for Partisan Gain

In addition to fake news propagated by profit seekers, innumerable websites and social media postings were and are still crafted for partisan gain alone, including by the Russian government. And there is a third category of bogus online information disseminators who blend profit with ideology and partisanship.* Aside from Fox News and Sinclair, they include the *National Enquirer*, Breitbart News, talk radio, InfoWars, the Daily Caller, Liberty Alliance, Truthfeed, and entrepreneurial fabricators such as Cameron Harris of Annapolis, Maryland, owner of the site ChristianTimesNewspaper.com. Like others, Harris was stunned by the gullibility of those conservatives drawn by his mendacity: "At first it kind of shocked me—the response I was getting. How easily people would believe it [bogus anti-Clinton screeds]."[24]

Some web authors are cyber sophisticates, utilizing innovations such as automated Twitter accounts or bots that disseminate programmed information in volume with very little human input. In fact, Professor Howard at Oxford University found that a fifth of the tweets his team examined in the last week of the election were generated by high volume users—fifty or more posts daily—a signal that they were likely automated bots. And by nearly a 3:1 margin (78,662 vs. 28,074), they disseminated pro-Trump, anti-Clinton messages, designed to attract attention with alluring captions beneath bizarre pictures.[25] Moreover, the location of the bots suggested to experts that they focused their political messages on users in important swing states such as Florida.[26]

The gullibility of grassroots conservatives and their tendency to self-select for right-wing news disseminators does not surprise Republican political professionals. Former Romney presidential campaign advisor Ted Newton explains that their conservative convictions "almost made them

---

*Pushing a partisan agenda can also be costly. The *Wall Street Journal*, for example, reported that the *National Enquirer* paid $150,000 to purchase exclusive rights to information about a woman's affair with Donald Trump, a report they promptly buried, squelched. (In contrast, on November 5, 2016, on the eve of the election, the *Enquirer* revealed to readers that Secretary Clinton was addicted to narcotics.) See Margaret Sullivan, "Enquirer Sticks a Fork in Rancid Campaign Journalism," *Washington Post*, November 6, 2016.

slaves to those news outlets. So there is a whole group of people who will only watch Fox, who will only read Breitbart News. And they are living in a bubble."[27] Retired conservative radio host Charlie Sykes describes many of his listeners in the same vein: "You can be in this alternative media reality and there's no way to break through it."[28] Other Republicans agree, including George W. Bush speechwriter David Frum: "Too often, conservatives dupe themselves. They wrap themselves in closed information systems based upon pretend information . . . [e.g.] tax cuts always pay for themselves . . . This is how to understand the Glenn Beck phenomenon. Every day, Beck offers alternative knowledge—an alternative history of the United States and the world, an alternative system of economics, an alternative reality."[29]

Between being targeted with fake news and their confirmation bias, the GOP grassroots is not well informed about political or economic issues, nor of the invaluable role government has played for two centuries in expanding American prosperity. Indeed, the GOP electoral base has become so fact-challenged as to alarm even some conservatives. Here is Jennifer Rubin, writing in May 2016: "Conservatives must end their infatuation with phony news, conspiracy theories and demonization of well-meaning leaders. It is time to grow up, turn off Sean Hannity, get off toxic social media and start learning about the world as it is . . . [It] has become pathological."[30]

Feeding American conservatives a diet of partisan Republican opinion with slanted and fake news is hugely profitable for Fox News, Breitbart News, entrepreneurs such as Vallorani, and talk radio hosts such as Rush Limbaugh. However, their success means that too many Americans have settled into comfort zones where facts are merely one option among many on the information dashboard: President Obama was not born in America; Serena Williams uses banned substances; 4 million people fraudulently voted for Hillary Clinton; New Jersey Muslims boisterously celebrated 9/11; President Obama wiretapped Trump Tower.

The gullibility regarding fake news that emerged in 2016 on the American right puts the lie to Alexis de Tocqueville's 1830s observation in *Democracy in America*: "I do not think that there is a single country in the world where, in proportion to the population, there are so few ignorant . . . individuals as in America."

Delegitimizing Fact-Based Journalism to Polarize the Electorate for Partisan Gain

Weaponized fake news has bolstered the GOP, and its fabulists present another barrier to ending the income bias. Recall Fox News's role in promoting the Tea Party at the behest of the Kochs and Rupert Murdoch. That role was reprised in recent years by the Mercer family in providing millions of dollars to the super PAC Make American Number 1 and the nationalist Breitbart News website.[31] The risks posed by such behavior to the quality of democracy are one reason that higher quality democracies explicitly limit their *fittest's* ability to bend politics. In *Harper v. Canada* (2004), for example, the Canadian Supreme Court expressed fears for any society where "the affluent . . . dominate the political discourse . . . This unequal dissemination of points of view undermines the voter's ability to be adequately informed of all views."[32]

The sheer scope of cyber entrepreneurialism in 2016 means the *fittest fifty* actually played only a modest role in the explosion of fake news. Nonetheless, its agenda has been greatly furthered by the ensuing GOP electoral successes.

The central role played by fake news in today's Republican Party is rooted in the aftermath of the 1964 Goldwater campaign when a narrative emerged, asserting the outcome reflected a liberal media bias. Richard Hofstadter wrote then of the paranoid beliefs of GOP grassroots, that "America has been largely taken away from them . . ."[33] That narrative has been embellished since. The George W. Bush administration mocked the "reality-based community" of the *New York Times*. "That's not the way the world works anymore . . . we create our own reality."[34] Mitt Romney's pollster in 2012, Neil Newhouse, declared: "We're not going to let our campaign be dictated by fact checkers."[35] President Trump has gone considerably further, making warfare on fact-checkers a central element of his administration's public outreach strategy. Doubts are raised. Independent purveyors of facts ranging from the *New York Times* to *Snopes* and Factcheck.org are labeled fake news sources. The mainstream media is routinely termed the "fake news industry" by President Trump himself, demonized as an "enemy of the American people . . . The press is out of control, the level of dishonesty is out of control."[36] President Trump also routinely punches down at "disgusting reporters . . . scum," asserting, "They're very, very dishonest people . . ."[37]

Scholars studying the use of fake news (it's called "agnotology") emphasize its goal to raise doubts about the truth by creating and then sustaining controversy regarding awkward facts. They explain that the GOP and President Trump's reliance on fake news mimics tactics used by the postwar tobacco industry anxious to obfuscate the fact that tobacco use caused cancer: All facts are preliminary; studies are merely anecdotal or statistical manipulations; experts disagreed; critics had hidden agendas; it's unsettled science; wait for the best people to get a real answer.[38]

This mimicry of the tobacco industry by President Trump in casting doubt on mainstream fact-based reporting has been astoundingly successful. Survey data from the Pew Research Center in March 2017 found that a sharp divide was opened in 2016 between how Democrats and Republicans perceive news organizations. Some 89 percent of Democratic adults agreed, for instance, that news organizations "keep political leaders from doing things that shouldn't be done." Only 42 percent of Republicans respondents agreed with this watchdog role, creating the widest gap by far in this survey series that began in 1985.[39]

One of the most notable statistics in this book is a Gallup finding that only one-third (32 percent) of Americans in 2016 toward the end of the election expressed "trust and confidence" in the mainstream media. That share has fallen by more than half from 72 percent in 1976 before Ronald Reagan launched the GOP assault on moderation in public affairs by abandoning the Fairness Doctrine.[40] With only one-third of Americans expressing confidence in fact-based reporting, the nation is no longer the collaborative postwar democracy that routinely reached compromise on difficult issues such as civil rights on the basis of a widely accepted body of common facts. Indeed, a Suffolk University–USA Today survey in March 2017 found that 34 percent of registered voters agreed that mainstream media outlets are "the enemy of the American people."[41] The GOP's war on the press has convinced one-in-three Americans that facts derived from investigative reporting are their enemy.

GOP officials' adoption of the destructive strategy of polarizing fake news signals how their powerfully aggressive pursuit of the *fittest fifty* agenda has overruled the Republicans' democratic—and conservative—roots. The intellectual father of modern conservatism, Milton Friedman, for example, acknowledged that facts are an inestimable pillar in sustaining a quality democracy. In his famous 1955 essay, he wrote that a "stable and democratic society is impossible without widespread acceptance of some common set of values and without a minimum degree of literacy and knowledge on the part of most citizens."[42]

In wielding fake news as a cudgel to demonize the mainstream press, the Republican Party and especially Donald Trump are precisely mimicking European and Japanese authoritarians in the 1930s; Richard Nixon in the 1970s; and more recently Silvio Berlusconi, Hugo Chavez, Vladimir Putin, and Recep Erdoğan. Sykes explains the vital role played by its partisan supporters on talk radio, Fox News, and the like in polarizing the nation:

> Instead, we opened the door for President Trump, who found an audience that could be easily misled . . . the more the fact-based media tries to debunk the president's falsehoods, the further it will entrench the battle lines . . . He can do this because members of the Trump administration feel confident that the alternative-reality media will provide air cover, even if they are caught fabricating facts or twisting words (like claiming that the "ban" on Muslim immigrants wasn't really a "ban"). Indeed, they believe they have shifted the paradigm of media coverage, replacing the traditional media with their own.[43]

Today's alternative-reality media includes conservative commentator Rush Limbaugh who regularly argues that "Fake News is the everyday [mainstream media] news . . . They just make it up."[44] The consequential diminution of factual information for Americans is lamented by Sykes: "As we learned this year [2016], we had succeeded in persuading our audiences to ignore and discount any information from the mainstream media. Over time, we'd succeeded in delegitimizing the media altogether—all the normal guideposts were down, the referees discredited . . . We destroyed our own immunity to fake news, while empowering the worst and most reckless voices on the right."[45]

Another conservative media figure, Oliver Darcy, adds:

I'm a conservative talk show host. All conservative hosts have basically established their brand as being contrasted to the mainstream
media. So we have spent 20 years demonizing the liberal mainstream
media . . . [A]t a certain point you wake up and you realize you have
destroyed the credibility of any credible outlet out there. The analogy
that I think of is somebody who has a baby alligator in their bathtub
and they keep feeding it and taking care of it. And it's really cute when
it's a baby alligator—until it becomes a grown-up alligator and comes
out and starts biting you."[46]

Their concern is echoed by other conservatives such as radio host John
Ziegler: "Over the years, we've effectively brainwashed the core of our
audience to distrust anything that they disagree with. And now it's gone
too far . . . The gatekeepers have lost all credibility in the minds of consumers . . . You can only be exposed to stories that make you feel good about
what you want to believe. Unfortunately, the truth is unpopular a lot."[47]

While being interviewed on Fox News by Megyn Kelly on January
21, 2014, a chastened Glenn Beck acknowledged that many of his gullible
viewers had become "fragile." He said, "I played a role unfortunately in
helping tear the country apart. And it's not who we are. I didn't realize
how really fragile the people were. I thought we were kind of a little more
in it together. And now I look back and I realize if we could have talked
about the uniting principles a little more, instead of just the problems . . ."[48]

In the wake of 2016, the hallmarks of twenty-first-century American
democracy are a social media industry promulgating division and a
Republican Party grown successful with fake news fostering polarization. You may deplore this new reality, but others welcome it, including
Russians eager to see America become the farce feared by Madison. The
Trump campaign's spinning of conspiracy theories while questioning
America's democratic process sowed distrust and discord, rather dramatically furthering Russian propaganda objectives. By mendaciously
claiming rigged elections and voter fraud, candidate and then President
Trump has utilized traditional Russian propaganda and misinformation
techniques to discredit American democracy. Moreover, he routinely
called attention to WikiLeaks information hacked by Russian cyber
spooks, credentialing, rewarding, and incentivizing Kremlin intervention. Traditional Republican conservatives such as Robert Kagan were

stunned by this de facto Trump–Putin collaboration: "It would have been impossible to imagine a year ago that the Republican Party's leaders would be effectively serving as enablers of Russian interference in this country's political system. Yet, astonishingly, that is the role the Republican Party is playing."[49]

On the world stage, America has championed the virtues of democracy, individual rights, and freedoms since World War II. Its economic and military might provide important sustenance to the higher quality democracies abroad whose political systems do actually spread the gains from growth broadly. A fretful Vladimir Putin has sought for nearly a decade to diminish the lure of such democratic governance. And his marquee success is the election of a president critical of the US democratic system and reluctant to reject white supremacists. American's image worldwide has suffered. Pew Research Center polling in June 2017 found the nation's favorability rating globally had fallen from 64 percent to 49 percent following Trump's first months in office. Pointing to his "arrogant" demeanor, Pew's 40,000 global respondents expressed more confidence in the murderous Putin (27 percent) than in Trump (22 percent).[50]

It is unclear if Putin is accountable for the election of Donald Trump. But Russian intervention certainly enhanced his relative appeal to American voters. How was that accomplished?

Russian Cyber Espionage in Support of Donald Trump

Vladimir Putin is hostile to democracy. He is especially annoyed by fact-checkers in the media at home or abroad. Unlike the GOP, however, Putin is able with impunity to do more domestically than merely demonize them in efforts to make facts miscible. More than a score of Russian investigative reporters have been murdered in unsolved crimes since 2009.[51] Others sit in jail at Putin's behest, falsely accused.

Abroad, the Russians have a history since 2009 of aggressive cyber intervention in the politics of the Baltic, Balkans, and Western democracies. This interference is motivated by concern for the well-being and position of Putin and his close colleagues, with the goal of discrediting democracies abroad sufficiently to blur their sharp contrasts with his kleptocracy. Putin's interest in discrediting democracy rose sharply following the Arab Spring, including the "color revolutions" in Ukraine and across

North Africa that displaced authoritarians. The Kremlin began to covertly aid the election of unconventional candidates in Europe and America to bring discredit on the democratic process. In 2014, Russia provided $10 million to Marine Le Pen's xenophobic, fascist French National Front.[52] In Holland in 2016, fake news disseminated by Russian intelligence officials masquerading as Ukrainians was responsible for Dutch voters rejecting a free trade agreement with Ukraine; it took another year to expose the Russians and achieve ratification. On TV and in public appearances, these *poseurs* demonized the new Ukrainian democracy, repeating Kremlin mendacities such as Ukrainian troops burned the Dutch flag or killed a three-year-old for wearing a crucifix.[53] Even so, most Russian misinformation was spread on social media platforms.

These and other similar events are elements of a pattern of "pervasive and endemic" Russian intervention in European elections documented by the Center for Strategic and International Studies in Washington and the Sofia, Bulgaria, Center for the Study of Democracy. Recent actions have focused on Eastern Europe in addition to America, France, and the Netherlands.[54] The Kremlin tactics featuring character assassination have scored considerable success, flipping governments to pro-Russian leaders in Armenia, Georgia, Hungary, and Moldova.[55]

This Russian strategy, including leaked emails, was replicated in America during 2016. For instance, its TV network RT broadcasting in America repeatedly smeared Secretary Clinton with fables such as "How 100 percent of the Clintons' 2015 'charity' went to . . . themselves."[56] The reach of this Kremlin propaganda became surprisingly broad among Americans. RT's English-language broadcasts streamed on Google's YouTube platform were more widely viewed, for instance, than CNN's streaming news coverage.[57] And pro-Trump ads surreptitiously purchased by Russians on social media were widely viewed. In January 2017, the American intelligence agencies explained the goals of such Russian intervention in the election this way:

> We assess Russian President Vladimir Putin ordered an influence campaign in 2016 aimed at the US presidential election . . . Russia's goals were to undermine public faith in the US democratic process, denigrate Secretary Clinton, and harm her electability and potential presidency.

> We further assess Putin and the Russian government developed a clear preference for President-elect Trump . . . Putin and the Russian government aspired to help President-elect Trump's election chances when possible by discrediting Secretary Clinton and publicly contrasting her unfavorably to him.[58]

This intervention actually began in 2015. Russian military websites, including Guccifer 2.0 (posing as Romanian freedom activists) and DCLeaks.com (posing as American freedom activists) joined RT in seeding anti-Clinton fake news on social media platforms. The impact of this cyber warfare was enhanced because of breakdowns at the US Federal Bureau of Investigation (FBI), which is responsible for countering covert Russian espionage. As reported on December 14, 2016, by the leading European business paper, the *Financial Times*, the FBI proved inept. Journalist David J. Lynch explained that the Russian cyber warriors exploited "short-handed Federal Bureau of Investigation counter-intelligence units."[59] And Luke Harding, Stephanie Kirchgaessner, and Mick Hopkins of the *Guardian* quoted the top British spy agency GCHQ conclusion that "It looks like the [US] agencies were asleep. They [the European agencies] were saying: 'There are contacts going on between people close to Mr. Trump and people we believe are Russian intelligence agents. You should be wary of this."[60] The sluggish FBI reaction hampered President Obama, reluctant to publicize the Russian intervention without hard facts during the election campaign. In fact, while the CIA had decided in August 2016 that the Kremlin was aiding candidate Trump, the undermanned FBI demurred for months. American voters were left in the dark about the de facto Russian–Trump collaboration deplored by Kagan and others.[61]

The Russian intervention included hacking of personal email accounts, websites, and at least twenty-one state election systems on behalf of candidate Trump, along with Russian propaganda being disseminated through thousands of ads and websites. Facebook hosted huge numbers of fake Russian accounts like the mythical Melvin Redick whose postings directed gullible Americans to anti-Clinton sites such as the Kremlin's DCLeaks.

At the center of Kremlin propaganda was the Russian Internet Research Agency. Its accounts generated Russian postings and advertisements viewed by 10 million Americans on Facebook alone—some bought with rubles. The surreptitious, incendiary posts featured divisive issues designed to generate anger and electoral enthusiasm among American conservatives, especially in swing states.

The moderate center of American democracy can prosper only when supported by what Madison termed "the power that knowledge gives"—a common body of widely accepted facts forming a foundation for reasoned public debate. [62] The next chapter reviews options for rebuilding that center by hewing to *originalism* in reducing the reach and impact of fake news.

CHAPTER 15

Closing the "Hate Factories": Avoiding the Farce Feared by Madison

Facebook: "The Hate Factory."[1]

—Jan Fleischhauer, *Der Spiegel,* October 2016

What they're doing [the POPS, or privately owned public spaces] is introducing all of these bad sites into our ecosystem and not having the means to monitor them appropriately and effectively.[2]

—Marc Goldberg, Trust Metrics, December 2016

Providers have used the social media like a newspaper or a radio station to disseminate their opinions and messages—without being subject to the provisions of the general press law. They should change quickly . . . Facebook should be like a publishing house.[3]

—German Christian Democrats party chairman Ruprecht Polenz, December 2016

MORE SO THAN IN any year in American history, 2016 brought to realization the framers' fear that voters would be misled by innuendo, half-truths, and character assassination conducted by an unsympathetic foreign power. In *Federalist 68*, Alexander Hamilton explicitly and forcefully warned of events that eerily unfolded in 2016, where the presidential contest was possibly determined by "cabal, intrigue, and corruption . . . chiefly from the desire in foreign powers to gain an improper ascendant in our councils. How could they better gratify this, than by raising a creature of their own to the chief magistracy of the union?"[4]

Hamilton's fear of an electorate duped by nefarious foreign powers was just one element of the framers' pervasive fears of misinformed citizens. In rather sharp contrast with original intent, the GOP's operational manifesto is garner political power by appealing to voters with an afactual alternative narrative centered on fake news. That strategy includes demonizing the fact-based information industry central to the framers' vision of a democracy sustained by an informed electorate.

The GOP manifesto rejects fact, truth, and political collaboration as pillars of American democracy. It is diametrically in opposition to the Constitution and original intent. Their manifesto has created a new era featuring an American electorate increasingly exemplifying what the framers feared.

Historians should look back with nostalgia at the relatively contained environment—comprised mostly of print and broadcast media—in which George Orwell and Alexander Solzhenitsyn labored to dissect and debunk the authoritarians' fake news of the 1930s and 1950s. Today's social media is a new and dangerous addition to the misinformation industry they confronted. More than 100 million Americans visit Facebook alone daily, far more than read newspapers and comparable to TV as an information source.[5]

The "Hate Factories"

With content filtration meek, the social media platforms or POPS have become populated by not only you and your neighbors, but also by partisans, Kremlin propagandists, terrorist recruiters, white supremacists, psychopaths, and other traffickers seeking political gain, revenge, or to demean US democracy. Twenty years ago they could only stand on a street corner and shout (unless owning a media property). Today they can broadcast to billions from their living rooms. Malicious and mendacious postings are a minority on social media but plentiful enough for Facebook to be labeled the "hate factory."[6] The lack of qualitative content censorship or filtration by the POPS has enabled this minority to expose democracies to the same dysfunction, antagonism, and disruption that followed the aggressive exploitation of the previous sensational new media innovation—radio—by European and Soviet authoritarians in the 1930s.

The POPS have been slow in addressing even pathological content on their platforms, with fake news, killings, revenge porn, animal abuse, and the like routinely going viral within moments of posting. Twitter for a time permitted then-Breitbart editor Milo Yiannopoulos and pharmaceutical entrepreneur Martin Shkreli to harass online (respectively) an actress and an investigative reporter, including doctored photos.[7] And, it permits physical assaults on customers by online sociopaths deploying flashing animation to precipitate epileptic seizures among the vulnerable—attacks that American police too rarely investigate.[8] Indeed, Twitter is an especially accommodating platform for psychopaths or partisans, easily accommodating anonymity. Moreover, its technical architecture is unusually vulnerable, enabling entrepreneurs to create hundreds of automated accounts or bots, propagating similar themes, striving to land on Twitter's "Trending Topics." Such coordination generates a Potemkin front of nonexistent persons providing puppet masters with a cyberspace sound truck. Samuel Woolley of Oxford University's Computational Propaganda Project explains: "Bots allow groups to speak much more loudly . . . to use Twitter as a megaphone . . . manufacturing consensus, or building the illusion of popularity for a candidate or a particular idea."[9] This practice is hugely popular because practitioners (and researchers) have discovered that viewers have great difficulty distinguishing bots from humans. Recall Oxford researchers concluded that about 20 percent of all political conversation they analyzed on Twitter in 2016 was merely bots.[10]

Twitter's efforts to strip terrorists and the like from its platform and rein in bots have been meek. In January 2017, angry relatives of the three Americans killed by ISIS (Islamic State of Iraq and Syria) attacks in Belgium and France sued Twitter for failing to delete members of the terrorist organization from its platform. The suit alleged that Twitter played "a uniquely essential role in the development of ISIS's image, its success in recruiting members from around the world, and its ability to carry out attacks and intimidate its enemies."[11] ISIS cyber experts continued to use Twitter to plan and direct attacks abroad in 2017.[12] Even more accommodating is Telegram, originally developed by Russian libertarians. Its military grade encryption and secret chat rooms have proven ideal for global communications by Islamic State terrorists who laud its features and encourage followers to use it.[13] Other POPS that have proven reluctant to censor neo-Nazis and the like are PayPal, GoFundMe, Patreon, and GoDaddy, facilitators of the racial confrontations in Charlottesville, Virginia, in August 2017.[14]

Facebook's track record is also discouraging. It failed to alert authorities in 2014 of information that could have prevented the murder by Islamist terrorists of British soldier Lee Rigby.[15] A suicide and murders in Minnesota, Virginia, and Cleveland have been streamed; and police in Uppsala, Sweden, during January 2017 investigated the streaming of a sexual assault.[16] Indeed, Facebook quite possibly influenced the presidential vote in 2016 by refusing to ban fake news postings; intimidated by conservatives in the month before the election, it actually fired its team of content monitors.[17] The Russian military meanwhile utilized Facebook marketing to craft pro-Trump and racist messaging. Posing as Americans, it fed propaganda hundreds of millions or billions of times to targeted voters before the election on Twitter, Facebook, and other POPS. Facebook on occasion has also mocked and intimidated critics of its permissiveness. BBC investigators uncovered Facebook postings involving child abuse in March 2017, for instance. After demanding the BBC investigators send it copies of the postings, Facebook officials refused to take them down, and instead played "gotcha"—reporting the investigators to the police.[18]

Voluntary Self-Regulation Failed

The POPS business model calls for maximizing user clicks by too readily dismissing ethical standards, journalistic safeguards, and a moral obligation to present the truth, censor hate speech, or (for PayPal and the like) deny funding for hate groups. Facebook has come to partner with fact-checkers to investigate complaints of offensive and bogus postings, deleting some or attaching alerts. And it does proactively veto some offensive postings including nudity. But like other POPS, user complaints about offensive postings or images are mostly addressed belatedly after they have already gone viral. Moreover, its filtration system has been slow to mobilize. Facebook officials in Germany concluded, for instance, that anonymous online threats by one or more sociopaths to attack a female actor's face with a chain saw "had not violated our community standards."[19] They refused to delete postings urging that war refugees be sent to gas chambers or that readers "pour petrol over them [Syrian refugees] and set them on fire." In each instance, Facebook responded that complaints about these posts "lack merit," and that its refusal to delete them was "no violation of German law by Facebook or its employees."[20] This business model shields psychopaths, Kremlin propaganda, and fake news from the sort of explicit content accountability that print journalists or broadcasters face under German law, where even printing malicious letters to the editor can cause a publication to be closed.[21]

Pushed by German officials, the POPS responded by agreeing in mid-2016 to voluntary self-filtration of content. The results were underwhelming. During the fourth quarter of 2016, only 40 percent of flagged content was even reviewed by the POPS within twenty-four hours, and only 28.3 percent of such content was removed.[22] Overall, Facebook deleted less than one-half of hate speech postings, despite the fact that German law obligates social media platforms to promptly delete postings inciting violence or slandering another person upon complaint.[23] In contrast, the more responsible YouTube platform removed 90 percent of objectionable content flagged by users within twenty-four hours.[24]

Justice Minister Heiko Maas summarized the experiment this way: "Too little illegal content is being deleted and it's not being deleted sufficiently quickly. The biggest problem is and remains that the networks don't take the complaints of their own users seriously enough."[25] His frustration led to the German January 2018 Network Enforcement law that imposes fines of up to €50 million on larger social media platforms failing to delete illegal or offensive speech, hate speech, or fake news within twenty-four hours.[26] The officials simply extended rules applicable to print and broadcasters to social media platforms as well. Structuring the censorship obligation in this manner mimics in some measure the successful American procedure under the Fairness Doctrine, although the German process remains reactive rather than *ex-ante*—a huge shortcoming.[27]

In France, it took similar severe pressure from officials fearing the impact of fake news and Russian propaganda on voters in 2017 for the POPS to begin aggressive monitoring of French-language postings. Some fifteen POPS, including Facebook and Google, eventually partnered with *Le Monde* in the CrossCheck initiative.

The situation is little better in America where cyber targets have redress only through cumbersome and expensive libel laws or privacy statutes. The successful suit by billionaire Peter Thiel fronted by Terry Bollea (Hulk Hogan), involving fake news disseminated by the website *Gawker*, consumed years, $10 million, hinged on a hometown jury, and defendants (owners of *Gawker)* who were Americans and thus reachable by US courts.[28]

Remediating the offensive content of the POPS is low on the agenda of the Trump administration. But American corporations including financial firms and Starbucks have increasingly become targets of cyberattacks. That has generated interest in corralling fake news that propagates globally at lightning speed (Costco no longer taking memberships; Xbox killed a teenager!). Some twelve of Snopes' top fifty fake news attacks were targeted at firms, reported the *Financial Times*.[29]

Leading European governments have become more proactive, insistent that the EU require dramatically better content accountability from the POPS. German Economic Minister Brigitte Zypries has called for laws against fake news and hate mongering, explaining that "soft" regulation "privatizes justice."[30] Referring to "evil material," Theresa May demanded in September 2017 that "Industry needs to go further and faster . . . developing technological solutions which prevent it being uploaded in the first place." This European pressure has forced the POPS to react more aggressively in evaluating questionable postings. New tools, algorithms, and thousands of censors have been added. The POPS have the technical and financial capability to censor ex-ante all content.[31] Thus far they have only selectively adopted *ex-ante* censorship, relying on algorithms that have proven easily gamed and by-passed.

Comprehensive content censorship is most likely to begin in Europe and with video content. Including YouTube, the POPS may perhaps soon be required to meet the same rules applicable to broadcasters. Hate speech, fake news, incitement to terror, and the like could be required to be rejected *ex-ante* through revisions to the audiovisual media services regulations.[32]

Expunging Fake News from All Media Platforms

The pathological, fake and partisan news carried by the POPS has darkened the visionary goals of entrepreneurs like Twitter cofounder Evan

Williams to make the world "a better place." To realize that vision, governments must cease abdicating content filtration to market forces. Their challenge is no different from confronting environmental polluters or drug dealers, who privatize profits while socializing the harmful costs of their practices and products. With social media, that cost is measured in the loss of individual privacy and contentment, as well as diminution in the quality of information available to citizens and voters. It is also measured in the steadily thinning newsrooms of the fact-based mainstream media struggling with online competitors who themselves eschew expensive investigative and watchdog reporting.

The time-honored solution of economists in situations like this where market forces underprice social costs is to raise that price with penalties or through regulation on suppliers. Adopting a nuanced and comprehensive approach drawing on that traditional economic principle is warranted to address the failures of the POPS market:

- Educators and parents should address the issue of fake news in schools, around the kitchen table, and elsewhere. For example, *Bamse,* the popular Swedish children's comic strip, has sought to teach youths to distinguish between fact and fake news, and to question all internet content.[33]
- Mainstream media should continue to aggressively identify fake news stories[34] and nourish fact-checking initiatives patterned on *Le Monde*'s Decodex and the BBC's RealityCheck.
- The public sector should require that content on POPS platforms not be poisonous, meet community standards, and be factual—ingredients central to a high quality democracy. That creates a bias toward ex-ante censorship. Policy advocacy/political ads should be limited, ex-ante filtered, and held to the same attribution standards as print and broadcast media, including identification of funders. Exceptions for individual political speech should be considered.
- In democracies imposing limits on electioneering spending, political information and opinion disseminated on social media threaten to derail the positive character of their political campaigns. Specific bans or limits on social media for all political speech in such countries are appropriate. Social media should not become a loophole

enabling corporate or independent entities to evade existing limits on political speech or issue advocacy during elections.

- Automated bots should be eliminated from cyberspace, following the pattern set by political parties in Germany.[35]
- The POPS such as PayPal that process payments should also be required to delete users promoting hate speech or fake news.
- All POPS should be required to obtain explicit user permission to disseminate their cyberspace data.

The German government is perhaps most advanced in this direction, aided by its existing thorough press law that lays out responsibilities and rights for information disseminators. *Handelsblatt* journalist Dietmar Neuerer explains the fundamental principle being promulgated is that derogatory information and opinion on social media is violative of the nation's free speech guarantee: "No one is entitled to freedom of expression, to violate the rights of others, for example, by inciting them to violence, or to slander them. These laws apply—they must be applied more consistently in social networks than before."[36]

Justice Minister Maas agrees: "The providers of social networks are responsible when their platforms are misused to spread hate crime or illegal false news."[37] Tabea Rößner, a leading Green Party official, explained their logic: "Social platforms were initially not press companies with editorial responsibility, [but have become a] crucial part of the opinion-forming process." The Christian Democratic Party's parliamentary chairman Ruprecht Polenz concurs: "Providers have used the social media like a newspaper or a radio station to disseminate their opinions and messages—without being subject to the provisions of the general press law. That should change quickly . . . Facebook should be like a publishing house."[38]

American internet experts agree in some measure. *Wired* journalist Emma Grey Ellis concluded in April 2017, for instance, that "The only way to kill revenge porn is to stop it being posted in the first place."[39] POPS's censorship of social media communications may offend many Americans, but it will not run afoul of their First Amendment rights shielding nearly all speech content. That right entitles one to opine on street corners and precludes the government from censoring your commentary on any media, including social media. But the media platforms themselves can legally act as censors in America and in Europe, as explained by law professors Margot Kaminski of Ohio State and Kate Klonick of Yale Law School.[40] Indeed, media platforms are routinely sued for not adequately censoring offending content. Media proprietors including the POPS are obligated neither to lend you megaphones nor to publish or otherwise broadcast your musings or opinion. Referring to media organizations, Kyle Pope, editor and publisher of the *Columbia Journalism Review,* explained, "It's totally within their rights to set ground rules," and to set standards in choosing what advertisements and news they air or publish.[41]

As an industry, the POPS differ only technologically from print or broadcast media platforms, and their content should be subject to *ex-ante* or ex-post review as appropriate. The original justification for the Fairness Doctrine requirement for broadcast censorship was the US role in fostering broadcasting technology. And the same compelling logic applies to cyberspace disseminators as well. Moreover, adoption of a filtration regime would align the POPS with common practice in many areas of American governance and society. Protocols and procedures to ensure dissemination of nonpartisan, fact-based information are common in the fields of national security, transportation, medicine, food and equipment safety, and a host of other applications that involve scientific investigation and development. They are intended to ensure that security and intelligence officials, judges, medical researchers, clinicians, pesticide safety investigators, transportation managers, environmental engineers, legislators, NASA engineers, and public officials are exposed to the wisdom derived from evidence-based, unbiased, and nonpartisan information. Voters, the ultimate stakeholders and arbiters of American governance, are entitled to no less.

Proactive censorship of cyberspace is controversial but will not disrupt the vast bulk of interpersonal communications. Indeed, POPS like Facebook and Google may seek to rebuild reputational damage in seizing the competitive advantage offered by providing users a credible platform rather than a grimy scrum. Content censorship is justified by the existential risks noted by Madison and others that are posed to democracy by a misinformed citizenry. The challenge is to find their aspirational information sweet spot—that universe where mostly factual information is enjoyed by citizens practicing free speech—free of distortion, free of self-serving filtration by government, and free of slander, hate speech, and fake news.

Admittedly, it is uncertain how technically comprehensive a regime to censor social media can be. Delistings by Facebook, PayPal, GoDaddy, Google, and others sent white supremacist websites scurrying to platforms such as Gab.ai, Hatrone, and WeSearchr during the latter half of 2017.[42] Desperate to remain accessible, the *Daily Stormer*, for instance, shifted to Tor (a browser for anonymous web surfing), then to a Russian server, then to CloudFlare from which it was also soon booted.[43] Flitting through the dark web certainly limits accessibility, which is important. Yet it will take the cooperation of state actors like Russia to achieve an effective cyber censorship regime, not to mention support by the Republican Party. Judging by behaviors in 2016, it seems evident that neither is inclined to see fake news and the like stripped from cyberspace. Quite the contrary.

The Dangers of Loopholes in Content Accuracy Standards

Ideally, content standards should apply impartially across all media platforms. Britain offers an example of the consequences of standards that are not comprehensively applied. It insists on a "due impartiality" standard for broadcasters but not for newspapers or social media.[44] That print loophole has been exploited by the *fittest,* including Rupert Murdoch. As a newspaper proprietor, he enjoys a judicially affirmed right (as in Australia and America) to discredit the disfavored and skew public opinion as much as his wallet and conscience allow. In one instance, Murdoch placed a large picture in color of political opponent Kevin Rudd professionally photoshopped in a Nazi uniform on the front page above the fold of Australia's most widely read newspaper weeks before an election.[45]

Such antics provide an important lesson. If any loophole is permitted, the outcome will mimic experience in Britain, with consequences all too familiar to Americans: "The type of opinionated and polarized news that is now a feature in US television and radio has for years been found in the UK print media," explained Jacob Rowbottom in the *New Republic:*

If "special interests" are often cast as the villains of US politics, media proprietors play an equivalent role in the UK. In the US, candidates, parties, and special interest groups spend huge sums of money to gain an advantage in the ad wars. By contrast, the most vicious political messages in the UK tend to be found in the pages of the tabloid news- papers . . . The newspapers . . . are the only outlet that can engage in electoral advocacy without restraint from either spending controls or content regulation. As a result, whoever controls the newspapers has a much greater capacity to steer the course of an election debate. Given the relatively small number of titles with a national audience and levels of concentration, this influence lies in the hands of a small number of companies. News Corporation alone has over a third of the market share for national newspapers. This explains why so many politicians went out of their way to win the favour of Rupert Murdoch and his lieutenants.[46]

This predicament highlights the challenge of integrating political and policy advocacy carried on social media with any system of limits on elec- tioneering and broadcast spending. Laws in higher quality democracies that limit campaign spending do not address social media advertising or communications as a rule. Thus, regulators in these countries face new challenges in crafting limits on the volume of political communications by any individual or organization over social media.[47]

A further challenge is posed by the emerging practices labeled psy- chometrics noted earlier, designed to sway voters using data surrepti- tiously seized from cyberspace. Russia, US politicians, and the Mercers garner data revealed by cyber interactions, what would seem to be an abuse of privacy by the POPS. Facebook for example, refused to sell most user information until 2012. Today, personal and credit card interactions are just another industry revenue stream, widely marketed without user permission. As exploited during the Brexit vote, noted earlier, this prized personal data enabled partisans to classify individual voters by their pet peeves and preferences. That is how some 600,000 targeted Brits came to be bombarded by a billion individualized, misleading, or even menda- cious appeals.[48]

The POPS should voluntarily end this abuse of privacy, ceasing to compile or market data on users. Lacking an effective response, the democracies should ban this invasive exploitation of social media users. This reform will need to be led by the higher quality democracies such as Germany, because the Trump administration is opposed. Soon after taking office, it torpedoed an Obama administration regulation requiring internet providers to obtain customer permission before tracking and commercializing their online habits.

Fact-Based Reporting Should Be Complemented with High-Quality Reporting

Another concern is the erosion of fact-based reporting as resources at mainstream media enterprises are drawn away by social media. Quality factual reporting is thriving in a few fact-based media organizations like the *New York Times* and *Washington Post,* which have successfully adapted to the cyber revolution. But, they are the exception. An example is the American Center for Public Integrity, including its branch the International Consortium of Investigative Journalists (ICIJ). Although they are the source of numerous exposés including the Panama Papers, which has reduced the use of international tax havens, they lack an adequate financial base.[49] Despite their fundamental value to societies, the same challenge exists for other investigators such as *ProPublica* or the Marshall Project's work on criminal justice.

Ideally, a regime requiring more socially responsible behavior by the POPS should include social media platforms directing resources to the expansion of what Richard Hasen terms the "checking" activity— fact-checking and unveiling the truth while holding dissemblers accountable.[50] That seminal obligation of mainstream journalism has inspired remarkable reporting on many occasions, including Karl Fleming and Claude Sitton reporting on institutionalized abuse and homicide during Jim Crow; Edward R. Murrow reporting on the demagogic Joseph McCarthy; or Bob Woodward and Carl Bernstein on Watergate. Such truth-telling requires an idealized "significant set of skills and traditions" explains University of Alabama law professor, Paul Horowitz: "Before a story is published, every line, every quote, every judgment call is subjected to checking and re-checking, debate and counter-debate, and institutional second guessing."[51] University of Chicago economist Luigi Zingales has argued that such an aggressive independent media—professional, objective, and free of bias—is vital in limiting abuse and corruption by government and powerful interests.[52]

The private and nonprofit sectors are actively searching for business models that support the preservation of objective journalism. And they are seeking innovative new ways to collaborate with social media platforms that increasingly dominate news dissemination. One successful if ad hoc approach has been for citizens to directly support online independent, investigative journalism, exemplified by the French venture *Mediapart* or by Philadelphia's H.F. Lenfest's support of *The Inquirer, The Daily News*, and Philly.com. Another example is eBay founder Pierre Omidyar, who donated $100 million in 2017 to support a number of independent investigative entities, including $4.5 million to the ICIJ. George Soros has also donated to efforts resisting fake news. And Wikipedia's founder Jimmy Wales is raising capital for a new global news organization called Wikitribune to expose fake news.[53] These efforts to enhance fact-based reporting and the checking function can be dramatically accelerated if the POPS themselves begin in-house investigative reporting. The more widespread the watchdog or checking activity on all American media platforms, including the POPS, the closer the nation will come to realizing the framers' intent for an informed electorate.

Restoring the Quality of American Democracy

A global retreat from democracy is well underway, with nations such as Hungary, Mozambique, Poland, and Turkey growing more authoritarian of late. Indeed, 2016 was the eleventh year in a row that the Freedom House matrix noted earlier documented that the reach of global democracy has diminished. This certainly reflects in some measure America's retreat from global leadership beginning with the humiliating 2000 election and the Iraq war of choice. That retreat is reflected in the Freedom House's rather dismal ranking of thirty-second place in 2016 for American democracy, as noted in chapter 8. It removed America from the top rank of democracies due to "the cumulative impact of flaws in the [US] electoral system, a disturbing increase in the role of private money in election campaigns, and the legislative process, legislative gridlock . . ."[54]

The last chapter provides recommendations to remediate these deficiencies. They are the steps needed to raise the quality of American democracy, enabling the nation to join the ranks of peer wealthy nations in prioritizing the prosperity of all its citizens.

CHAPTER 16

Epilogue

If we must be governed by those whom the billionaires choose to fund, then the social contract really has been ruptured.[1]

—Charles Fried, Reagan administration
solicitor general, April 2014

THE LAST MILLENNIUM OF political thought, revolution, and evolution has produced a handful of wealthy societies that have managed to derail capitalism's default setting of plutocratic rule. Many have crafted high-quality Aristotelian democracies where individual political rights are respected and equal to all others: Not the United States.

Many feature expansive voting rights and proportional representation where every vote is meaningful: Not the United States.

Many feature voter sovereignty where policy outcomes reflect majoritarian preferences clearly heard and readily heeded by lawmakers: Not the United States.

Many are responsive to middle-class aspirations for steadily rising prosperity. Just as Adam Smith dared hope in 1776 in *An Inquiry into the Nature and Causes of the Wealth of Nations*, they have harnessed the wondrous mechanism of capitalism to widely broadcast the gains of growth: Not the United States.

Many moderate passions in the pursuit of the common good, rejecting tribalism: Not the United States.

Today, the low quality of America's democracy is primarily a consequence of transitory majorities of conservative justices on the Supreme Court beginning with *Buckley v. Valeo* in 1976. For partisan gain, they have rejected *originalism* in the key area of political corruption—epitomized by the Roberts Court's *McCutcheon v. FEC* (2014) decision, in which the majority concluded that political donations to purchase "ingratiation and access . . . is a central feature of democracy." Thus, they have proudly made industrial-scale vote buying and the ensuing cynicism and tribalism the central features of American democracy.

The *Buckley* era has empowered the *fittest fifty* to move the nation backward, toward the default setting of capitalism. Average Americans are now firmly in the grip of Piketty's endless inegalitarian spiral. The consequence, according to Brookings Institution researchers, is that a majority have come to believe that the American dream is dead, that "hard work and determination are no guarantee of success."[2] Their grim prognosis will not soon or easily be lifted, notes Robin Wigglesworth, US Markets Editor of the *Financial Times*: "In the long term it is not inconceivable that the political landscape shifts away from corporate interests and the US re-embraces the "trust-busting" zeal of Teddy Roosevelt. But it certainly looks a distant prospect today."[3]

Improving Political Equality Begins with the Supreme Court

Ending the spiral to resuscitate the American dream begins with the Supreme Court, where all issues involving pay-to-play and political equality fall within its purview. Its powers under judicial review are a settled matter. That means the corruption of pay-to-play is more amenable to remediation over time, for example, than the slaveocracy that confronted Abraham Lincoln in 1861. True, the antimajoritarian US electoral and governance architectures pose the same barriers to political equality today as in the spring of 1861. But judicial review offers a lifeline to future reformers that was unavailable to Lincoln because the Constitution unquestionably embraced slavery. In contrast, both the founding fathers and the framers' original intent unquestionably was to deny a constitutional shield to the political corruption inherent with pay-to-play.

Raising the quality of American democracy hinges on more than ending pay-to-play. While meaningfully amending the Constitution is problematic, the Supreme Court can unilaterally implement needed seminal reforms enhancing political equality. Indeed, other democracies have rather routinely improved the quality of their governance by revamping antiquated practices, including nations such as the UK, whose democracy predates the US. To elevate individual political rights so that citizens are fairly heard and heeded, for instance, upgrades by higher quality democracies have featured adoption of unicameral legislative systems to render irrelevant malapportioned legislative bodies like the US Senate. Moreover, the upgrades have facilitated adoption of proportional representation electoral systems, which in the process eliminated the severely antidemocratic phenomenon of wasted votes caused by single-member legislative districts, inevitably gerrymandered. And many have eliminated winner-take-all (plurality) electoral systems in favor of binary runoff structures. These reforms were adopted precisely to avoid American-style outcomes where majoritarian opinion is degraded and popular vote losers leapfrog over winners to become national leaders, sometimes by judicial edict, as in banana republics.

These upgrades abroad have ensured that public authority to act and the consequences for such acts are clear to voters, avoiding an American-style miasma of diffused political accountability. The complexity and tangled authority forced by the US Constitution guarantees opaqueness in an age when higher quality democracies emphasize transparency.

A Supreme Court Agenda to Build a Higher Quality Democracy

An aspirational agenda for a visionary Supreme Court beyond ending pay-to-play includes the following items:

Supreme Court Appointment

Life tenure populates the Court with justices whose formative years, education, and career experiences often leaves them quite far removed from their legal contemporaries or society. Term-limiting Supreme Court justices is the best remedy. Another upgrade would require legislative supermajority confirmation of all judicial appointments, including the Supreme Court. Over some years, that step would populate the American judiciary with less strident or partisan justices. In contrast, the conservative Justice Gorsuch was confirmed in 2017 by a bare majority of senators representing a minority of Americans. At a minimum, justices of the Supreme Court should adopt the same ethical code of conduct applicable to all other federal judges. It should become de rigeur to place assets in blind trusts. And recusal should be triggered in cases involving familial or commercial connections or cases involving interests with whom justices interact meaningfully.

The Campaign Finance System

Recriminalizing vote buying will require complementary reforms to the American campaign finance system, drawn from the spending limits and electioneering funding practices of higher quality democracies.

Voting Rights

Ending the income bias should incentivize voter participation. That can be encouraged with steps to expand voting rights by reversing rulings of the Roberts Republicans, including *Crawford* and *Shelby County,* which disenfranchised millions of citizens.

The Senate

Article V of the Constitution poses a formidable barrier to democratizing the Senate. An option is to draw on Australian law. Its Senate suffers irreparably from American-style malapportionment (it has a US-style equal state-representation structure), but Australians ameliorate its undemocratic feature in this fashion: A relatively large number of senators (12) represent each state, importantly selected through a proportional representation electoral system. Australia also provides representation in the Senate for its national capital, Canberra.

Electoral College

The antidemocratic Electoral College should be neutered, its members voting only for the winner of the national presidential popular vote. This reform is being implemented by the National Popular Vote Interstate Compact, encouraging states to enact statutes pledging to cast their electoral votes for the popular vote winner.[4] Such action by states with at least 270 electoral votes would de facto eliminate the Electoral College, although state statutes can always be repealed at a later date.

Reforming State and Local Judicial Systems

All state and local judicial appointments should be based on merit, appointed by supermajority votes of legislators. The Supreme Court should insist that judgeships be professionalized, drawing on the potent mechanism in higher quality democracies: The judiciary is a formal, professional career track, featuring educational thresholds and periodic evaluations. For example France's rigorous training to become a judge is open only to lawyers and lasts twenty-seven months. Only 5 percent of aspirants become judges. Cornell international law professor, Mitchel Lasser, explains that judges abroad "have spent years in school taking practical and theoretical courses on how to be a judge. They are professionals. The rest of the world is stunned and amazed at what we do, and vaguely aghast that our state judges can rise to their positions through elections rather than highly specialized, demanding training."[5] Additionally, judicial recusal from cases involving familial or commercial connections should be mandated, as should the use of blind trusts for all state and local judges.

Reforming State and Local Electoral Systems

With a federal government dominated by the GOP at the moment, steps toward political equality can only be taken at state and local levels. The Brennan Center estimates that five million eligible voters are affected by voter ID laws and the like, their votes potentially lost to partisan disenfranchisement.[6] Yet, that figure is dwarfed by the sixty million or so Americans whose votes were wasted in 2016, cast for losers in single member legislative districts. Their preferences are ignored, the voters unrepresented because of the undemocratic American electoral structure. In contrast, all voters' voices are heard in higher quality democracies abroad through their PR electoral systems. The Supreme Court should mandate PR for all American legislative elections.

Another reform is binary runoff elections (or the increasingly popular ranked-choice mechanism) in instances involving a single office, such as mayor or governor. States can also abolish gerrymandering on their own initiative by adopting independent entities to design legislative districts; it is possible that the Supreme Court's *Gill v. Whitford* ruling, due in 2018, could even mandate that states minimize gerrymandering. And they can upgrade by adopting a further handful of reforms, including open primaries (as in Louisiana, Washington state, and California), election day registration, and automatic voter registration of applicants for drivers' licenses, as in Oregon, California, West Virginia, and Vermont; that innovation tripled new registrations in Oregon (nine other states and the District of Columbia have approved the reform). Finally, states and communities can draw on experience in Connecticut, Maine, New York City, and the like and adopt electioneering spending caps complemented by public funding of elections.

Fact-Based Media

In today's media market, factual information struggles to compete with alluring and flamboyant fake news, with more Americans consequently coming to distrust than trust mainstream media. The seminal responsibility of media as sources of factual information for voters distinguishes them as a class uniquely valuable to democracy. There are three steps appropriate to restore the centrality sought by James Madison of nonpartisan, fact-based information to American democracy. First, the Fairness Doctrine should be resurrected, applicable to both broadcasters and the POPS, each media form the product of public investment. Proprietors in both media industries should be held accountable for meeting community standards, for the accuracy of the information they disseminate, and for reflecting the doctrine in their presentation of political and policy issues. That means fake news, abusive content, hate speech, violent content, and content that fails community standards should be denied access to the public space provided by broadcasters and the POPS. Nor should online payment proprietors permit access by entities that disseminate such content. While these steps would leave the vast bulk of information on the POPS unaffected, objectionable content would be denied the public space. Meeting required quality standards as truth-tellers would include broadcasters and the POPS evaluating all content *ex-ante*, the veracity of material verified. The success of the Fairness Doctrine teaches the powerful lesson that dissemination of factual information sustained by content filtration does not equate to Orwellian censorship.

Second, social media should end collection of personal information from users without explicit and clear permission.

Third, the POPS should support investigative journalism and ideally initiate their own factual reporting.

Upgrading American Democracy

The goal of these reforms is to upgrade the quality of American democracy by easing the political grip of the *fittest fifty*. They view the US economy as a zero-sum game where the gain of others in the form of higher wages, for instance, is only achieved at their expense. Adam Smith recognized this syndrome in 1776, noting that "masters [employers] are always and everywhere in a sort of tacit, but constant and uniform combination, not to raise the wages of labor. . . ."[7] Many have proven unwilling to support the same opportunities for others that America availed them. Most are market literalists, yet ignore the tapestry woven by Adam Smith, who insisted that capitalism flourishes best when featuring regulation encouraging responsible business stewardship and citizenship. The *fittest fifty* reject the seminal role envisaged by Smith and the higher quality democracies for the business community as guarantors of a broadly based prosperity.

America confronts formidable structural challenges to productivity and growth, as explored by economists such as Northwestern University professor Robert J. Gordon.[8] Those challenges are rendered forbidding by opposition from the *fittest fifty* and their GOP acolytes to higher wages and to the types of public investment that have been instrumental to growth in the past like education and R&D. They view demands for higher wages, an end to offshoring of high-wage jobs, closing foreign tax havens, and meeting government safety, health, labor, and environmental standards as impositions. Fierce opposition to taxes by the GOP on behalf of the *fittest fifty*, for example, is the reason American families confront the highest out-of-pocket child care costs of any wealthy democracy. According to the OECD, Americans spend 28 percent of net family incomes for toddler child care—nearly double the share in Australia and triple the 9 percent share in France or Germany.[9]

Embracing the *fittest fifty* agenda has seen the Republican Party forsake political moderation. Their extreme tactics in pursuit of this agenda have emptied the American political center, diminishing the ballast provided by a broad moderate core of swing voters. The virtues of prudence, acknowledged limits, invective-free debate, balancing competing principles, openness to new facts, and respect for opponents have become scarce in American politics. Public policy devised by facts-driven debate, dialogue, compromise, and the crowning virtue of majoritarian opinion fairly heard and heeded have been subsumed by intemperance and a Machiavellian pursuit of political gain.

Pay-to-play and the ensuing polarization has made American democracy the farce feared by James Madison. The US government now resembles that of India, as noted by Tom Colebatch in the *Sydney Morning Herald*: "Look at the United States, and India, where partisan politics has ruled out any serious attempt to reform even the most obvious problems."[10]

This Australian columnist is one in a chorus of foreign observers perceiving America as a nation in decline. With middle-class economic opportunity eroding and politics bedeviled by pay-to-play, American exceptionalism has faded apace with its shrinking middle class. Vote buying, economic immobility, stagnant wages, and the loss of a moderate, fact-based political center mock that pretension. Here is an assessment by *Spiegel* journalists: "[It] has reached a point in its history when the obvious can no longer be denied: The reality of life in America so greatly contradicts the claim—albeit one that has always been exaggerated—to be the 'greatest nation on earth,' that even the most ardent patriots must be overcome with doubt."[11] And these comments were written before the 2016 election.

The only preceding period in American history of such political division was the antebellum era, when slave owners insisted that their constitutional rights be respected. Then as now, America lacked a visionary

Supreme Court. The issues may be different—today plutocrats seek economic gain by lowering the quality of democracy rather than economic gain by perpetuating slavery. But the outcome is the same. Political and economic equality are suppressed, democracy demeaned.

Here is how neoconservative Robert Kagan explains the consequence of Republicans pursuing the *fittest fifty* agenda: "The Party's wild obstructionism—the repeated threats to shut down the government . . . the insistence that compromise was betrayal . . . taught Republican voters that government, institutions, political traditions, party leadership and parties themselves were things to be overthrown, evaded, ignored, insulted, laughed at."[12]

Charles Darwin would recognize the pathology immediately. In the *Descent of Man*, he described the disadvantage of such tribal division: "An advancement in the standard of morality will certainly give an immense advantage to one tribe over another. A tribe including many members who, from possessing in a high degree the spirit of patriotism, fidelity, obedience, courage and sympathy, were always ready to aid one another, and to sacrifice themselves for the common good, would be victorious over most other tribes . . ."[13]

Higher quality democracies abroad are characterized by unity of purpose, compromise, and collaboration. Their communitarian comity yields more advantageous societies that better fulfill the potential for citizens to meet their aspirations and achieve happiness. High-quality democracies are ballasted by large centers of moderate voters. They flourish because governance is focused on the greater good. Voter aspirations for tranquility and widespread prosperity combine with political equality to translate into government policy. Their citizens are able to overcome a natural distrust of others and actualize the moral sentiments in mankind's better angels. That is how these democracies are able to perform on a higher plane than America and suppress the darker aspects of mankind's nature and of capitalism. It is how they succeed where America fails in sustaining societies that realize the greatest good for the greatest number.

Turnover on the Supreme Court will eventually put that *desideratum* in reach of America. Recriminalization of vote buying in particular will begin the process of replacing a pathology that Harvard biology professor E.O. Wilson terms "individual selection" with a society featuring empathy and shared mutual aid.[14]

Like the Warren Court's support of civil rights, it will take courage for future Court majorities to subordinate the *fittest* to Aristotle's landless. But in doing so, these giants will begin the process of rebuilding the moderate center of American democracy and realizing the full promise of the founding fathers' remarkable preamble to the Declaration of Independence.

☆ NOTES ☆

Introduction: Removing the Dead Hand of Pay-to-Play

1. US District Court, D. New Mexico, September 2001, www.leagle.com/decision /20011426160FSupp2d1266_11314/HOMANS%20v.%20CITY%20OF%20 ALBUQUERQUE
2. Chief Justice John Roberts, *Arizona Free Enterprise Club's Freedom Club PAC v. Bennett*, quoted in Richard L. Hasen, *Plutocrats United* (New Haven, CT: Yale University Press, 2016), 86.
3. Nicholas Kulish, "And on Your Left, Behind Those Walls, Lobbyists Are at Work," *New York Times*, November 23, 2012.
4. Larry M. Bartels, *Unequal Democracy* (New York: Russell Sage Foundation; Princeton, NJ: Princeton University Press), 283–84.
5. John Ferling, *Jefferson and Hamilton* (New York: Bloomsbury, 2013), 350.
6. Ibid., 182.
7. Robert C. Post, *Citizens Divided* (Cambridge, MA: Harvard University Press, 2014), 11.
8. Herbert J. Storing, ed. "Federal Farmer, no. 4, October 12, 1787," in *The Complete Anti-Federalist*. 7 vols. Chicago: University of Chicago Press, 1981, press-pubs.uchicago.edu/founders/documents/a5s5.html
9. Matthew C. Simpson, "The Founding Fathers' Power Grab: Was the Constitution Designed to Make the United States Less Democratic?" *New Republic*, September 29, 2016.
10. Ezra Klein, "Disclosing the Deeper Ills of Campaign Finance," *Washington Post*, July 28, 2012.
11. Daniel Lazare, *The Frozen Republic* (New York: Harcourt, 1996), 180.
12. Dana Lanskyd, "Proceeding to a Constitution: A Multi-Party Negotiation Analysis of the Constitutional Convention of 1787" *Harvard Negotiation Law Review*, 5 Harv. Negotiation L. Rev. 167. (Spring 2000), 279–284.
13. Michael Gerson, "The Senate Has Lost Its Way," *Washington Post,* April 4, 2014.
14. Samuel Bowles and Herbert Gintis, *Democracy and Capitalism* (New York: Basic Books, 1987), 52–3.

15. Gaillard Hunt, ed. "James Madison, Letter to W.T. Barry, August 4, 1822," in *The Writings of James Madison,* vol. 9, 103 (1910). *Respectfully Quoted: A Dictionary of Quotations,* 1989, www.bartleby.com/73/969.html

16. Thomas Piketty (blog), "WID.world: New Data on Inequality and Collapse of Low Income" (World Wealth and Income Data Base), *Le Monde,* January 11, 2016, piketty.blog.lemonde.fr/2017/01/11/wid-world-une-nouvelle-base -de-donnees-mondiales-sur; see also (paywall) Facundo Alvaredo, Lucas Chancel, Thomas Piketty, Emmanuel Saez, and Gabriel Aucman, "Global Inequality Dynamics: New Findings from WID.world" (February 2017), National Bureau of Economic Research, no. 23119, http://wid.world /document/f-alvaredo-l-chancel-t-piketty-e-saez-g-zucman-global -inequality-dynamics-new-findings-wid-world-2017/.

17. Tibor Scitovsky, *The Joyless Economy: The Psychology of Human Satisfaction,* rev. ed. (New York: Oxford University Press, 1992), 8.

18. Jeremy Grantham, "This Time Seems Very, Very Different," *GMO newsletter,* June 2017, www.gmo.com/docs/default-source/public-commentary/gmo -quarterly-letter.pdf?sfvrsn=44

19. Ibid.

20. See Roberto S. Foa and Yascha Mounk, "The Danger of Deconsolidation," *Journal of Democracy* 27:3 (July 2016), 13.

21. Global Perception Index, Transparency International, archive.transparency .org/policy_research/surveys_indices/cpi/previous_cpi

22. Gallup, "75% in US See Widespread Government Corruption," September 15, 2015, www.gallup.com/poll/185759/widespread-government-corruption .aspx?g_source=gallup%20world%20poll%202010&g_medium=search&g _campaign=tiles

23. See Joan C. Williams, "What So Many People Don't Get About the American Working Class," *Harvard Business Review* (November 10, 2016), hbr .org/2016/11/what-so-many-people-dont-get-about-the-u-s-working-class; and Stanley Greenberg, "The Democrats' 'Working-Class Problem,'" *The American Prospect,* June 1, 2017.

24. See comments of Evercore ISI industry analyst Arndt Ellinghorst in Richard Milne, "Volkswagen: System Failure," *Financial Times,* November 4, 2015.

25. Nancy Folbre, "Not Really Made in China (or the United States)," *New York Times,* August 19, 2013.

26. Jim Tankersley, "How Trump Won: The Revenge of Working-Class Whites," *Washington Post,* November 9, 2016.

27. Thomas Mann and Norman J. Ornstein, "Let's Just Say It: The Republicans Are the Problem," *Washington Post,* April 27, 2012.

28. Paul Krugman, "Things Can Only Get Worse," *New York Times,* January 23, 2017.

29. Maureen Dowd, "Trapped in Trump's Brain," *New York Times,* February 19, 2017.

30. Aram Goudsouzian, "Doomed Nixon Illuminated by New Research," *Washington Post,* March 26, 2017.
31. "Partisanship and Political Animosity in 2016," Pew Research Center, June 22, 2016, www.people-press.org/2016/06/22/partisanship-and-political -animosity-in-2016/
32. Dan Balz, "Trump's Right: He Didn't Break It. But Can He Fix It?" *Washington Post*, January 20, 2017.
33. John Sides, "The Astonishing Decline of the American Swing Voter," *Washington Post*, November 3, 2015.

Chapter 1: Faux Democracy: America's Decline to History's Dismal Default Setting

1. Stein Ringen, "Is American Democracy Headed to Extinction?" *Washington Post*, March 30, 2014.
2. Joseph Stiglitz, *The Great Divide* (New York: Norton, 2015), 125.
3. Gemma Tetlow and Alan Smith, "Squeezed Midwest vs. Squeezed Midlands: How US and UK Incomes Compare," *Financial Times*, December 18, 2016, www.ft.com/content/1adde6e6-c3a7-11e6-81c2-f57d90f6741a
4. Lauren Leatherby, "Five Charts Show Why Millennials Are Worse Off Than Their Parents," *Financial Times*, August 29, 2017.
5. Robert Jones, Daniel Cox, Juhem Navarro-Rivera, E.J. Dionne, Jr, and William A. Galston, "Do Americans Believe Capitalism and Government Are Working?" PRRI, April 28, 2014, https://www.prri.org/spotlight/brookings -institution-releases-new-report-faith-in-equality-economic-justice-and -the-future-of-religious-progressives/
6. See Lauren Gensler, "Only Half of American 30-Year-Olds Are Making More Than Their Parents Did," *Forbes*, December 9, 2016, www.forbes .com/sites/laurengensler/2016/12/09/american-dream-income-mobility-raj -chetty-study/#4c1def0f2405
7. Dana Milbank, "American Optimism Is Dying," *Washington Post*, August 12, 2014.
8. Max Ehrenfreund, "Young Workers Earned More in 1975 Than Today," *Washington Post*, April 21, 2017.
9. Fatih Guvenen, Greg Kaplan, Jae Song, and Justin Weidner, "Lifetime Incomes in the United States Over Six Decades," *Nation Bureau of Economic Research*, April 2017.
10. Florence Jaumotte and Carolina Osorio Buitron, "Power from the People," *Finance & Development International Monetary Fund*, 52:1 (March 2015), www.imf.org/external/pubs/ft/fandd/2015/03/jaumotte.htm
11. Robert P. Jones, Daniel Cox, Betsy Cooper, and Rachel Lienesch, "Anxiety, Nostalgia and Mistrust," American Values Survey, Public Religion

Research Institute, November 17, 2015, publicreligion.org/site/wp-content /uploads/2015/11/PRRI-AVS-2015.pdf

12. See George Tyler, *What Went Wrong* (Dallas, TX: BenBella Books, 2013), chart 18.1.

13. Ashley Ward and Matthew Parkinson, "International Comparisons of UK Productivity, Final Estimates 2015," Office of National Statistics, April 4, 2017, www.ons.gov.uk/economy/economicoutputandproductivity /productivitymeasures/bulletins/internationalcomparisonsofproductivity finalestimates/2015

14. Karl Brenke and Alexander S. Kritikos, "Hourly Wages in Lower Deciles No Longer Lagging Behind When It Comes to Wage Growth," German Institute for Economic Research, *DIW Economic Bulletin* 21.2017, 210, 211, https://www.diw.de/documents/publikationen/73/diw_01.c.559085.de/diw _econ_bull_2017-21-1.pdf

15. Robert Reich, *Saving Capitalism* (New York: Vintage, 2015), 127.

16. Jordi Angusto, "World Imbalances and the Decline in Wages," *Social Europe Journal* (June 1, 2017), https://www.socialeurope.eu/world -imbalances-decline-wages

17. Stephan Kaufman, "Reallöhne in Deutschland deutlich gestiegen," *Berliner Zeitung*, February 4, 2016, www.berliner-zeitung.de/wirtschaft /statistisches-bundesamt-realloehne-in-deutschland-deutlich-gestiegen, 10808230,33714080.html; and DPA, "German Real Wages of Workers Continue to Rise," *Handelsblatt,* June 23, 2016.

18. See "Pressemitteilungen 2016," Hans-Böckler Stiftung, November 30, 2016, boeckler.de/cps/rde/xchg/hbs/hs.xsl/63056_105887.htm

19. BLS, Manufacturing 1996–2012 (XLS), table 1.1., www.bls.gov/fls /#compensation. See also "Hourly Compensation Costs in Manufacturing," Statistisches Bundesamt (DuStatis), www.destatis.de/EN/FactsFigures /CountriesRegions/InternationalStatistics/Topic/Tables/BasicData _LaborCosts.html; and also BLS, Manufacturing 1996–2012 (XLS), table 1.2., www.bls.gov/fls/#compensation. Updated data for 2013 provided by the Conference Board, "International Comparisons of Hourly Compensation Costs in Manufacturing," table 1, www.conference-board.org/ilcprogram /index.cfm?id=28277

20. Deutsche Presse-Agentur, "Country Workers Get 5.6 Percent More Content," *Handelsblatt,* March 9, 2013, handelsblatt.com/politik/deutschland /tarifverhandlungen-laender-angestellte-bekommen-5-6-prozent-mehr -gehalt/7902896.html

21. Mehreen Khan, "UK Loses Mantle as World's Fastest Growing Advanced Economy in 2016," *Financial Times*, February 22, 2017, www.ft.com /content/4f8fad29-a66b-37a2-9240-01ae7f6b80be

22. Liz Alderman and Steven Greenhouse, "Serving Up Fries, for a Living Wage," *New York Times*, October 28, 2014.

23. Miles Corak, "Economic Mobility," *Pathways,* The Stanford Center on Poverty and Inequality, May 11, 2016, inequality.stanford.edu/sites/default /files/Pathways-SOTU-2016-Economic-Mobility-3.pdf

24. Harold Meyerson, "A Plan to Raise Pay," *Washington Post*, September 18, 2014.

25. Alfred Stepan and Juan Linz, "Comparative Perspectives on Inequality and the Quality of Democracy in the US," *Perspective on Politics* 9:4 (December 2011), 843.

26. Gemma Tetlow and Alan Smith, "Squeezed Midwest vs. Squeezed Midlands: How US and UK Incomes Compare, *Financial Times*, December 18, 2016, www.ft.com/content/1adde6e6-c3a7-11e6-81c2-f57d90f6741a

27. See Neil Irwin, "How Being More Like France Might Help Labor Markets," *New York Times,* June 21, 2016.

28. Ronald Janssen, "Labour Market Deregulation and Productivity: IMF Finds No Link," *Social Europe Journal,* April 15, 2015, www.social europe.eu/2015/04/labour-market-deregulation-productivity-imf-finds -no-link/

29. Marie Charrel, "Ben Bernanke: Donald Trump Exploited the Frustrations of the Americans Left Behind," *Le Monde,* June 27, 2017.

30. Harold Meyerson, "Warren's Friends on the Right," *Washington Post*, December 18, 2014.

31. Jill Lepore, "Richer and Poorer," *New Yorker*, March 16, 2015.

32. Ben Bernanke, "When Growth Is Not Enough," European Central Bank Forum on Central Banking, June 26, 2017, www.brookings.edu/wp-content /uploads/2017/06/es_20170626_whengrowthisnotenough.pdf

33. "Populist Platform 1892: Preamble," *Primary Sources: Workshops in American History*, https://www.learner.org/workshops/primarysources/corporations /docs/popplat.html

34. Matthew C. Klein, "The Myth of the German Jobs Miracle," *Financial Times*, July 11, 2017.

35. Steven Greenhouse, "Share of the Work Force in a Union Falls to a 97-Year Low," *New York Times*, January 24, 2014.

36. Reuters, "KKR Schickt Pro-Sieben-Chef in den Aufsichtsrat," *Handelsblatt*, April 7, 2017, translate.google.com/translate?u=http%3A%2F%2Fwww.ha ndelsblatt.com%2Funternehmen%2Fmanagement%2Fkonsumforsc her-gfk-kkr-schickt-pro-sieben-chef-in-den-

37. Marc Hujer, "What Potatoes Say About the State of US Democracy," *Der Spiegel*, August 17, 2012.

38. Editorial, "US Republican 'Cranks' Threaten Growth: Swan," *Brisbane Times*, September 21, 2012.

39. See "Measuring US Against the World Economic Scene," quoted in Eduardo Porter, "Inequality in America: The Data Is Sobering," *New York Times*, July 13, 2013.

40. Bureau of Labor Statistics data, www.bls.gov/webapps/legacy/cpswktab1 .htm

41. Neil Irwin, "Job Growth in Past Decade Was in Temp and Contract," *New York Times*, March 31, 2016. See also Eduardo Porter, "The Workers Trump Forgot," *New York Times*, March 1, 2017.

42. Eduardo Porter, ibid.

43. Ibid.

44. Annie Lowrey, "Recovery Has Created Far More Low-Wage Jobs Than Better-Paid Ones," *New York Times*, April 28, 2014.

45. Martin Wolf, "Why Inequality Is Such a Drag on Economies," *Financial Times*, September 30, 2013.

46. Harold Meyerson, "What Clinton Must Do," *Washington Post*, April 16, 2015.

47. Rakesh Kochhar, "Middle Class Fortunes in Western Europe," Pew Research Center, April 24, 2017, www.pewglobal.org/2017/04/24/middle -class-fortunes-in-western-europe/

48. "The Middle Class Lost Ground in Nearly Nine-in-Ten Metropolitan Areas Examined," Pew Research Center, May 11, 2016, www.pew socialtrends.org/2016/05/11/americas-shrinking-middle-class-a-close-look -at-changes-within-metropolitan-areas/?utm_source=Pew+Research+ Center&utm_campaign=1173200409-Weekly_May_12_20165_12 _2016&utm_medium=email&utm_term=0_3e953b9b70-1173200409 -399361261

49. Rakesh Kochhar, "Middle Class Fortunes."

50. Eduardo Porter, "Richer But Not Better Off," *New York Times*, October 30, 2016.

51. Ibid.

52. "Social Justice in the OECD," Bertelsmann Foundation, 2011, www .bertelsmann-stiftung.de/en/press/press-releases/press-release/pid /viele-wohlstandsstaaten-sozial-ungerecht/

53. UNDP, "Sustaining Human Progress," *Human Development Report, 2014*, hdr.undp.org/sites/default/files/hdr14-report-en-1.pdf

54. Current research on the rule of oligarchs includes Carles Boix and Luis Garicano, "Democracy, Inequality, and Country-Specific Wealth," Yale University, 2002, www.yale.edu/leitner/pdf/PEW-Boix.pdf; Adam Przeworksi, Michael E.Alvarez, Jose A. Cheibub, and Fernando Limngi, *Democracy and Development: Political Institutions and Well-Being in the World, 1950–1990*, (London, UK: Cambridge University Press), 2000; and Daron Acemoglu and James A. Robinson, "Why Did the West Extend the Franchise? Democracy, Inequality, and Growth in Historical Perspective," *Quarterly Journal of Economics* 115:4 (2000), 1167–99.

55. Larry M. Bartels, *Unequal Democracy*, 283–4.

56. See Ian Morris, *Why the West Rules—For Now* (New York: Farrar, Straus & Giroux, 2010), 259–60. The discussion of Aristotle borrows from some

material in George R. Tyler, *What Went Wrong* (Dallas, TX: BenBella Books, 2013), 26–28.

57. Stein Ringen, "Is American Democracy Headed to Extinction?" *Washington Post*, March 28, 2014.

58. See for example, Daron Acemoglu, Simon Johnson, and James A. Robinson, "The Colonial Origins of Comparative Development: An Empirical Investigation," *The American Economic Review* 91:5 (December 2001), 1369–1401.

59. Stein Ringen, "Is American Democracy Headed to Extinction?" *Washington Post*, March 30, 2014.

60. Trade Union Advisory Committee of the OECD, "The Role of Collective Bargaining as Part of a Comprehensive Strategy to Reduce Income Inequality," Background paper for G20 sub-group on Labor Income Share and Inequalities, May 6, 2015, https://www.fes.de/gewerkschaften/common /pdf/2015_TUAC_on_Inequality.pdf

61. Joseph Stiglitz, "Is Inequality Inevitable?" *New York Times,* June 29, 2014.

62. Steven Pearlstein, "Can We Save American Capitalism?" *Washington Post*, September 2, 2012.

63. Daron Acemoglu and James Robinson, *Why Nations Fail* (New York: Penguin/Random House, 2013), 311, 317.

64. Frank Specht, "Hour for the Union Fright," *Handelsblatt*, January 24, 2017, translate.google.com/translate?u=http%3A%2F%2Fwww.handelsblatt. com%2Funternehmen%2Fmanagement%2Fmitbestimmung-in-konzern en-sternstunde-fuer-den-gewerkschaftsschreck%2F19293026.html&hl=en &langpair=auto|en&tbb=1&ie=utf-8

65. Deutsche Presse-Agentur (DPA), "Expansion Abroad Secures Jobs in the Home Country: Jobs for Highly Qualified People Are Hardly Shifted," *Handelsblatt*, October 17, 2016, translate.google.com/translate?u=http%3A%2F%2Fwww .handelsblatt.com%2Funternehmen%2Fmittelstand%2Fwachstumsmaerkte %2Fglobalisierung-in-dax-konzernen-expansion-ins-ausland-sichert-jobs -in-der-heimat%2F14696124.html&hl=en&langpair=auto|en&tbb=1&ie =utf-8

66. David Wessel, "Big US Firms Shift Hiring Abroad," *Wall Street Journal*, April 29, 2011.

67. Martin A. Sullivan, "Testimony Before the House Ways and Means Committee," January 20, 2011, http://waysandmeans.house.gov/Uploaded Files/sullivan_written_testimony_WM_Jan_20.pdf

68. Tyler, *What Went Wrong* (Dallas, TX: BenBella, 2013), 362–3.

69. Frank Specht, "Hour for the Union Fright." *Handelsblatt*.

70. Cara Waters, "High Court Finds Quest Was Engaged in Sham Contracting 'Mischief,'" *Sydney Morning Herald*, December 3, 2015, www.smh.com.au /small-business/managing/high-court-finds-quest-engaged-in-sham -contracting-mischief-20151202-gle1fe.html

71. See Thomas Piketty, "Productivity in France and Germany," *Le Monde,* January 7, 2017, translate.google.com/translate?u=http%3A%2F%2Fwww.lemonde .fr%2Feconomie%2F1.html&hl=en&langpair=auto|en&tbb=1&ie=utf-8

72. Scott N. Paul, "Trump, Tariffs and Jobs," *New York Times,* December 8, 2016.

73. Larry Fauver and Michael E. Fuerst, "Does Good Corporate Governance Include Employee Representation? Evidence from German Corporate Boards," *Journal of Financial Economics* 82, December 2006.

74. Robert P. Jones, Daniel Cox, Betsy Cooper, and Rachel Lienesch, "Anxiety, Nostalgia and Mistrust," American Values Survey, Public Religion Research Institute, November 17, 2015, publicreligion.org/site/wp-content /uploads/2015/11/PRRI-AVS-2015.pdf

75. "Beyond Distrust: How Americans View Their Government," Pew Research Center, November 23, 2015, www.people-press.org/2015/11/23 /beyond-distrust-how-americans-view-their-government

76. John Asker, Joan Farre-Mensa, and Alexander Ljungqvist, "Comparing the Investment Behavior of Public and Private Firms," National Bureau of Economic Research, Working Paper 17394, September 2011.

77. See E.J. Dionne Jr, "A Start on Closing the Divide," *Washington Post,* June 19, 2017.

78. Eric Lichtblau and Alexandra Stevenson, "Behind Cruz Campaign's Striking Start, a Donor of Few Words," *New York Times,* April 11, 2015.

79. Acemoglu and Robinson, *Why Nations Fail,* 113.

80. Thomas Piketty, *Capital in the Twenty-First Century* (Cambridge, MA: Harvard University Press, 2014), 23–4, 514.

81. Among the many books reflecting this theme are Larry Bartels, *Unequal Democracy* (Princeton, NJ: Princeton University Press, 2010); Robert H. Frank, *The Darwin Economy* (Princeton, NJ: Princeton University Press, 2011); Thomas Frank, *What's the Matter with Kansas?* (New York: Henry Holt, 2005) and *Listen Liberal* (New York: Metropolitan Books/Henry Holt, 2017); James K. Galbraith, *The Predator State* (New York: Free Press, 2009); Lawrence Lessig, *Republic, Lost* (New York: Twelve, 2015); Michael Lind, *Up from Conservatism* (New York: Free Press, 1997); Robert Reich, *Aftershock* (New York: Vintage, 2013), *Supercapitalism* (New York: Vintage, 2008), and *Saving Capitalism* (New York: Vintage, 2016); Joseph Stiglitz, *The Price of Inequality* (New York: W.W. Norton & Company, 2013); and Luigi Zingales, *A Capitalism for the People* (New York: Basic Books, 2012).

Chapter 2: Documenting Low-Quality American Democracy: The Income Bias and International Evidence

1. Bartels, *Unequal Democracy,* 283–4.

2. Martin Gilens and Benjamin Page, "Testing Theories of American Politics: Elites, Interest Groups and Average Citizens," *Perspective on Politics* 32,

doi: 10.1017/S1537592714001595; www.polisci.northwestern.edu/people /documents/TestingTheoriesOfAmericanPoliticsFINALforProduction 6March2014.pdf

3. Branko Milanovic, "Inequality and Democratic Capitalism," *Globalist* reprinted from the Barcelona news magazine *La Vanguardia Dossier,* March 15, 2013, www.theglobalist.com/inequality-and-democratic-capitalism /http://www.theglobalist.com/storyid.aspx?storyid=9934

4. Ringen, "Is American Democracy Headed to Extinction?"

5. The political science literature on the policy influence of wealthier citizens is extensive, including scholars such as G. William Domhoff, Philip A. Burch, Thomas Ferguson, Kay Lehman Schlozman, Sidney Verba, Henry Brady, Jeffrey Winters, George Stigler, Mancur Olson, Anthony Downs, Jacob Hacker, and Paul Pierson. A useful summary of findings and competing schools of thought is available in the study by Gilens and Page (see note 8).

6. Martin Gilens, *Affluence and Influence* (New York: Russell Sage Foundation; Princeton, NJ: Princeton University Press, 2012), 10, 234, 239.

7. Ibid., 8, 10.

8. Martin Gilens and Benjamin Page, "Testing Theories of American Politics: Elites, Interest Groups and Average Citizens," *Perspective on Politics,* March 7, 2014, scholar.princeton.edu/sites/default/files/mgilens/files/gilens_and_ page_2014_-testing_theories_of_american_politics.doc.pdf

9. Ibid.

10. Ibid.

11. Ibid.

12. Lee Drutman, "Why Corporate Cash Doesn't Dominate Elections," *Washington Post,* March 30, 2015.

13. Gilens and Page, "Testing Theories of American Politics," 32–35.

14. Arloc Sherman, Robert Greenstein, and Kathy Ruffing, "Contrary to 'Entitlement Society' Rhetoric, Over Nine-Tenths of Entitlement Benefits Go to Elderly, Disabled or Working Households," Center on Budget and Policy Priorities, February 11, 2012, www.cbpp.org/research/contrary-to -entitlement-society-rhetoric-over-nine-tenths-of-entitlement-benefits -go-to

15. Ibid.

16. Benjamin I. Page, Larry M. Bartels, and Jason Seawright, "Democracy and the Policy Preferences of Wealthy Americans," *Perspective on Politics,* March 2013, 57, faculty.wcas.northwestern.edu/~jnd260/cab/CAB2012%20-%20 Page1.pdf

17. "Rural Poll Released Today," Center for Rural Affairs, June 25, 2013, www.cfra.org/news/130625/rural-poll-released-today; and Nate Birt, "Ten Things Rural America Wants Washington to Know," AG Web, June 25, 2013, http://www.agweb.com/article/ten_things_rural_america _wants_washington_to_know/

18. Noam Scheiber and Dalia Sussman, "Inequality Troubles Americans Across Party Lines, a Poll Finds," *New York Times*, June 4, 2015, Question 10.
19. See "The Many Ways to Measure Income Inequality," Pew Research Center, September 22, 2015, www.pewresearch.org/fact-tank/2013/12/18/the-many-ways-to-measure-economic-inequality/
20. See "Income Distribution and Poverty," OECD, stats.oecd.org/Index.aspx?DataSetCode=IDD; for other comparisons, see Andrea Brandolini and Timothy M. Smeeding, "Inequality Patterns in Western Democracies: Cross-Country Differences and Changes Over Time," in *Democracy, Inequality, and Representation*, ed. Pablo Beramendi and Christopher J. Anderson (New York: Russell Sage Foundation, 2008), fig. 2.1.
21. Jonathan David Ostry, Andrew Berg, and Charalambos G. Tsangarides, "Redistribution, Inequality and Growth," International Monetary Fund, February 17, 2014, www.imf.org/external/pubs/cat/longres.aspx?sk=41291.0
22. Ali Alichi, Kory Kantenga, and Juan Solé, "Income Polarization in the United States," WP/16/121, The International Monetary Fund, June 2016, http://www.imf.org/external/pubs/ft/wp/2016/wp16121.pdf
23. James Druckman and Lawrence Jacobs, "Segmented Representation: The Reagan White House and Disproportionate Responsiveness," in *Who Gets Represented*, ed. Peter K. Enns and Christopher Wlezien (New York: Russell Sage Foundation, 2011), chapter 6.
24. Binyamin Appelbaum, "Least Affluent Families' Incomes Are Declining, Fed Survey Shows," *New York Times*, September 5, 2014.
25. Nicholas Kristof, "It's Now the Canadian Dream," *New York Times*, May 15, 2014.
26. Emmanuel Saez and Gabriel Zucman, "Wealth Inequality in the United States Since 1913: Evidence from Capitalized Income Data," National Bureau of Economic Research, October 2014, http://eml.berkeley.edu/~saez/saez-zucmanNBER14wealth.pdf
27. Gretchen Morgenson, "Ending Tax Breaks for Ultrawealthy May Not Take Act of Congress," *New York Times*, May 6, 2016.
28. See Robert Shapiro, "The US and the Real Outrage About the Panama Papers," *Globalist*, May 2, 2016, www.theglobalist.com/united-states-finale-reforms-economy-republicans/
29. Christoper Caldwell, "The Billionaires Bending American Politics to Their Will," *Financial Times*, September 12, 2014.
30. Bartels, *Unequal Democracy*, 256, 269.
31. Ibid., 271–2.
32. Thomas Mann and Norman Ornstein, *It's Even Worse Than It Looks* (New York: Basic, 2012), 190.
33. Robert J. Kaiser, *Act of Congress* (New York: Knopf, 2013), 273–4.
34. Editorial, "The Biggest Losers as Interest Rates Rise," *New York Times*, January 7, 2017.

35. Steven Rattner, "Airport Lines and Budget Lies," *New York Times*, July 9, 2016.

36. Gina Kolata, "So Many Research Scientists, So Few Professorships," *New York Times*, July 14, 2016.

37. "Revenue Statistics, 2015," OECD, December 3, 2015, www.oecd.org/ctp /tax-policy/revenue-statistics-19963726.htm

38. John Dizard, "Fear and Regulatory Loathing Makes America the Top Tax Haven, *Financial Times,* March 27, 2016. See also Nassim Khadem, "Australia a Safe Haven for Illicit Funds, US Overtakes Caymans as Tax Shelter for Rich," *Sydney Morning Herald*, November 3, 2015, www.smh.com.au /business/the-economy/australia-a-safe-haven-for-illicit-funds-us -overtakes-cayman-as-tax-shelter-for-rich-20151102-gkokks.html

39. Editorial, "The Biggest Losers as Interest Rates Rise," *New York Times*, January 7, 2017.

40. Nelson D. Schwartz, "On Capitol Hill, Partisan Heat, Not Economic Light," *New York Times*, June 23, 2016.

41. Norman J. Ornstein and Thomas E. Mann, *It's Even Worse Than It Looks*, 18.

42. Matea Gold and Robert Barnes, "GOP Groups Intensify Efforts to Aid Trump from Outside," *Washington Post*, April 3, 2017.

Chapter 3: The *Buckley* Era: Constitutionally Shielding Vote Buying

1. Warren Buffett, CNN, April 3, 2015, www.youtube.com/watch?v=eBGDL bhnSOU

2. Ciara Torres-Spelliscy, "The History of Corporate Personhood," Brennan Center for Justice, April 7, 2014, www.brennancenter.org/blog /hobby-lobby-argument

3. Laurie Bennett, "The Kochs Aren't the Only Funders of Cato," *Forbes*, March 12, 2012, www.forbes.com/sites/lauriebennett/2012/03/13/the-kochs -arent-the-only-funders-of-cato/

4. Ezra Klein, "The DISCLOSE Act Won't Fix Campaign Finance," *Washington Post*, July 27, 2012.

5. Ruth Marcus, "Clinton, Sanders and Why This Is a Dangerous Moment for Democrats," *Washington Post,* February 5, 2016.

6. Acemoglu and Robinson, *Why Nations Fail*, 319–23.

7. Nicholas Confessore, "In Republican Circles, Talk of a Campaign Aimed at Stopping Trump," *New York Times*, September 5, 2015.

8. Wendall Potter and Nick Penniman, *Nation on the Take* (London, UK: Bloomsbury Publishing, 2016), 31.

9. Robert E. Mutch, *Buying the Vote* (New York: Oxford University Press, 2014), 150.

10. Ibid.
11. Zephyr Teachout, *Corruption in America* (Cambridge, MA: Harvard University Press), 14.
12. Ezra Klein, "Disclosing the Deeper Ills of Campaign Finance," *Washington Post*, July 28, 2012.
13. Teachout, *Corruption in America*, 38.
14. Ibid., Appendix one.
15. Lawrence Lessig, *Republic, Lost* (New York: Twelve, 2011), 241.
16. Teachout, *Corruption in America*, 7.
17. Carl Hulse, "Is the "Supreme Court Naïve About Corruption? Ask Jack Abramoff," *New York Times*, July 6, 2016.
18. Lessig, *Republic, Lost*, 249.
19. Ron Fein, "Goldwater Would Have Hated 'Citizens United,'" *Washington Post*, October 15, 2014.
20. Dana Milbank, "A Ruling for the People, at Least the Artificial Ones," *Washington Post*, July 1, 2014.
21. Ben Bernanke, "People, Not Companies Should Have to Face a GFC Prosecution, says Ben Bernanke," *Sydney Morning Herald*, October 5, 2015.
22. Richard Painter, "The Conservative Case for Campaign Finance Reform," *New York Times*, February 3, 2016.
23. As quoted by Robert Reich, "Social Darwinism Is Here to Stay," *Christian Science Monitor*, April 4, 2012.
24. James MacGregor Burns, *Packing the Court* (New York: Penguin Press, 2009), 109.
25. Ibid., 252.
26. Lawrence Goldstone, *Inherently Unequal: The Betrayal of Equal Rights by the Supreme Court, 1865–1903* (New York: Walker, 2011), 70.
27. *McConnell v. FEC* (2003), Opinion of Scalia, 257–8. See also Thomas Frank, "Zephyr Teachout's 'Corruption in America,'" *New York Times Sunday Book Review*, October 16, 2014.
28. Teachout, *Corruption in America*, 241.
29. Matea Gold, "Wealthy Political Donors Seize on New Latitude to Give to Unlimited Candidates," *Washington Post*, September 2, 2014.
30. Robert E. Mutch, *Buying the Vote*, 149.
31. See Andrew Jacobs, "Brazil's Graft-Prone Congress, a Circus That Has Its Own Clown," *New York Times*, May 16, 2016.
32. See "Political Finance Database," Institute for Democracy and Electoral Assistance, www.idea.int/political-finance/
33. Ciara Torres-Spelliscy, "The History of Corporate Personhood," Brennan Center for Justice, April 7, 2014, www.brennancenter.org/blog/hobby-lobby-argument
34. Adam Winkler, "Corporate Personhood and the Rights of Corporate Speech," *Seattle University Law Review* 30:863 (2007), 865. See also *Wheeling Steel*

Corporation v. Glander US 562 (1949) in Brad Delong, "A Short Dialogue on *Santa Clara County v. Southern Pacific Railroad Company*," DeLong, Long Form, January 15, 2007, http://delong.typepad.com/delong_long _form/2007/02/hoisted-from-the-archives-do-judges-make-or-discover -the-law-a-short-dialogue-on-santa-clara-county-v-southern-pacific-ra .html#more

35. MacGregor Burns, *Packing the Court*, 107.
36. Ibid., 96.
37. Malcolm Gladwell, *Outliers* (Boston, MA: Little Brown, 2008), 56.
38. Editorial, "The Horror of Lynchings Lives On," *New York Times*, December 4, 2016.
39. Ciara Torres-Spelliscy, "The History of Corporate Personhood."
40. Howard Jay Graham, "The 'Conspiracy Theory' of the Fourteenth Amendment: 2," 48:2 *Yale Law Journal* (December 1938), 18, Scribd., www .scribd.com/document/147445180/Fourteenth-Amendment-Diversity -Corporation-Cannot-Sue-Rundle-v-Delaware
41. Richard L. Aynes, "Unintended Consequences of the Fourteenth Amendment and What They Tell Us About Its Interpretation," University of Akron School of Law, January 2006, section V, ideaexchange.uakron.edu/cgi/viewcontent .cgi?article=1020&context=ua_law_publications
42. William O. Douglas and Hugo Black, "*Wheeling Steel Corp. v. Glander* Dissent, United States Supreme Court No. 447 (1949, FindLaw, http://caselaw .findlaw.com/us-supreme-court/337/562.html)
43. Ibid.

Chapter 4: The Donor Class Buys Itself a Political Party

1. David M. Kennedy, "Malefactors of Megawealth," *New York Times Sunday Book Review,* October 21, 2007.
2. Joseph Stiglitz, "Inequality Is Not Inevitable?" *New York Times*, June 27, 2014.
3. Theda Skocpol and Vanessa Williamson, *The Tea Party and the Remaking of Republican Conservatism* (New York: Oxford University Press, 2012), 102.
4. Robert Reich, "And Now the Richest .01 Percent" (Robert Reich's blog), November 18, 2014, www.robertreich.org
5. Eduardo Porter, "Big Business Is Losing Clout in a Republican Party Moving Right," *New York Times*, September 4, 2013.
6. "The Influence of Money Has Broken Our Government," *Issue One*, January 9, 2017.
7. Bill Turque, "GOP Plank: Leave Campaign Spending Alone," *Washington Post*, August 30, 2012.
8. Jin-Hyuk Kim, "Corporate Lobbying Revisited," *Business and Politics* 10:2 (2008) (Berkeley Electronic Press), Published online as U Colorado

CU Scholar, May 1, 2008, http://scholar.colorado.edu/cgi/viewcontent
.cgi?article=1001&context=econ_facpapers

9. David Gelles, "They Tilt Right, but Top CEOs Don't Give to Trump," *New York Times,* May 27, 2016.

10. Nicholas Confessore, Sarah Cohen, and Karen Yourish, "From Only 158 Families, Half the Cash for '16 Race," *New York Times,* October 11, 2015.

11. "Beyond Distrust: How Americans View Their Government," Pew Research Center, November 23, 2015, section 2, http://www.people-press.org/2015/11/23/beyond-distrust-how-americans-view-their-government/

12. Jane Mayer, "In the Withdrawal from the Paris Climate Agreement, the Koch Brothers' Campaign Becomes Overt," *New Yorker,* June 5, 2017.

13. Nicholas Confessore, "Father of Koch Brothers Helped Build Nazi Oil Refinery, Book Says," *New York Times,* January 11, 2016.

14. Skocpol and Williamson, *The Tea Party,* 9, 84.

15. Sheryl Gay Stolberg and Mike McIntire, "A Federal Budget Crisis Months in the Planning," *New York Times,* October 6, 2013.

16. Jurek Martin, "American Business Can't Afford Not to Stand Up to the Tea Party," *Financial Times,* October 22, 2013.

17. Frank Rich, "The Billionaires Bankrolling the Tea Party," *New York Times,* August 28, 2010; Nick Corasaniti, "Fox's Impact, Absent Ailes," *New York Times,* July 23, 2016.

18. Skocpol and Williamson, *The Tea Party,* 172.

19. Dana Milbank, "The GOP's Darwinism," *Washington Post,* January 1, 2014.

20. Michael Dimock, Carroll Doherty, and Jocelyn Kiley, "Whither the GOP? Republicans Want Change, but Split Over Party's Direction," Pew Research Center, July 31, 2013.

21. Joe Rothstein, "What's the Matter with North Carolina? (Nothing a New Pope Wouldn't Fix)," *US Politics Today,* EINnews.com, July 1, 2013, uspolitics.einnews.com/column/156819184/what-s-the-matter-with-north-carolina-nothing-a-new-pope-wouldn-t-fix

22. Jane Mayer, "State for Sale: Art Pope's Conquest of North Carolina," *New Yorker,* October 10, 2011.

23. T.W. Farnam, "Americans for Prosperity Puts Big Money on Legislative Races in Arkansas," *Washington Post,* October 1, 2012.

24. Colin Woodard, "Olympia Snowe, Fighting for Common Ground. We Can Fix the Stalemate in Congress," *Washington Post,* June 9, 2013.

25. Seth Masket and Michael Miller, "Does Public Election Funding Create More Extreme Legislators? Evidence from Arizona and Maine," *State Politics and Policy Quarterly,* 2014, http://mysite.du.edu/~smasket/Masket_Miller_SPPQ.pdf

26. Syed Zaidi, "Senators Murkowski and Wyden Initiate Bipartisan Disclosure Proposal," Money in Politics This Week, Brennan Center for Justice, January 18, 2013, http://www.brennancenter.org/blog/money-politics-week-19.

27. Michael Wines, "5 Numbers That Give Clearer View of Election," *Washington Post*, March 18, 2017.

28. Editorial, "Virginia's Carnival of Cakewalks," *Washington Post*, November 6, 2015.

29. Sara Fitzgerald, letter to editor, "Voters Will Be Watching the VA Legislators Who Nixed Redistricting Reform," *Washington Post*, February 19, 2017.

30. Kenneth Vogel, "Koch World 2014," Politico.com, Jan. 24, 2014.

31. Robert Reich, *Saving Capitalism* (New York: Vintage, 2015), 173.

32. Matea Gold, "The Koch-Backed Ground Game: Door-to-Door-to-Database," *Washington Post*, July 30, 2015; Stephen Foley, "Lunch with the FT: Charles Koch," *Financial Times*, January 8, 2016; and Matea Gold, "Some Grinding Noises in the Koch Machine, *Washington Post*, August 2, 2016.

33. Kenneth P. Vogel and Jeremy W. Peters, "In Alabama Win, Model of New Bannon Alliance," *New York Times*, September 29, 2017.

34. Barney Jopson, "US Billionaire Bankrolls Attacks on Jeb Bush Over Climate Change," *Financial Times*, April 7, 2015.

35. Skocpol and Williamson, *The Tea Party*, 157.

36. Ross Douthat, "Donald Trump, Traitor to His Class," *New York Times*, August 30, 2015.

37. Rich, "The Billionaires."

38. Demetri Sevastopulo, "Republican Hopefuls Find Deep Pockets for Most Expensive Campaign," *Financial Times*, April 20, 2015.

39. Dana Milbank, "Citizens Disenfranchised," *Washington Post*, April 28, 2015.

40. Potter and Penniman, *Nation on the Take*, 38.

41. Andrew Ross Sorkin, "A Bloomberg Run? Drums Are Beating," *New York Times,* October 20, 2015.

42. Mathew Garrahan, "Fox News Election Coverage Tops ESPN Primetime Ratings," *Financial Times*, December 28, 2016, www.ft.com /content/6e631e68-cd4c-11e6-864f-20dcb35cede2

43. Matea Gold and Tom Hamburger, "Will Donors, Lobbyists Help 'Drain the Swamp'?" *Washington Post*, November 13, 2016.

44. See Jane Mayer, *Dark Money* (New York: Doubleday, 2016.); Thomas Frank, *Listen Liberal* (New York: Metropolitan Books/Henry Holt, 2017); Steven Pearlstein "Sorry, Reagan, Big Government Is Good for America," *Washington Post*, March 27, 2016; and E.J. Dionne, Jr, *Why the Right Went Wrong* (New York: Simon & Schuster, 2016).

45. Kenneth Vogel, *Big Money* (New York: Public Affairs Books, 2014), 16.

46. Tilman Klumpp, Hugo Mialon, and Michael Williams, "The Business of American Democracy: Citizens United, Independent Spending, and Elections," *Social Science Research Network*, July 2014, papers.ssrn.com/sol3 /papers.cfm?abstract_id=2312519; see also Tilman Klumpp, Hugo Mialon, and Michael Williams, "Yes, 'Citizens United' Helped the GOP," *Washington Post*, April 8, 2016.

47. David Callahan and J. Mijin Cha, "Stacked Deck," *Demos*, March 2013, 18, 23.

48. Gail Collins, "Billion Dollar Babies," *New York Times*, March 5, 2014.

49. Matthew Miller and Peter Newcomb, "Billionaires Worth $3.7 Trillion Surge as Gates Wins 2013," *Bloomberg News*, January 2, 2014, www .bloomberg.com/news/articles/2014-01-02/billionaires-worth-3-7-trillion -surge-as-gates-wins-2013

50. Tom Metcalf and Jack Witzig, "In a Year of Political Turmoil, Things Look Pretty Good for Billionaires," *Washington Post*, January 3, 2017.

51. Nicholas Confessore, "A Wealthy Governor and His Friends Are Remaking Illinois," *New York Times*, November 29, 2015.

52. Confessore et al., "From Only 158 Families, Half the Cash for '16 Race."

53. Piketty, *Capital*, 440, 443–445.

54. "In Florence, the Rich Families of the Fifteenth Century Are Still," *Le Monde*, May 21, 2016.

55. Coral Davenport and Eric Lipton, "How GOP Leaders Came to View Climate Change as Fake Science," *New York Times*, June, 2017.

56. Stuart Stevens, "How to Get Better at Running for President," *New York Times*, October 18, 2015.

57. Mann and Ornstein, *It's Even Worse Than It Looks*, 132.

58. Ibid., xv, 216.

59. Thomas L. Friedman, "Elephants Down Under," *New York Times*, March 28, 2012.

60. Ross Douthat, "Mr. Trump, Establishment Sellout," *New York Times*, May 21, 2017.

61. Jeff Merkley, "Make the Republicans Go Nuclear," *New York Times*, February 3, 2017.

Section 2: Reducing the Role of Money to Improve the Quality of American Democracy

1. David Cay Johnson, *Perfectly Legal* (New York: Penguin Random House, 2004), 308.

Chapter 5: The Roberts Republicans: A Partisan Court of Sumner Darwinians

1. Richard Posner, "The Supreme Court Is a Political Court, the Republicans' Actions Are Proof," *Washington Post*, March 9, 2016.

2. Stanley Greenberg, "Why Voters Tune Out Democrats," *New York Times*, August 5, 2011.

3. Neal Devins and Lawrence Baum, "Split Definitive: How Party Polarization Turned the Supreme Court into a Partisan Court," William and Mary Law School Research Paper No. 09-276, May 2, 2014; and Hasen, *Plutocrats United*, 180.

4. Jeffrey Rosen, "Supreme Court, Inc.," *New York Times Magazine*, March 16, 2008.

5. Editorial, "A Coup Against the Supreme Court," *New York Times*, November 7, 2016.

6. Linda Greenhouse, "What the Chief Justice Should Have Said," *New York Times*, January 8, 2017.

7. Kim Soffen, "Trump's Judicial Influence Could Go Far Beyond Putting Gorsuch on the Supreme Court," *Washington Post*, February 1, 2017.

8. Eric Lipton and Jeremy W. Peters, "Conservatives Press Overhaul in the Judiciary," *New York Times*, March 19, 2017.

9. See the comments of Ed Whelan, president of the conservative think tank the Ethics and Public Policy Center, in E.J. Dionne Jr., "The Court Fight Is About Democracy," *Washington Post*, March 21, 2016.

10. Richard Posner, "A Supremely Politicized Court," *Washington Post*, March 10, 2016.

11. Adam Liptak, "Judges Who Are Elected Like Politicians Tend to Act Like Them," *New York Times*, October 4, 2016.

12. Ari Berman, *Give Us the Ballot* (New York: Farrar, Straus & Giroux, 2015), 309.

13. Sari Horwitz, "Justice Dept. Shifts on Texas Voting Law," *Washington Post*, February 28, 2017.

14. Ari Berman, "Iowa's New Voter-ID law Would Have Disenfranchised My Grandmother," *Nation*, April 13, 2017.

15. ———, "Wisconsin's Voter ID Law Suppressed 200,000 Votes in 2016 (Trump Won by 22,748)," *Nation*, May 9, 2017, www.thenation.com/article/wisconsins-voter-id-law-suppressed-200000-votes-trump-won-by-23000/

16. Ibid.

17. Berman, *Give Us the Ballot,* 210, 213.

18. Robert E. Mutch, *Buying the Vote*, 179–80.

19. Pippa Norris, "How Common Is the Belief That an Election Can Be Rigged?" NPR radio interview with Robert Siegel, October 20, 2016, www.npr.org/2016/10/20/498736800/how-common-is-the-belief-that-an-election-can-be-rigged

20. Lawrence Goldstone, *Inherently Unequal: The Betrayal of Equal Rights by the Supreme Court, 1865–1903* (New York: Walker, 2011), 126.

21. Ibid., 175.

22. Editorial, "A Meaningful Move on Voting Rights," *New York Times*, May 31, 2017.

23. David Cole, "Shutting Americans Out of the Ballot Booth," *Washington Post*, March 6, 2016.

24. James Q. Whitman, *Hitler's American Model: The United States and the Making of Nazi Race Law* (Princeton, NJ: Princeton University Press, 2017).

25. Editorial, "A Meaningful Move on Voting Rights."

26. Editorial, "Restoring the Vote in Va.," *Washington Post*, June 12, 2017.

27. Quoted by Adam Liptak, "The Polarized Court," *New York Times*, May 10, 2014.

28. Robert Barnes, "Politics Is Certainly Part of the High Court," *Washington Post*, July 18, 2016.

29. Liptak, "The Polarized Court."

30. David Cay Johnson, *Free Lunch* (New York: Portfolio, 2008), 93.

31. Lee Epstein, William E. Landes, and Richard A. Posner, *The Behavior of Federal Judges* (Cambridge, MA: Harvard University Press, 2013), chapter 3. See also Erwin Chemerinsky, *The Case Against the Supreme Court* (New York: Viking 2014), 190.

32. MacGregor Burns, *Packing the Court*, 101.

33. Liz Kennedy, "Citizens Actually United: The Bi-Partisan Opposition to Corporate Political Spending and Support for Common Sense Reform," *Demos*, October 25, 2012, www.demos.org/publication/citizens-actually -united-bi-partisan-opposition-corporate-political-spending-and-support

34. David Savage, "Supreme Court Makes Age Bias Suits Harder to Win," *Los Angeles Times*, June 19, 2009.

35. Herman Schwartz, "The Death of the Class Action Lawsuit," *Nation*, September 24, 2015, www.thenation.com/article/the-death-of-the-class-action-lawsuit/

36. Reich, *Saving Capitalism*, 80.

37. Editorial, "So No One's Responsible?" *New York Times*, June 14, 2011.

38. Reich, *Saving Capitalism*, 80.

39. Adam Liptak, "Supreme Court Sides with Tobacco Company in RICO Case," *New York Times*, June 21, 2016.

40. ———, "Justice Stevens Suggests Solution for 'Giant Step in the Wrong Direction,'" *New York Times*, April 22, 2014.

41. Cristian Farias, "Antonin Scalia's Death Just Cost This Company $835 million," *Huffington Post Politics*, February 26, 2016, http://www.huffingtonpost .com/entry/antonin-scalia-dow-chemical_us_56d0d4bfe4b03260bf76efa4

Chapter 6: Rejection of Political Equality by the Constitution

1. Matthew C. Simpson, "The Founding Fathers' Power Grab. Was the Constitution Designed to Make the United States Less Democratic?" *New Republic*, September 29, 2016.

2. Ferling, *Jefferson and Hamilton* (New York: Bloomsbury, 2013), 361.

3. Robert C. Post, *Citizens Divided* (Cambridge, MA: Harvard University Press,2014), 8.
4. Matthew Spalding, "How to Understand Slavery and the American Founding," The Heritage Foundation, August 26, 2002, http://www.heritage. org/research/reports/2002/08/how-to-understand-slavery-and-americas
5. *Slavery and the Making of America: Commonwealth v. Nathaniel Jennison* (1783), PBS, http://www.pbs.org/wnet/slavery/experience/legal/feature 3b.html. See also Lexis/Nexis, "Minutes from the case of Commonwealth v. Nathaniel Jennison, which abolished slavery in Massachusetts" [Source Note: Proceedings of the Massachusetts Historical Society: (1873–1875), Boston, 1875], https://www.lexisnexis.com/academic/1univ/hist/aa/aas_ case.asp
6. Ferling, *Jefferson and Hamilton*, 3, 181–2.
7. Joseph J. Ellis, *The Quartet* (New York: Vintage Books, 2016), 130.
8. Simpson, "The Founding Fathers' Power Grab."
9. Ellis, *The Quartet*, 144.
10. Ferling, *Jefferson and Hamilton*, 188, 216.
11. Michael Waldman, "The Fight to Vote," 5.

Chapter 7: Political Bribery Decriminalized: Vote Buying as "Free Speech"

1. Adam Liptak, "Judges on the Campaign Trail," *New York Times,* September 28, 2014.
2. Lawrence Norden, Brent Ferguson, and Douglas Keith, "Five to Four," Brennan Center for Justice, January 13, 2016, www.brennancenter.org/sites /default/files/publications/Five_to_Four_Final.pdf
3. See Eric Lipton, "For Freshman in the House, Seats of Plenty," *New York Times,* August 11, 2013.
4. Ibid.
5. See Benjamin Edwards, "Pruning Wall Street's Thicket of Conflicts," *New York Times,* December 29, 2016.
6. Norden et al., "Five to Four."
7. Teachout, *Corruption in America* (Cambridge, MA: Harvard University Press), 225.
8. Lessig, *Republic, Lost* (New York: Twelve, 2011), 8.
9. Ibid.
10. Liptak, "Judges on the Campaign Trail."
11. Trevor Potter, "The Court's Changing Perception of Corruption," The Campaign Legal Center, May 7, 2015, www.campaignlegalcenter.org/news /blog/court-s-changing-conception-corruption
12. Joe Nocera, "Rethinking Campaign Finance," *New York Times,* May 17, 2014.

13. Jeffrey Birnbaum, "Builder Group Resumes Campaign Contributions," *Washington Post*, May 6, 2008.

14. Jill Lepore, "The Crooked and the Dead," *New Yorker*, August 25, 2014.

15. Sam Roberts, "Bribery and Corruption, or 'Honest Graft'?" *New York Times*, June 19, 2016.

16. Debbie Freeman, "New Study: Companies Making Campaign Contributions to Tax-Writing Members of Congress Pay Lower Tax Rates," Arizona State University, December 1, 2014, wpcarey.asu.edu/news-releases/2014-12-01/new-study-companies-making-campaign-contributions-tax-writing-members. Original study at Jennifer Brown, Katharine Drake, and Laura Wellman, "The Benefits of a Relational Approach to Corporate Political Activity: Evidence from Political Contributions to Tax Policymakers," *American Accounting Association Journal*, 2015, aaajournals.org/doi/pdf/10.2308/atax-50908; see also Eric Jay Toll, "Pay to Play with Congress Pays Off in Company Tax Breaks," *Phoenix Business Journal*, December 1, 2014.

17. Ashley Parker, "Big Donors Seek Larger Roles in Presidential Campaigns," *New York Times*, September 29, 2015.

18. See J. Silverman and G. Durden, "Determining Legislative Preferences on the Minimum Wage: An Economic Approach," *Journal of Political Economy*, 84 (April 1976); Sam Peltzman, "Constituent Interest and Congressional Voting," *Journal of Law and Economics* 27 (April 1984) 181–210; John Frendreis and Richard Waterman, "PAC Contributions and Legislative Behavior: Senate Voting on Truck Deregulation," *Social Science Quarterly* 66 (June 1985).

19. Rui J. de Figueiredo and Geoff Edwards, "Does Private Money Buy Public Policy? Campaign Contributions and Regulatory Outcomes in Telecommunications," Institute of Government Studies, University of California, Berkeley, Working Paper 2005, 40, bcep.haas.berkeley.edu/papers/figueiredo_edwards.pdf

20. Debbie Freeman, "New Study."

21. Ran Duchin and Denis Sosyura, "TARP Investments: Financials and Politics," University of Michigan, Ross School of Business, October 2010, webuser.bus.umich.edu/dsosyura/Research%20Papers/TARP%20Investments%20October%202010.pdf; see also Norbert Haring, "Self-Service for Banks," *Handelsblatt*, September 30, 2010.

22. Steven Brill, "On Sale: Your Government. Why Lobbying Is Washington's Best Bargain." *Time*, July 12, 2010.

23. David Kocieniewski, "Companies Push for Tax Breaks on Foreign Cash," *New York Times*, June 19, 2011.

24. Raquel Alexander, Steven Mazza, and Susan Scholz, "Measuring Rates of Return for Lobbying Expenditures: An Empirical Analysis under the American Jobs Creation Act," April 8, 2009. Available at SSRN: ssrn.com/abstract=1375082 or http://dx.doi.org/10.2139/ssrn.1375082; see also

Dan Eggen, "Investments Can Yield More on K Street, Study Indicates," *Washington Post*, April 12, 2009.

25. Jeffrey Brown and Jiekun Huang, "All the President's Friends: Political Access and Firm Value," CATO Research Briefs, April 2017, https://www.cato.org/publications/research-briefs-economic-policy/all-presidents-friends-political-access-firm-value

26. Thomas Stratmann, "What Do Campaign Contributions Buy? Deciphering Causal Effects of Money and Votes," *Southern Economic Journal* 57:3 (January 1991), 618, www.jstor.org/stable/1059776, or www.jstor.org/stable/1059776?seq=2#fndtn-page_scan_tab_contents

27. Adam Liptak, "Rendering Justice, With One Eye on Re-election," *New York Times*, May 25, 2008, www.nytimes.com/2008/05/25/us/25exception.html

28. Editorial, "Judges, with Hat in Hand," *New York Times*, January 19, 2015.

29. Erik Eckholm, "Outraged by Court in Kansas, GOP Sets Out to Reshape It," *New York Times*, April 2, 2016.

30. Adam Liptak and Janet Roberts, "Campaign Cash Mirrors a High Court's Rulings," *New York Times*, October 1, 2006.

31. Catherine Rampell, "In Kansas, Schools Do Less with Less," *Washington Post*, May 1, 2015.

32. John Eligon, "Court Budget Intensifies Kansas Dispute Over Powers Caveat," *New York Times*, June 6, 2015. See also John Eligon, "Kansas Legislature Threatens Showdown with Court Over School Financing," *New York Times*, October 9, 2015.

33. Bryan Lowry and Dion Lefler, "Democrats Make Gains in Kansas Legislature," *Wichita Eagle*, November 8, 2016, www.kansas.com/news/politics-government/election/article113472308.html

34. In *Caperton v. A. T. Massey Coal Co.* (2009), the Roberts Court ruled that this donation and subsequent vote was not bribery. They did conclude that Judge Benjamin should have recused.

35. Billy Corriher and Brent DeBeaumont, "Dodging a Billion-Dollar Verdict," Center for American Progress, August 14, 2013, https://www.americanprogress.org/issues/courts/reports/2013/08/14/72199/dodging-a-billion-dollar-verdict/

36. "Public Financing of Judicial Campaigns," American Bar Association, Standing Committee on Judicial Independence, February 2002, ix, www.americanbar.org/content/dam/aba/migrated/judind/pdf/commission report4_03.authcheckdam.pdf

37. "New Poll: Vast Majority of Voters Fear Campaign Cash Skews Judges' Decisions," Brennan Center for Justice, October 29, 2013, www.brennan center.org/press-release/new-poll-vast-majority-voters-fear-campaign-cash-skews-judges-decisions

38. Joanna Shepherd, "Justice at Risk, An Empirical Analysis of Campaign Contributions and Judicial Decisions," American Constitution Society,

June 2013, table 5, www.acslaw.org/ACS%20Justice%20at%20Risk%20
%28FINAL%29%206_10_13.pdf

39. Michael Kang and Joanna Shepherd, "The Partisan Price of Justice: An
    Empirical Analysis of Campaign Contributions and Judicial Decisions,"
    86:69 (June 12, 2012), *New York University Law Review*, 104, www.nyulaw
    review.org/sites/default/files/pdf/NYULawReview-86-1-Kang-Shepherd.pdf

40. As quoted by Robert Reich, *Saving Capitalism*, 78.

41. Robert A. Dahl, *Polyarchy: Participation and Opposition* (New Haven, CT:
    Yale University Press, 1971), 1; Liptak and Roberts, "Campaign Cash."

42. Liptak and Roberts, "Campaign Cash."

43. Vernon Valentine Palmer and John Levendis, "The Louisiana Supreme
    Court in Question: An Empirical and Statistical Study of the Effects of
    Campaign Money on the Judicial Function," *Tulane Law Review* 82, (2008),
    law.tulane.edu/uploadedFiles/Tulane_Journal_Sites/Tulane_Law_Review
    /docs/824palmer27.pdf

44. Geri Palast, "Justice at Stake," *AmericanViewpoint*, January 2002, www
    .justiceatstake.org/media/cms/JASJudgesSurveyResults_EA8838C0504A5
    .pdf

45. Ibid.

46. National Center for State Courts, various years, www.judicialselection.us
    /judicial_selection/reform_efforts/opinion_polls_surveys.cfm?state

47. "New Poll: Vast Majority of Voters Fear Campaign Cash Skews Judges'
    Decisions," Brennan Center for Justice, October 29, 2013, www.brennan
    center.org/press-release/new-poll-vast-majority-voters-fear-campaign
    -cash-skews-judges-decisions

48. Liptak and Roberts, "Campaign Cash."

Chapter 8: The *Buckley* Era: Cynicism and Diminished Faith in Democracy

1. Lessig, *Republic, Lost*, 243.

2. "Voters Think Congress Cheats to Get Elected," *Rasmussen Report*,
   September 3, 2014, www.rasmussenreports.com/public_content/archive
   /mood_of_america_archive/congressional_performance/voters_think
   _congress_cheats_to_get_reelected

3. Marc Fisher, "Wisconsin Gov. Scott Walker's Recall Vote: Big Money Fuels
   Small-Government Fight Money Fuels," *Washington Post*, March 26, 2012.

4. Bill Bishop, "Trust," *Washington Post*, March 5, 2017.

5. "Beyond Distrust: How Americans View Their Government," Pew Research
   Center, November 23, 2015, http://www.people-press.org/2015/11/23
   /beyond-distrust-how-americans-view-their-government/

6. Lessig, *Republic, Lost*, 243.

7. Nicholas Confessore and Megan Thee-Brenan, "Poll Shows Americans Favor an Overhaul of Campaign Financing," *New York Times*, June 3, 2015; "Americans' Views on Money in Politics," *New York Times/CBS News Poll*, June 2, 2015, https://www.nytimes.com/interactive/2015/06/02/us/politics /money-in-politics-poll.html

8. Richard L. Fox and Jennifer L. Lawless, "Turned Off by Politics," *Washington Post*, November 24, 2013.

9. John F. Burns, "Rude Britannia," *New York Times*, July 24, 2011.

10. "Perspectives from Business on Campaign Finance Reform," Committee for Economic Development, July 31, 2013, www.ced.org/events/single /perspectives-from-business-on-campaign-finance-reform

11. Robert Reich, *Saving Capitalism* (New York: Vintage, 2016),181; Rasmussen Reports, "Voters Still Say Congress Is for Sale," telephone poll, February 22, 2016, August 7–8, 2010, October 29, 2010, and July 27, 2011.

12. Liz Kennedy, "Citizens Actually United: The Bi-partisan Opposition to Corporate Political Spending and Support for Common Sense Reform," *Demos*, October 25, 2012 www.demos.org/publication /citizens-actually-united-bi-partisan-opposition-corporate-political -spending-and-support

13. Global Perception Index, Transparency International, www.transparency. org/cpi2015#results-table

14. Gallup, "75% in US See Widespread Government Corruption," September 15, 2015, www.gallup.com/poll/185759/widespread-government-corruption .aspx?g_source=gallup%20world%20poll%202010&g_medium=search&g _campaign=tiles

15. "Freedom in the World," Freedom House, 2016, freedomhouse.org/report /freedom-world-2016/table-scores

16. World Value Survey, Wave 6, 2011 (question V140), http://www.worldvalues survey.org/WVSDocumentationWV6.jsp

17. Roberto S. Foa and Yascha Mounk, "The Danger of Deconsolidation," *Journal of Democracy* 27:3 (July 2016), 13.

18. Sharon LaFraniere and Adam Goldman, "Guest List at Donald Trump Jr.'s Russian Meeting Expands Again," *New York Times*, July 18, 2017.

19. Campbell Robertson and Mitch Smith, "What's the Big Deal? If Putin Meddled, Trump Voters Ask," *New York Times*, January 8, 2017.

20. Karen Douglas, "You Just Can't Trust 'Em," *International Politics and Society*, May 22, 2017, www.ips-journal.eu/in-focus/conspiracy-theories/article /show/you-just-cant-trust-em-2057

21. Roberto S. Foa and Yascha Mounk, "The Danger of Deconsolidation," *Journal of Democracy* 27:3 (July 2016), fig. 2.

22. Ibid.

Chapter 9: International Dismay with the Variant of Capitalism Produced by Low-Quality American Democracy

1. Chris Bryant, Brian Groom, Michael Steen, and James Wilson, "Germany Shows How to Score On and Off the Football Pitch," *Financial Times*, May 24, 2013.

2. Alfred Stepan and Juan J. Linz, "Comparative Perspectives on Inequality and the Quality of Democracy in the United States," *Perspectives on Politics* 9:4 (December 2011), www.researchgate.net/publication/231755068 _Comparative_Perspectives_on_Inequality_and_the_Quality_of _Democracy_in_the_US; journals.cambridge.org/download.php?file=%2 FPPS%2FPPS9_04%2FS1537592711003756a.pdf&code=f88ba5210eb24423 c3e652438a6bb5dd

3. Sarah O'Connor, "Amazon Unpacked," *Financial Times,* February 8, 2013.

4. Eva Roth, "Working Conditions at an Online Mail-Order: How Amazon Defends Against Accusations of Wage Dumping (Versandhandel Wie sich Amazon gegen Vorwürfe des Lohndumpings wehrt)," *Berliner Zeitung*, December 12, 2015, www.berliner-zeitung.de/wirtschaft/arbeitsbedin gungen-bei-einem-online-versandhandel-wie-sich-amazon-gegen -vorwuerfe-des-lohndumpings-wehrt,10808230,32909328.html

5. Cameron Atfield, "Unions Promise 'CUB-Style' Campaign Against Coca-Cola If Demands Are Not Met," *Sydney Morning Herald*, February 1, 2017, www.smh.com.au/business/workplace-relations/unions-promise-cubstyle -campaign-against-cocacola-if-demands-are-not-met-20170201-gu34sm .html

6. Denis McShane, "European Works Councils—Another Brexit Victim," *Social Europe*, January 5, 2017, www.socialeurope.eu/2017/01 /european-works-councils-another-brexit-victim/

7. Rebecca Page, "Co-determination in Germany—A Beginner's Guide," *Arbeitspapier* 33, Hans Böckler Stiftung, June, 2011, https://www.boeckler .de/pdf/p_arbp_033.pdf

8. For international data on real gross fixed capital formation (Thomson Reuters Datastream) see Valentina Romei, "The Scale of the European Investment Crisis and Why It Matters," *Financial Times*, October 6, 2016.

9. Michael A. Fletcher, "Studies Track High Cost of Fast-Food Pay," *Washington Post*, October 16, 2013.

10. Harold Meyerson, "Saying No to Wal-Mart," *Washington Post*, July 17, 2013.

11. Susan Berfield, "Are American Taxpayers Subsidizing Walmart's Low Wages?" *BusinessWeek*, June 3, 2013.

12. See "The Walmart Tax Subsidy," Americans for Tax Fairness, April 2015, americansfortaxfairness.org/files/Taxpayers-and-Walmart-ATF1.pdf

13. Ibid.

14. The most comprehensive source of detailed public information on Walmart's failed attempt to enter the continental market are the "Wal-Mart Pages" a series which appeared periodically on the United Food and Commercial Workers website. The series included, "Ridicule and Anger Instead of Results and Profits," April 12, 2005; "Critical Wal-Mart Documentary Is Well Received at Berlin Film Festival," February 2003; "Wal-Mart Throws in the Towel in Germany as Social Dumping Did Not Work," July 28, 2006; "Social Dumping Does Not Pay: Wal-Mart Lost 4.5 Billion Dollars on Its German Fiasco." August 7, 2006; and "Wal-Mart Says No to Personnel Representatives Training in Germany, May Have to Answer in Court," September 4, 2006.

15. Agence France-Presse, "Molex Displays Record Results," *Figaro*, October 27, 2010; and AFP, "The Government Calls for a Boycott of PSA and Renault Molex," *Figaro*, October 27, 2010.

16. Rachel Mendleson, "Electro-Motive Lockout: Caterpillar to Close London, Ont. Plant, Company Says," *Huffington Post Canada*, April 4, 2012, http://www.huffingtonpost.ca/2012/02/03/electro-motive-lockout-ca_n_1252510.html

17. See Andrew Edgecliffe-Johnson, "Davos Confronted by Peak of Distrust," *Financial Times,* January 26, 2009.

18. Edelman Trust Barometer, 2006 Annual Survey, http://edelman.edelman1.netdna-cdn.com/assets/uploads/2014/01/2006-Trust-Barometer-Global-Results.pdf

19. Ibid.

20. Professor Tony Royle at the University of York is the leading European expert on McDonald's and author of *Working for McDonald's in Europe* (New York: Routledge, 2000). His analyses have also appeared in a variety of professional journals including "Just Vote No! Union-Busting in the European Fast-Food Industry: The Case of McDonald's," *Industrial Relations Journal* 33 (2002), 262–76, homepages.se.edu/cvonbergen/files/2013/11/Just-Vote-No_Union-busting-in-the-European-Fast-food-Industry_The-Case-of-McDonalds.pdf and ssm.com/abstract=320668; Tony Royle, "Worker Representation Under Threat? The McDonald's Corporation and Effectiveness of Statutory Works Councils in Seven European Union Countries," *Comparative Labor Law and Policy Journal* 22:2/3 (February 2003), https://www.researchgate.net/publication/228224650_Worker_Representation_Under_Threat_The_Mcdonald%27s_Corporation_and_the_Effectiveness_of_Statutory_Works_Councils_in_Seven_European_Union_Countries

Section 3: Achieving Political Equality

1. Amanda Taub, "Warning Signs 'Flashing Red' for Democracies," *New York Times,* November 29, 2016.

Chapter 10: Other Wealthy Democracies Corral Oligarchs

1. Editorial, "Britain's Parties Should Be Funded by the State," *Financial Times*, February 19, 2015.
2. Janan Ganesh, "The Transatlantic Delusions of the Westminster Wing," *Financial Times*, April 10, 2015.
3. Jacob Rowbottom, "How Campaign Finance Laws Made the British Press So Powerful," *New Republic*, July 25, 2011, newrepublic.com/article/92507 /campaign-finance-united-kingdom-news-corporation
4. Ruth Marcus, "Old School in Old Europe," *Washington Post*, September 25, 2013.
5. Editorial, "Britain's Parties Should Be Funded by the State."
6. Clancy Yates, "Political Donations in Spotlight After NAB Move," *Sydney Morning Herald*, October 11, 2016.
7. "Freedom in the World, 2015," Freedom House, freedomhouse.org/report /freedom-world-2015/table-country-ratings
8. Tobias Döring and Christof Kerkmann, "As Companies Get Involved in the Election Campaign," *Handelsblatt*, September 20, 2013, www.handelsblatt .com/politik/deutschland/bundestagswahl-2013/bundestagswahl -wieunternehmen-im-wahlkampf-mitmischen-seite-all/8822520-all.html
9. Jess Garland, "Deal or No Deal: How to Put an End to Party Funding Scandals," UK Electoral Reform Commission, February 2015, www.electoral -reform.org.uk/images/dynamicImages/file/Deal%20or%20No%20Deal %2017%20Feb%20FINAL.pdf
10. Hugh Carnegy, "Sarkozy Quits Top Legal Council Over Election Funding Decision," *Financial Times*, July 4, 2013.
11. Guy Chazan, "Berlin Seeks to Strip Far-Right Party's State Funding," *Financial Times,* April 6, 2017.
12. Tobias Döring and Christof Kerkmann, "As Companies Get Involved in the Election Campaign," *Handelsblatt*, September 20, 2013, www.handelsblatt .com/politik/deutschland/bundestagswahl-2013/bundestagswahl -wieunternehmen-im-wahlkampf-mitmischen-seite-all/8822520-all.html
13. Jess Garland, "Deal or No Deal: How to Put an End to Party Funding Scandals," UK Electoral Reform Commission, February 2015, footnote 19, www.electoral-reform.org.uk/sites/default/files/Deal%20or%20No%20 Deal%2017%20Feb%20FINAL.pdf
14. Stephen Castle, "An Affinity for American Style Politics Meets Tight Spending Rules in Britain," *New York Times*, May 5, 2015.
15. Bob Hepburn, "US Election Spending an Obscene Joke," *The Star* (Toronto), November 12, 2014, www.thestar.com/opinion/commentary/2014/11/12 /us_election_spending_an_obscene_joke_hepburn.html
16. Castle, "An Affinity for American Style Politics."

17. Rowbottom, "How Campaign Finance Laws Made the British Press So Powerful."
18. Castle, "An Affinity for American Style Politics."
19. Jess Garland, "Deal or No Deal: How to Put an End to Party Funding Scandals."
20. Dan Levin, "In British Columbia, Some See a 'Wild West' of Canadian Political Cash," *New York Times,* January 15, 2017.
21. For a summary by officials at Elections Canada, see Tim Mowrey and Alain Pelletier, "Election Financing in Canada," May 2002, www.elections.ca /content.aspx?section=res&dir=eim/issue5&document=p2&lang=e
22. Andrew Heard, "Canadian Election Laws and Policies," 2015 (Simon Fraser University, blog) at 2011, www.sfu.ca/~aheard/elections/laws.html
23. Elections Canada, "Broadcasting Guidelines," August 3, 2015, www.elections .ca/content.aspx?section=abo&dir=bra/bro/2015&document=index&lang =e 24
24. Ruth Marcus, "Old School in Old Europe," *Washington Post,* September 25, 2013.
25. Elections Canada, "Political Financing," The Electoral System of Canada, www.elections.ca/content.aspx?section=res&dir=ces&document=part6& lang=e
26. ———, "Limits on Contributions," www.elections.ca/content.aspx?section =pol&document=index&dir=lim&lang=e
27. ———, "Political Financing."
28. ———, "Third Party Election Advertising Expense Limits," http://www .elections.ca/content.aspx?section=pol&document=index&dir=thi /limits&lang=e
29. ———, "Broadcasting Guidelines," August 3, 2015.
30. Ian Austen, "Trudeau Faces Questions of Whether Donors Are Given Special Access," *New York Times,* November 25, 2016.
31. Elections Canada, "Political Financing."
32. Canada Elections Act, section 351, Justice Laws website, Government of Canada, laws.justice.gc.ca/eng/acts/e-2-01/page-41.html
33. *Harper v. Canada,* 2004 SCC 33, para. 79, from Michael Karanicolas, "Regulation of Paid Political Advertising: A Survey," Center for Law and Democracy, March 2012, www.law-democracy.org/wp-content /uploads/2012/03/Elections-and-Broadcasting-Final.pdf
34. Urs Geiser, "Party Pockets Lined by Business Interests," Swissinfo. ch, February 21, 2012, www.swissinfo.ch/eng/party-pockets-lined-by -business-interests/32160592
35. Anne-Sylvaine Chassany, "Nicolas Sarkozy Suffers Setback Over €18 m Campaign Funding Scandal," *Financial Times,* February 16, 2016; "French Presidential Spending Rules," *Le Monde,* December 21, 2012.

36. Giulia Segreti, "Austerity Hits Italian Campaign Spending," *Financial Times*, February 24, 2013.
37. Kulish, "And on Your Left, . . . Lobbyists Are at Work."

Chapter 11: Recriminalizing Vote Buying

1. Teachout, *Corruption in America*, 20.
2. David Crossland, "The Regional CDU Seems Arrogant and Aloof," *Der Spiegel*, February 23, 2010.
3. Greg Jaffe, "Which Speech Comes Closest to Lincoln's Gettysburg?" *Washington Post*, July 24, 2016.
4. Robert Barnes, "High Court: States May Ban Judicial Candidates from Personal Fundraising," *Washington Post* April 29, 2015.
5. Richard Posner, *How Judges Think* (Cambridge, MA: Harvard University Press, 2010), 1.
6. MacGregor Burns, *Packing the Court*, 150.
7. Ibid., 180.
8. Matea Gold and Paul Kane, "Republicans Building Firewall Between Congress and Trump," *Washington Post*, March 24, 2016; Matea Gold, "Some Grinding Noises in the Koch Machine," *Washington Post*, August 2, 2016.
9. Michael Waldman, *The Right to Vote* (New York: Simon & Schuster, 2016), 11.
10. Teachout, *Corruption in America*, 20.
11. Trevor Potter, "The Court's Changing Perception of Corruption," The Campaign Legal Center, May 7, 2015, www.campaignlegalcenter.org/news /blog/court-s-changing-conception-corruption; Linda Greenhouse, "The Supreme Court: The Ruling; Justices, in a 5:4 Decision, Back Campaign Finance Law That Curbs Contributions," *New York Times*, December 11, 2003.
12. Teachout, *Corruption in America*, 3, 8.
13. Ibid., 200.
14. Ibid., 114.
15. Ibid., 116.
16. Adam Winkler, "Corporate Personhood and the Rights of Corporate Speech," *Seattle University Law Review* 30:863 (2007), http://digital commons.law.seattleu.edu/cgi/viewcontent.cgi?article=1908&context=sulr
17. Robert C. Post, *Citizens Divided* (Cambridge, MA: Harvard University Press, 2014), 41.
18. See, for example, Robert Dahl, *Polyarchy: Participation and Opposition* (New Haven, CT: Yale University Press, 1971), 1; Richard Hasen, *Plutocrats United*, 165; Zyphyr Teachout, *Corruption in America*, 280–82; and Bruce Cain, "Moralism and Realism in Campaign Finance Reform," *University of Chicago Legal Forum* (1995): 111–140, http://chicagounbound.uchicago.edu /cgi/viewcontent.cgi?article=1180&context=uclf

19. Adam Liptak, "Justice Stevens Suggests Solution for 'Giant Step in the Wrong Direction,'" *New York Times*, April 22, 2014.
20. Teachout, *Corruption in America*, 282.
21. Richard Hasen, *Plutocrats United*, 121–22; Robert Post, *Citizens Divided*, 48.
22. Guido Calabresi, "*Ognibene, et al. v. Parkes, et al.*," US Court of Appeals for the Second Circuit, Docket Nos. 09-0994-cv (Lead) 09-1432-cv (Con), January 2012, bradlander.nyc/sites/default/files/images/Ognibene%20-%202d%20Cir%20aff%20of%20SJ%20(slip%20op%20)%20-%20(%23%20Legal%203278303).pdf
23. Ibid.
24. Post, *Citizens Divided*, 37.
25. Stephen Breyer, "Dissent, *McCutcheon v. Federal Election Commission*," Supreme Court Syllabus, April 2, 2014, www.supremecourt.gov/opinions/13pdf/12-536_e1pf.pdf
26. Calabresi, "*Ognibene, et al.*"
27. Hasen, *Plutocrats United*, 147.
28. Ibid.
29. Kenneth Mayer, Timothy Werner, and Amanda Williams, "Do Public Funding Programs Enhance Electoral Competition?" *The Marketplace of Democracy: Electoral Competition and American Politics*, edited Michael P. McDonald and John Samples, (Washington, DC: Brookings Institution, 2006), 245–67, works.bepress.com/mayer/15/
30. Kihong Eom and Donald A. Gross, "Contribution Limits and Disparity in Contributions Between Gubernatorial Candidates," *Political Research Quarterly* 59:1 (March 2006): 99–110, www.uspirg.org/sites/pirg/files/reports/Campaign_Contribution_Limits_USPIRG.pdf
31. John Sides and Eric McGhee, "Redistricting Didn't Win Republicans the House," *Washington Post* (Wonkblog) February 17, 2013, www.washingtonpost.com/blogs/wonkblog/wp/2013/02/17/redistricting-didnt-win-republicans-the-house/
32. Kyle Kondik and Geoffrey Skelly, "Incumbent Reelection Rates Higher Than Average in 2016," *Sabato's Crystal Ball*, December 15, 2016, http://www.centerforpolitics.org/crystalball/articles/incumbent-reelection-rates-higher-than-average-in-2016/
33. Michael G. Miller, "*Subsidizing Democracy: How Public Funding Changes Elections and How It Can Work in the Future* (Ithaca, NY: Cornell University Press, 2013), 80.
34. Hasen, *Plutocrats United*, 86.
35. Seth Masket and Michael Miller, "Does Public Election Funding Create More Extreme Legislators? Evidence from Arizona and Maine," *State Politics and Policy Quarterly* (2014), mysite.du.edu/~smasket/Masket_Miller_SPPQ.pdf
36. Michael G. Miller, *Subsidizing Democracy* (Ithaca, NY: Cornell University Press, 2014), 86, 43, 83, 86. See also Kenneth Mayer, Timothy Werner,

and Amada Williams, "Do Public Funding Programs Enhance Electoral Competition?," (Washington, DC: Brookings Institution, 2006), 245–67.

37. Richard Hasen, *Plutocrats United* (New Haven, CT: Yale University Press, 2016), 120–21.
38. US District Court, D. New Mexico, September, 2001, www.leagle.com /decision/20011426160FSupp2d1266_11314/HOMANS%20v.%20CITY%20 OF%20ALBUQUERQUE; see also Hasen, *Plutocrats United*, 120–21.
39. "Beyond Distrust: How Americans View Their Government," Pew Research Center, November 23, 2015, www.people-press.org/2015/11/23 /beyond-distrust-how-americans-view-their-government
40. Greg Stohr, "Bloomberg Poll: Americans Want the Supreme Court to Turn Off the Money Spigot," September 28, 2015, http://www.newsmax.com /Newsfront/turn-off-political-spending/2015/09/28/id/693597/
41. *New York Times*/CBS News poll, May 28–31, 2015, www.scribd.com /doc/267409090/cbs-news-new-york-times-money-and-politics-poll; www .nytimes.com/interactive/2015/06/01/us/politics/document-poll-may-28-31 .html
42. *New York Times*/CBS poll News Survey, May 28–31, 2015, 32, www.scribd .com/doc/267409090/cbs-news-new-york-times-money-and-politics-poll
43. Erwin Chemerinsky, *The Case Against the Supreme Court*, (New York: Viking 2014), 250.
44. Liz Kennedy, "Citizens Actually United."
45. "Model for Success: Amend the Constitution, Reclaim the American Dream," 2015, http://reclaimtheamericandream.org/success-amend/

Chapter 12: Rehabilitating America's Flawed Democracy: A Framework for Ending Vote Buying

1. Rob Garver, "US No Longer a 'Full Democracy,' But It's Not Trump's Fault," *Fiscal Times*, January 25, 2017, http://www.thefiscaltimes.com/2017/01/25/US -No-Longer-Full-Democracy-It-s-Not-Trump-s-Fault-Report
2. John Paul Stevens (Dissent, *Randall v. Sorrell*), Legal Information Institute, Cornell University Law School, www.law.cornell.edu/supct/html/04-1528 .ZD.html
3. Hasen, *Plutocrats United*, 11.
4. Ruth Marcus, "Old School in Old Europe," *Washington Post,* September 25, 2013.
5. Trevor Potter, "The Court's Changing Perception of Corruption," The Campaign Legal Center, May 7, 2015, http://www.campaignlegalcenter.org /news/blog/court-s-changing-conception-corruption; Linda Greenhouse, "The Supreme Court: The Ruling; Justices, in a 5-to-4 Decision, Back

Campaign Finance Law That Curbs Contributions," *New York Times*, December 11, 2003.

6. Sir Christopher Kelly (chair), "Political Party Finance," Committee on Standards in Public Life, London, November 2011, 44, 46, www.gov.uk /government/uploads/system/uploads/attachment_data/file/228646/8208 .pdf

7. Nicholas Kulish, "And on Your Left, Behind Those Walls, Lobbyists Are at Work," *New York Times*, November 23, 2012.

8. Carnegy, "Sarkozy Quits Top Legal Council"; Scheherazade Daneshkhu, "Nicolas Sarkozy Paves Way for Political Comeback," *Financial Times*, July 5, 2013.

9. Scheherazade Daneshkhu, "Nicolas Sarkozy Paves Way for Political Comeback," *Financial Times*, July 5, 2013.

10. "Beyond Distrust: How Americans View Their Government," Pew Research Center, November 23, 2015, http://www.people-press.org/2015/11/23 /beyond-distrust-how-americans-view-their-government/

11. Michael G. Miller, *Subsidizing Democracy: How Public Funding Changes Elections and How It Can Work in the Future* (Ithaca, NY: Cornell University Press, 2013), 145.

12. Ibid.

13. Maine "Clean Elections" Initiative Question 1 (2015), Ballotpedia, http://ballot-pedia.org/Maine_%22Clean_Elections%22_Initiative,_Question_1_(2015)

14. Michael Malbin, Peter Brusoe, and Bendan Glavin, "Small Donors, Big Democracy: New York City's Matching Funds as a Model for the Nation and States," *Election Law Journal* (November 1, 2012), www.cfinst.org/pdf /state/NYC-as-a-Model_ELJ_As-Published_March2012.pdf

15. Miller, *Subsidizing Democracy*, 145.

16. Ibid., 148–156.

17. Potter and Penniman, *Nation on the Take*, 201.

18. Ibid., 157.

19. Elections Canada, "Political Financing," The Electoral System of Canada, http://www.elections.ca/content.aspx?section=res&dir=ces&document =part6&lang=e

20. Ron Fein, "Goldwater Would Have Hated 'Citizens United,'" *Washington Post*, October 15, 2014.

21. Jacob Rowbottom, "How Campaign Finance Laws Made the British Press So Powerful," *The New Republic*, July 25, 2011, https://newrepublic.com /article/92507/campaign-finance-united-kingdom-news-corporation

22. See Fredreka Schouten and Mary Troyan, "Secret Donors Aid Elected Leaders on Pet Projects," *USA Today*, May 6, 2016.

23. Andrew Heard, "Canadian Election Laws and Policies," Simon Fraser University, blog post, 2011, www.sfu.ca/~aheard/elections/laws.html

24. Aaron Chatterji and Michael Toffel, "The Power of CEO Activism," *New York Times*, April 3, 2016.

25. Potter and Penniman, *Nation on the Take*, 209. See also Anthony York, "List Unmasks Secret Donors to California Initiative Campaigns," *Los Angeles Times*, October 24, 2013; Jim Rutten, "Koch Brothers' Massive Spending Bad for Democracy, California's Republican Party," Tim Rutten, *Los Angeles Daily News*, January 30, 2015.

26. Chisun Lee and Lawrence Norden, "The Secret Power Behind Local Elections," *New York Times*, June 26, 2016.

27. Chris Bryant and Joshua Chaffin, "MEP Resigns Over Claims of Lobbyist Payments," *Financial Times*, March 20, 2011.

28. Chris Bryant, "Press Sting Hits Romanian Schengen Ambitions," *Financial Times*, February 11, 2011, www.docfoc.com/parliamentary-ethics-a-question -of-trust-codes-of-conduct

29. See Simon Wren-Lewis, "Why Are the UK and the US More Vulnerable to Right Wing Populism?" *Social Europe Journal*, May 26, 2017, www.social europe.eu/2017/05/uk-us-vulnerable-right-wing-populism/; and Kenneth Vogel, "Ex-Aides Aim to Expand the President's Voting Base, *New York Times*, August 17, 2017.

30. Carole Cadwalladr, "The Great British Brexit Robbery; How Our Democracy Was Hijacked," *Guardian*, May 7, 2017, www.theguardian .com/technology/2017/may/07/the-great-british-brexit-robbery -hijacked-democracy

31. Danielle Kurtzleben, "Canada Reminds Us That American Elections Are Much Longer," *It's All Politics*, National Public Radio, October 21, 2015, www.npr.org/sections/itsallpolitics/2015/10/21/450238156/canadas -11-week-campaign-reminds-us-that-american-elections-are-much-longer

32. Orestis Omran and Stefan Passantino, "Campaign Finance in the US and the UK: A Comparative Assessment," May 8, 2015, *JDSupra Business Advisor*, www.jdsupra.com/legalnews/campaign-finance-in-the-us-and-the-uk -a-43421/

33. Danielle Kurtzleben, "Canada Reminds Us."

34. Andrew Heard, "Canadian Election Laws and Policies."

35. Elections Canada, "Broadcasting Guidelines," http://www.elections.ca /content.aspx?section=abo&dir=bra/bro/2015&document=index&lang=e

36. Ibid.

37. Matea Gold, "You've Got Questions About Campaign Money This Year. We've Got Answers," *Washington Post*, October 31, 2014.

38. Miller, *Subsidizing Democracy*, 1.

39. Mutch, *Buying the Vote*, 166–167.

40. Editorial, "An Idea Worth Saving," *New York Times*, May 6, 2012.

41. David Ignatius, "A Manifesto to Mend Our Politics," *Washington Post*, April 22, 2016.

42. Laurie Roberts, "Small Donors Will Fund Tallahassee 2016 Elections," issue one, March 22, 2016.

43. Liz Kennedy, "Citizens Actually United."

44. Money in Politics National Survey, November 3, 2009, reported by Ross Ramsey, "Americans Worry About Sources of Political Cash," *Texas Tribune*, November 16, 2009.

45. "History of Reform Efforts," National Center for State Courts, various years, www.judicialselection.us/judicial_selection/reform_efforts/opinion_polls _surveys.cfm?state

46. "Public Financing of Judicial Campaigns," American Bar Association, Standing Committee on Judicial Independence, February 2002, 63–4, http://www.americanbar.org/content/dam/aba/migrated/judind/pdf /commissionreport4_03.authcheckdam.pdf

47. Geri Palast, "Justice at Stake," *American Viewpoint*, January 2002, www .justiceatstake.org/media/cms/JASJudgesSurveyResults_EA8838C0504A5 .pdf

48. Potter and Penniman, *Nation on the Take*, 201; Emily Cadei, "Amid Billion-Dollar Campaign, Two States Weigh Untested Alternative to Campaign Fundraising, *Newsweek*, October 19, 2016.

49. Editorial, "In Seattle, a Campaign Finance Plan That Voters Control," *New York Times*, November 7, 2015.

50. "Nearly Two-Thirds of Incoming Legislature Elected Using Clean Elections," Maine Citizens for Clean Elections, November 22, 2016, www .mainecleanelections.org/sites/default/files/press_releases/%5Bcurrent -date%3Acustom%3AY%5D/161121_MCCE_PressRelease_16CELegislators _FINAL.pdf

51. "Models for Success: Empower Small Donors, Public Campaign Funding," Reclaim the American Dream, 2016, reclaimtheamericandream.org /success-public/

52. "State Awards $8 Million in Public Election Funds to Legislative Candidates," *CTPost*, September 14, 2016, www.ctpost.com/local/article/State-awards-8 -million-in-public-election-funds-9223583.php

53. "Small Donor Solutions for Big Money: The 2014 Elections and Beyond," *Public Campaign*, January 13, 2015, http://everyvoice.org/wp-content /uploads/2015/04/2014SmallDonorReportJan13.pdf

54. Michael G. Miller, *Subsidizing Democracy*, 106.

55. See Kenneth R. Mayer, Timothy Werner, and Amanda Williams, "Do Public Funding Programs Enhance Electoral Competition?" in The Marketplace of Democracy: Electoral Competition and American Politics, *ed. Michael McDonald and John Sample (Washington, DC: Brookings Institution, 2006)*, users.polisci.wisc.edu/behavior/Papers/mayerwernerwilliams2004 .pdfhttp://citeseerx.ist.psu.edu/viewdoc/download?doi=10.1.1.571.7006& rep=rep1&type=pdf; Neil Malhotra, "The Impact of Public Financing on

Electoral Competition: Evidence from Arizona and Maine," *State Politics and Policy Quarterly*, 2008; and Miller, *Subsidizing Democracy*.

56. Mayer et al., "Do Public Funding Programs Enhance Electoral Competition?"
57. Bill Turque, "On the Heels of New Law, Montgomery Candidates Line Up for Individual Donations," *Washington Post*, June 8, 2017.
58. "Small Donor Solutions for Big Money: The 2014 Elections and Beyond," *Public Campaign*, January 13, 2015, http://everyvoice.org/wp-content /uploads/2015/04/2014SmallDonorReportJan13.pdf
59. Ibid.
60. Editorial, "Voice of the People, Squelched in Florida," *Washington Post*, April 17, 2017.
61. Miller, *Subsidizing Democracy*, 123.
62. Ibid., fig. 6.2.
63. Lawrence Norden, Brent Ferguson, and Douglas Keith, "Five to Four," Brennan Center for Justice, January 13, 2016, http://www.brennancenter. org/sites/default/files/publications/Five_to_Four_Final.pdf
64. "2013 Post-Election Report," New York City Campaign Finance Board; Potter and Penniman, *Nation on the Take*, 199.
65. Lee Drutman, "Maine Passes Ranked-Choice Voting, South Dakota Approves Campaign Vouchers," *Vox*, November 9, 2016, www.vox.com /polyarchy/2016/11/9/13574478/maine-ranked-choice-voting-south -dakota-campaign-vouchers
66. Pippa Norris, "Why American Elections Are Flawed (And How to Fix Them)," Faculty Research Working Paper Series 16-038, September 30, 2016, https://research.hks.harvard.edu/publications/getFile.aspx?Id=1431
67. Ibid.
68. Garver, "US No Longer a 'Full Democracy.'"
69. Pippa Norris, "The New Research Agenda Studying Electoral Integrity," *Electoral Studies* 32:4 (December 2013), www.sciencedirect.com/science /article/pii/S0261379413001157
70. Wolfgang Merkel, "Trump and Democracy in America," *Social Europe Journal*, November 21, 2016, www.socialeurope.eu/2016/11 /trump-democracy-america/
71. Don Beyer, "Let's Change How We Elect House Members," *Washington Post*, June 28, 2017.
72. See Adam Liptak, "When Does Gerrymandering Cross a Line?" *New York Times*, May 16, 2017.
73. Emily Baselong, "Department of Justification," *New York Times Magazine*, March 5, 2017.
74. Nils-Christian Bormann and Matt Golder, "Democratic Electoral Systems Around the World, 1946–2011," *Electoral Studies* 32:2 (June 2013), www .sciencedirect.com/science/article/pii/S0261379413000073

75. Fatima Hussein, "Republicans Limiting Early Voting in Marion County, Letting It Bloom in Suburbs," *IndyStar*, August 10, 2017, http://www.indystar.com/story/news/2017/08/10/silencing-vote-data-shows-unequal-barrier-indiana-polls/435450001/

76. Michael Wines, "5 Numbers That Give Clearer View of Election," *Washington Post*, March 18, 2017.

77. Sharad Goel, Marc Meredith, Michael Morse, David Rothschild, and Houshmand Shirani-Mehr, "One Person, One Vote: Estimating the Prevalence of Double Voting in US Presidential Elections," 5harad.com, January 13, 2017, https://5harad.com/papers/1p1v.pdf

78. Christopher Ingraham, "Kan. Voter Vetting Program Often Errs," *Washington Post*, July 21, 2017.

79. Sharad Goel et al., "One Person, One Vote."

80. Andrew Chung, "US Supreme Court to Hear Ohio's Bid to Revive Voter Purge Policy," *Reuters*, May 30, 2017.

81. Ari Berman, "Votings Rights in the Age of Trump," *New York Times*, November 22, 2016.

82. Editorial, "The Absurdity of Voting Obstacles," *New York Times*, August 31, 2017.

83. Lee Drutman, "Maine Passes Ranked-Choice Voting, South Dakota Approves Campaign Vouchers," *Vox*, November 9, 2016, www.vox.com/polyarchy/2016/11/9/13574478/maine-ranked-choice-voting-south-dakota-campaign-vouchers

84. See George Tyler, "The Best News Democrats Will Hear All Summer," *Social Europe Journal*, August 11, 2014, www.socialeurope.eu/2014/08/best-news-us-democrats-will-hear-summer/

85. Ibid., for an analysis of the California system.

Section 4: Original Intent to Prevent Fake News

1. Dan Balz, "Trump's Right: He Didn't Break It. But Can He Fix It?" *Washington Post*, January 20, 2017.

2. John Sides, "The Astonishing Decline of the American Swing Voter," *Washington Post*, November 3, 2015.

Chapter 13: Original Intent: A Fact-Based Media

1. *Red Lion Broadcasting Co., Inc., et al. v. Federal Communications Commission et al.*, Supreme Court of the United States, 395 US 367, June 9, 1969, law2.umkc.edu/faculty/projects/ftrials/conlaw/redlion.html

2. Jim Rutenberg, "Behind the Scenes, Billionaires' Growing Control of News," *New York Times*, May 28, 2016.

3. Alexander Keyssar, *The Right to Vote* (New York: Basic, 2009), 15.

4. Dana Lanskyd, "Proceeding to a Constitution: A Multi-Party Negotiation Analysis of the Constitutional Convention of 1787," *Harvard Negotiation Law Review*, 5 Harv. Negotiation L. Rev. 167. (Spring 2000), 279–284.

5. Michael Gerson, "The Senate Has Lost Its Way," *Washington Post*, April 4, 2014.

6. Gaillard Hunt, ed., "James Madison, letter to W.T. Barry, August 4, 1822," in *The Writings of James Madison,* vol. 9: 103 (1910); *Respectfully Quoted: A Dictionary of Quotations*, 1989, http://www.bartleby.com/73/969.html

7. Thomas Jefferson on Politics and Government, Topic "51. Freedom of the Press," Thomas Jefferson Letter to Walter Jones, 1814. (Memoral Edition 14:46), https://famguardian.org/subjects/politics/thomasjefferson/jeff1600.htm

8. Robert G. Parkinson, "Fake News? That's a Very Old Story," *Washington Post*, November 26, 2016.

9. David Greenberg, "Spin," *Washington Post*, March 20, 2016.

10. Sophie Hylands, "The Invisible Government: Edward Bernays, Public Relations and Propaganda," *New Histories*, November 4, 2013, newhistories .group.shef.ac.uk/wordpress/wordpress/the-work-of-edward-bernays/

11. Izabella Kaminska, "A Lesson in Fake News from the Info-Wars of Ancient Rome," *Financial News*, January 19, 2017.

12. Jan-Werner Müller, "The Problem with 'Illiberal' Democracy," *Social Europe Journal*, January 27 2016.

13. *Red Lion Broadcasting.*

14. Guido Calabresi, "*Ognibene, et al.*"

15. Penny Pagano, "Reagan's Veto Kills Fairness Doctrine," *Los Angeles Times*, June 21, 1987, articles.latimes.com/1987-06-21/news/mn-8908 _1_fairness-doctrine

16. *Red Lion Broadcasting.*

17. Penny Pagano, "Reagan's Veto."

18. Karanicolas, "Regulation of Paid Political Advertising: A Survey," Centre for Law and Democracy, March 2012, 2, www.law-democracy.org/wp-content /uploads/2012/03/Elections-and-Broadcasting-Final.pdf

19. As quoted by Hasen, *Plutocrats United*, 132.

20. Corwin Smidt, "Polarization and the Decline of the American Floating Voter," *American Journal of Political Science,* 2015, http://onlinelibrary .wiley.com/doi/10.1111/ajps.12218/epdf?r3_referer=wol&tracking_action =preview_click&show_checkout=1&purchase_referrer=search.aol .com&purchase_site_license=LICENSE_DENIED_NO_CUSTOMER

21. "Trump, Clinton Voters Divided in Their Main Sources of News for Election News," Pew Research Center, January 17, 2017, http:// www.journalism.org/2017/01/18/trump-clinton-voters-divided-in-their -main-source-for-election-news/pj_2017-01-18_election-news-sources _0-01/

22. Dan Cassino, "Ignorance, Partisanship Drive False Beliefs About Obama, Iraq," Fairleigh Dickinson Public Mind Poll, January 7, 2015, publicmind .fdu.edu/2015/false/

23. Nicholas Confessore, "Father of Koch Brothers Helped Build Nazi Oil Refinery, Book Says," *New York Times*, January 11, 2016.

24. "Political Polarization and Media Habits," Pew Research Center, October 21, 2014, http://www.journalism.org/2014/10/21/political-polarization -media-habits/

25. Amy Mitchell, "Which News Organization Is the Most Trusted? The Answer Is Complicated," Pew Research Center, October 30, 2014, http:// www.pewresearch.org/fact-tank/2014/10/30/which-news-organization -is-the-most-trusted-the-answer-is-complicated/

26. Dan Cassino, "Ignorance, Partisanship."

27. On January 17, 2017, Fox News claimed a terrorist attack had occurred in Sweden, inspiring President Trump to repeat the bogus claim. See Liam Stack and Christina Anderson, "Sweden's Defense and National Security Adviser? 'We Don't Know This Guy,'" *New York Times*, February 27, 2017.

28. Editorial, "Polling the Tea Party," *New York Times,* April 14, 2010.

29. Paul Farhi, "How a Giant Company Helped Donald Trump's Campaign," *Washington Post*, December 23, 2016.

30. Glenn Kessler, "With Five of the Year's Biggest Pinocchios, Trump Shatters His Own Record," *Washington Post*, December 18, 2016.

31. Paul Krugman, "The Insecure American," *New York Times*, May 29, 2015.

32. Gretchen Morgenson, "The Impunity That Main St. Didn't Forget," *New York Times*, November 13, 2016.

33. Ylan Q. Mui, "The Shocking Number of Americans Who Can't Cover a $400 Expense Emergency," *Washington Post*, May 27, 2016.

34. Editorial, "Poverty Shouldn't Be a Crime," *Washington Post*, November 13, 2016.

35. Georgia Wilkins and Gareth Hutchens, "Joe Hockey Says Tax Cheats Are 'Thieves'," *Sydney Morning Herald*, October 10, 2014.

36. Neil Chenoweth, "Rupert Murdoch's News Corp Is TO's Top Tax Risk," *AFR Weekend*, May 11, 2015, www.afr.com/news/policy/tax /rupert-murdochs-news-corp-is-atos-top-tax-risk-20150510-ggy6cfs

37. Harold Meyerson, "Americans See a Rigged System," *Washington Post*, November 19, 2015.

Chapter 14: Fake News Exacerbates Political Polarization, Tribalism, and the Income Bias

1. Michael D. Shear and David Sanger, "Putin Led Scheme to Aid Trump, Report Says," *New York Times,* January 7, 2017; Charles Blow, "Trump and

the Tainted Presidency," *New York Times* January 9, 2017; and Greg Miller and Adam Entous, "Report: Putin Ordered Cyber-Intrusion," *Washington Post*, January 7, 2017.

2. Jeremy Peters, "Wielding Claims of 'Fake News,' Conservatives Take Aim at Mainstream Media," *Washington Post*, December 26, 2016.

3. Paul Mozur and Mark Scott, "Leverage for Globe's Gullible: Facebook's Fake News Problem," *New York Times*, November 18, 2016.

4. Amy Mitchell, Jeffrey Gottfried, Michael Barthel, and Elisa Shearer, "The Modern News Consumer," Pew Research Center, July 7, 2016, www.journalism.org/2016/07/07/the-modern-news-consumer/

5. Shannon Bond, "Big TV Companies and Publishers Offer Shelter from YouTube Storm," *Financial Times*, March 30, 2017, www.ft.com/content/8d7735cc-14c4-11e7-80f4-13e067d5072c

6. Jonathan Taplin, *Move Fast and Break Things* (New York: Little Brown, 2017).

7. David Streitfeld, "The Internet Is Broken: @ev Is Trying to Salvage It," *New York Times*, May 20, 2017.

8. Maeve Duggan, "Online Harassment," Pew Research Center, October 22, 2014, http://www.pewinternet.org/2014/10/22/part-2-the-online-environment/

9. Hayley Tsukayama, "Facebook to Crack Down on 'Revenge Porn' Images," *Washington Post*, April 6, 2017.

10. Brooke Donald, "Stanford Researchers Find Students Have Trouble Judging the Credibility of Information Online," Stanford Graduate School of Education, November 22, 2016, stanford.edu/news/stanford-researchers-find-students-have-trouble-judging-credibility-information-online

11. David Blood, "Fake News Is Shared as Widely as the Real Thing," *Financial Times*, March 27, 2017.

12. Greg Gordon and David Goldstein, "Twitter Study Shows Pro-Trump Tweets Swamped Clinton's in Michigan," *McClatchy*, March 26, 2017.

13. Jim Rutenberg, "Mark Zuckerberg and Facebook Must Step Up to Defend Truth," *New York Times*, November 21, 2016.

14. See Neil Irwin, "Fake News? Welcome to 'False Remembering,'" The Upshot, *New York Times*, January 26, 2017.

15. Tim Harford, "Hard Truths About Fake News," *Financial Times*, March 1, 2017.

16. Andrew Higgins, Mike McIntire, and Gabriel J.X. Dance, "Inside a Fake News Sausage Factory: 'This Is All About Income.'" *New York Times*, November 25, 2016.

17. Dan Tynan, "How Facebook Powers Money Machines for Obscure 'Political' Newsites," *The Guardian*, August 24, 2016, www.theguardian.com/technology/2016/aug/24/facebook-clickbait-political-news-sites-us-election-trump

18. Higgins et al., "Inside a Fake News Sausage Factory."

19. Anna Nicolaou, "Alt-News Sites Face Post-Election Identity Crisis," *Financial Times*, November 25, 2016.

20. Roger Cohen, "Am I Imagining This?" *New York Times*, February 10, 2017.

21. Richard Waters, Matthew Garrahan, and Tim Bradshaw, "Harsh Truths About Fake News for Facebook, Google and Twitter," *Financial Times,* November 21, 2016, www.ft.com/content/2910a7a0-afd7-11e6-a37c-f4a01f1b0fa1

22. Skocpol and Williamson, *The Tea Party*, 12, 118.

23. Nancy Folbre, "Defining Economic Interest," Economix, *New York Times*, August 8, 2011.

24. Scott Shane, "How to Make a Masterpiece in Fake News," *New York Times*, January 19, 2017.

25. Gideon Resnick, "How Pro-Trump Twitter Bots Spread Fake News," *Daily Beast*, November 17, 2016, www.thedailybeast.com/articles/2016/11/17/how-pro-trump-twitter-bots-spread-fake-news.html; Gordon and Goldstein, "Twitter Study Shows Pro-Trump Tweets"; and Waters et al., "Harsh Truths About Fake News."

26. Ibid.

27. Oliver Darcy, "Donald Trump Broke the Conservative Media," *Business Insider*, August 26, 2016, www.businessinsider.com/conservative-media-trump-drudge-coulter-2016-8?utm_source=referral&utm_medium=aol

28. Ibid.

29. David Frum, "Post-Tea-Party Nation," *New York Times Magazine*, November 12, 2010.

30. Jennifer Rubin, "Remaking Conservatism," *Washington Post*, May 9, 2016.

31. Max Kutner "Meet Robert Mercer, the Mysterious Billionaire Benefactor of Breitbart," *Newsweek*, November 21, 2016, www.newsweek.com/2016/12/02/robert-mercer-trump-donor-bannon-pac-523366.html; See also Robert O'Harrow, Jr., "Trump Adviser Stephen Bannon Received Salary from Charity While Steering Breitbart News," *Washington Post*, November 23, 2016.

32. Robert C. Post, *Citizens Divided*, 79.

33. Charles Sykes, "We Can't Ignore the Fringe," *New York Times*, June 18, 2017.

34. Editorial, "Truth and Lies in the Age of Trump," *New York Times*, December 11, 2016.

35. Kevin Kruse, "The Real Loser: Truth," *New York Times*, November 6, 2012.

36. Michael Grynbaum, "Trump Calls News Media, 'The Enemy of the American People,'" *New York Times*, February 17, 2017.

37. See Jim Rutenberg, "'Alternative Facts' and the Costs of Trump's Reality," *New York Times*, January 23, 2017; Jeffrey Toobin, "When Truth Is Not Enough," *New Yorker*, December 19 and 26, 2016; and Masha Gessen, "Into the Trumpian Fog," *New York Times*, January 15, 2017.

38. Tim Harford, "The Problem with Facts," *Financial Times Magazine*, March 9, 2017.

39. Michael Barthel and Amy Mitchell, "Americans' Attitudes About the News Media Deeply Divided Along Partisan Lines," Pew Research Center, May 10, 2017, http://www.journalism.org/2017/05/10/americans-attitudes-about -the-news-media-deeply-divided-along-partisan-lines/

40. Art Swift, "Trust in Mass Media Sinks to New Low," Gallup, September 14, 2016, www.gallup.com/poll/195542/americans-trust-mass-media-sinks -new-low.aspx

41. Callum Borchers, "1 in 3 Voters Agree with Trump That the Media Is 'the Enemy of the American People,'" *Washington Post*, March 8, 2017.

42. Milton and Rose Friedman, *Capitalism and Freedom* (Chicago: University of Chicago Press, 1962), 87.

43. Charles Sykes, "Why Nobody Cares the President Is Lying," *New York Times*, February 4, 2017.

44. Jeremy Peters, "Wielding Claims of 'Fake News,' Conservatives Take Aim at Mainstream Media," *Washington Post*, December 26, 2016.

45. Charles J. Sykes, "Where the Right Went Wrong," *New York Times*, December 18, 2016.

46. Darcy, "Donald Trump Broke the Conservative Media."

47. Peters, "Wielding Claims of 'Fake News.'"

48. Quoted by Charles M. Blow, "The Penance of Glenn Beck," *New York Times*, January 24, 2014.

49. Robert Kagan, "Running Interference for Russia," *Washington Post*, March 7, 2017.

50. Richard Wike, Bruce Stokes, Jacob Poushter, and Janell Fetterolf, "US Image Suffers as Publics Around World Question Trump's Leadership," Pew Research Center, June 26, 2017, www.pewglobal.org/2017/06/26/u-s-image -suffers-as-publics-around-world-question-trumps-leadership/

51. Stephen Pogány, "The Fourth Estate and the Twilight of Liberal Democracy," *Social Europe Journal*, January 18, 2017, www.socialeurope.eu/2017/01 /fourth-estate-twilight-liberal-democracy-part-one/

52. Michale Stothard, "Le Pen Borrows from Father's Company to Fund Presidential Campaign," January 1, 2017, www.ft.com/content/c06f74ce -d010-11e6-9341-7393bb2e1b51

53. Andrew Higgins, "Fake News, Fake Ukrainians: How a Group of Russians Tilted a Dutch Vote," *New York Times*, February 16, 2017.

54. John Walcott and Warren Strobel, "Russia Has Playbook for Covert Influence in Eastern Europe: Study," *Reuters*, October 13, 2016, www.reuters.com /article/us-russia-security-usa-idUSKCN12D13Q

55. Andrew Byrne, "Orban Joins Putin in Attack on Russian Sanctions," *Financial Times*, February 2, 2017, https://www.ft.com/content/f1f4482a -e96b-11e6-893c-082c54a7f539

56. Jim Dwyer, "A 1964 Lesson in Fake News Still Applies," *New York Times*, January 11, 2017.

57. Craig Timberg, "Research Ties 'Fake News' to Russia," *Washington Post*, November 25, 2016.

58. Michael D. Shear and David Sanger, "Putin Led Scheme to Aid Trump, Report Says," *New York Times*, January 7, 2017; Charles Blow, "Trump and the Tainted Presidency," *New York Times*, January 9, 2017; and Greg Miller and Adam Entous, "Report: Putin Ordered Cyber-Intrusion," *Washington Post*, January 7, 2017.

59. David J. Lynch, "Russian Spies Adopt New Tactics to Battle Old Enemy," *Financial Times*, December 14, 2016.

60. Luke Harding, Stephanie Kirchgaessner, and Mick Hopkins, "British Spies Were First to Spot Trump Team's Links with Russia," *Guardian*, April 13, 2017.

61. Eric Lichtblau, "CIA Tracked Russian Prying in the Summer," *New York Times*, April 7, 2017.

62. Gaillard Hunt, ed. "James Madison, Letter to W.T. Barry, August 4, 1822," in *The Writings of James Madison*, vol. 9, 103 (1910); *Respectfully Quoted: A Dictionary of Quotations*, 1989, http://www.bartleby.com/73/969.html

Chapter 15: Closing the "Hate Factories": Avoiding the Farce Feared by Madison

1. Jan Fleischhauer, "The Hate Factory: When Free Speech and German Law Collide on Facebook," *Der Spiegel*, October 6, 2016, www.spiegel.de/international/business/facebook-under-pressure-for-violating-german-speech-laws-a-1115271.html

2. Sapna Maheshwari, "In Fake News, Ads Are Costly to Conscience," *New York Times*, December 27, 2016.

3. Dietmar Neuerer, "Facebook Should Adhere to False Declarations," *Handelsblatt*, December 16, 2016.

4. Michael Gerson, "Find Truth of Russian Meddling," (Albany) *Times Union*, December 13, 2016, http://www.timesunion.com/tuplus-opinion/article/Michael-Gerson-Find-truth-of-Russia-s-meddling-10793938.php.

5. Max Read, "Donald Trump Won Because of Facebook," *New York Magazine*, November 9, 2016.

6. Jennifer Baker, "Fakebook," *International Politics and Society*, March 16, 2017, www.ips-journal.eu/regions/europe/article/show/fakebook-1917/

7. "Entrepreneur Martin Shkreli Suspended by Twitter for Harassing Journalist," *Le Monde*, January 9, 2017.

8. Max Ehrenfreund and Antonio Olivo, "Seizure-Inducing Tweet Leads to a New Kind of Prosecution for a New Era,"*Washington Post*, March 17, 2017.

9. Farhad Manjoo, "How Twitter Is Being Gamed to Feed Misinformation," *New York Times*, May 31, 2017.

10. Ibid.

11. Alex Heath, "Families of Americans Killed by ISIS Are Suing Twitter for Allegedly Providing 'Tremendous Utility and Value' to the Terrorist Organization," *Business Insider,* January 9, 2017, www.businessinsider.com/twitter-sued-isis-victims-families-france-belgium-attacks-2017-1

12. Rukmini Callimachi, "Not 'Lone Wolves' After All: How ISIS Guides World's Terror Plots from Afar," *New York Times*, February 4, 2017.

13. Joby Warrick, "Terror Groups Find Their 'App of Choice': Telegram," *Washington Post*, December 24, 2016.

14. Tracy Jan and Elizabeth Dwoskin, "Silicon Valley Aims to Limit Online Reach of Hate Groups," *Washington Post*, August 17, 2017.

15. David Bond, "Facebook, Twitter and Google Face Criticism Following London Attack," *Financial Times,* June 4, 2017.

16. Christina Anderson, "Swedish Police Investigate Report of Rape on Facebook Live," *New York Times,* January 24, 2017.

17. Max Read, "Donald Trump Won Because of Facebook."

18. Angus Crawford, "Facebook Failed to Remove Sexualized Images of Children," *BBC News*, March 7, 2017, http://www.bbc.com/news/technology-39187929

19. Jan Fleischhauer, "The Hate Factory."

20. Guy Chazan, "Zuckerberg and Facebook Face German Probe Over Racist Post," *Financial Times,* November 4, 2016, www.ft.com/content/c10aa4f8-08a5-11e7-97d1-5e720a26771b

21. Guy Chazan, "Germany Cracks Down on Social Media Over Fake News," *Financial Times*, March 14, 2017, www.ft.com/content/c10aa4f8-08a5-11e7-97d1-5e720a26771b

22. Jennifer Baker, "Fakebook."

23. Chazan, "Zuckerberg and Facebook."

24. Melissa Eddy and Mark Scott, "Germany Tells Sites to Delete Hate or Pay Up," *New York Times*, July 1, 2017.

25. Chazan, "Germany Cracks Down."

26. Dietmar Neuerer, "Digital Economy Runs Storm Against Maas Law," *Handelsblatt,* April 5, 2017, translate.google.com/translate?u=http%3A%2F%2Fwww.handelsblatt.com%2Fpolitik%2Fdeutschland%2Fhasskommentare-bei-facebook-digitalwirtschaft-laeuft-sturm-gegen-maas-gesetz%2F19619212.html&hl=en&langpair=auto|en&tbb=1&ie=utf-8

27. Dietmar Neuerer, "Digital economy runs storm against Maas Law," *Handelsblatt,* April 5, 2017, http://translate.google.com/translate?u=http%3A%2F%2Fwww.handelsblatt.com%2Fpolitik%2Fdeutschland%2Fhasskommentare-bei-facebook-digitalwirtschaft-laeuft-sturm-gegen-maas-gesetz%2F19619212.html&hl=en&langpair=auto|en&tbb=1&ie=utf-8

28. Toobin, "When Truth Is Not Enough."

29. Hannah Kuchler, "Companies Scramble to Combat 'Fake News,'" *Financial Times*, August 22, 2017.
30. Jennifer Baker, "Fakebook."
31. Hannah Kuchler, "Facebook Turns to AI to Help Block Terror Posts," *Financial Times*, June 16, 2017.
32. Duncan Robinson, "Social Networks Face Tougher EU Oversight on Video Content," *Financial Times*, May 25, 2017, www.ft.com/content /d5746e06-3fd7-11e7-82b6-896b95f30f58?tagToFollow=
33. Richard Milne, "Swedish Comic Strip Teaches That Internet Voles Are Full of Fake News," *Financial Times*, January 20, 2017, www.ft.com/content /b6d4b0d0-df12-11e6-9d7c-be108f1c1dce
34. Simon Kuper, "Why the French Have Switched Off Political News," *Financial Times*, February 16, 2017.
35. Dana Priest and Michael Birnbaum, "In Europe, Fake News from Russia Is Old News," *Washington Post*, June 26, 2017.
36. Dietmar Neuerer, "Nationwide BKA Raid Against Hassposter," *Handelsblatt*, June 20, 2017, www.handelsblatt.com/politik/deutschland/nutzer-von -facebook-und-co-bundesweite-bka-razzia-gegen-hassposter/19955278.html
37. Anthony Faiola and Stephanie Kirchner, "Germany Fights 'Fake News,' Hate Speech on Social Sites," *Washington Post*, April 6, 2017.
38. Neuerer, "Facebook Should Adhere."
39. Emma Grey Ellis, "Facebook's New Plan May Curb Revenge Porn, but Won't Kill It," *Wired*, April 6, 2017, www.wired.com/2017/04/facebook -revenge-porn/
40. Margot E. Kaminski and Kate Klonick, "Speech in the Social Public Square," *New York Times*, June 27, 2017.
41. Niraj Chokshi, "CNN Turns Down 'Fake News' Ad from Trump Campaign," *New York Times*, May 2, 2017.
42. Tracy Jan and Elizabeth Dwoskin, "Silicon Valley Aims to Limit Online Reach of Hate Groups," *Washington Post*, August 17, 2017.
43. Nellie Bowles, "Pursuing Man Behind a Nazi Site," *New York Times*, August 21, 2017.
44. Rowbottom, "How Campaign Finance Laws Made the British Press So Powerful."
45. "Murdoch Row Amid Australian Election Campaign," *BBC News*, August 8, 2013, www.bbc.com/news/world-asia-23598223
46. Rowbottom, "How Campaign Finance Laws Made the British Press So Powerful."
47. Simon Kuper, "How Facebook Is Changing Democracy: Targeting Specific Voters Is More Effective and Cheaper Than Speaking to the Public on TV," *Financial Times*, June 15, 2017.
48. Ibid.

49. Nicholas Fandos, "Watchdog That Shepherded Panama Papers Now Constrained by Finances," *New York Times*, June 6, 2016.
50. Hasen, *Plutocrats United*, 136, 144.
51. Paul Horowitz, *First Amendment Institutions* (Cambridge, MA: Harvard University Press, 2013), 155.
52. Luigi Zingales, "A Strong Press Is Best Defense Against Crony Capitalism," *Financial Times*, October 18, 2015.
53. David Bond, "Wikipedia's Jimmy Wales to Set Up Global News Website," *Financial Times*, April 26, 2017.
54. "Freedom in the World," Freedom House, 2016, https://freedomhouse.org /report/freedom-world-2016/table-scores; see also Arch Puddington and Tyler Roylance, "Populists and Autocrats: The Dual Threat to Global Democracy," Freedom in the World, 2017, Freedom House, April 2017, freedomhouse.org/report/freedom-world/freedom-world-2017

Chapter 16: Epilogue

1. Charles Fried, letter to editor, *New York Times*, April 4, 2014.
2. Robert Jones, Daniel Cox, Juhem Navarro-Rivera, E.J. Dionne, Jr, and William A. Galston, *Do Americans Believe Capitalism and Government Are Working?* (Washington, DC: Brookings Institution, 2013).
3. Robin Wigglesworth, "Survival of US Profitability Miracle Depends on Wages," *Financial Times*, June 10, 2017.
4. Amy Sherman, "The Electoral College vs. the Popular Vote: Could States Do an End-Run Around the Current System?" *PolitiFact Florida*, November 17, 2016, www.politifact.com/florida/article/2016/nov/17 /electoral-college-vs-popular-vote-could-states-a/
5. Adam Liptak, "Rendering Justice with One Eye on Reelection," May 25, 2008.
6. Wendy R. Weiser and Lawrence Norden, "Voting Law Changes in 2012," Brennan Center for Justice, October 3, 2011, http://www.brennancenter.org /publication/voting-law-changes-2012
7. Adam Smith, *An Inquiry into the Nature and Causes of the Wealth of Nations*, (New York: Bobbs-Merrill, 1961), 66.
8. Robert J. Gordon, *The Rise and Fall of American Growth* (Princeton, NJ: Princeton University Press, 2017), 642.
9. Valentina Romel, "Datawatch: Childcare Costs Are a Burden in the UK," *Financial Times*, November 22, 2016.
10. Tim Colebatch, "Adapt or Die—RBAs Bitter Medicine," *Sydney Morning Herald*, June 13, 2012.
11. Ullrich Fichtner, Hans Hoyng, Marc Hujer, and Gregor Peter Schmitz, "Notes on the Decline of a Great Nation," *Der Spiegel*, November 5, 2012,

www.spiegel.de/international/world/divided-states-of-america-notes-on
-the-decline-of-a-great-nation-a-865295.html

12. Robert Kagan, "The GOP's Frankenstein Monster," *Washington Post*,
February 25, 2016.

13. Ralph Gomory, "Put Human Nature Back in Business," *Washington Post*,
June 28, 2013.

14. Ibid.

☆ ACKNOWLEDGMENTS ☆

A NUMBER OF COLLEAGUES AND reviewers have been instrumental in shaping and refining the manuscript, with three warranting particular notice. I am especially indebted to Clyde Prestowitz, President of the Economic Strategy Institute and author most recently of *Betrayal of American Prosperity* (New York: Free Press, 2010), for sharing his thoughts and keen insights. James Klumpner, former chief economist at both the Senate and House Budget Committees, has been an invaluable sounding board and sober critic. And political scientist Ian Fried with the Washington-based Close Up Foundation has provided keen conceptual advice.

I am grateful for the support of my agent, Howard Koon, and for the admirable editorial and production support of Eric Wechter, J.P. Connolly, Vy Tran, Jessika Rieck, Lindsay Marshall, Sarah Avinger, Alicia Kania, and Adrienne Lang. I want to also acknowledge the enthusiasm and support of BenBella's publisher, Glenn Yeffeth.

☆ INDEX ☆

Abramoff, Jack (lobbyist), 58
Acemoglu, Daron (economist), *Why Nations Fail*, 27–29, 33, 56
Adams, James Truslow, 16
Adelson, Sheldon, 52, 73–77, 85, 103, 138, 146, 168
Ailes, Roger, 194
Albuquerque, public funded elections, 1, 157–158, 165, 171, 173
  Homans v. City of Albuquerque, 157
Allcott, Hunt (political scientist), 202
Amazon, 125–126
  Rugeley, UK, 126
  Germany, 126
American Bar Association, 108, 172
American Center for Public Integrity (International Consortium of Investigative Journalists), 226
American Populist Party, 22
Americans for Tax Fairness, 128
American Values Survey, 50
Aristotle, 2, 26–27, 33, 59, 93, 238
Arizona, public funding of campaigns, 156, 172–176
Articles of Confederation, 2, 3, 96, 150
Australia,
  political donations, 139
  reformed senate, 232
Australian Tax Office, 21st Century Fox, 197

Bamse, 221
Barnes, Robert (journalist), 89
Barone, Guglielmo (historian), 77
Barr, Andy (congressman), 99, 101

Bartels, Larry (economist, political scientist), 48–50
Baum, Lawrence (law professor), 84
Beck, Glenn, 195, 205, 210
Benjamin, Brent (West Virginia Supreme Court justice), 108
Berlusconi, Silvio, 209
Bernanke, Ben (former chairman, Federal Reserve), 22, 59
Bernays, Edward, 191
Bertelsmann Foundation (German), 26
Bildt, Nils, 195
binary runoff, 145, 163, 184, 231, 234
Bingham, John (congressman), 64
Black, Hugo (Supreme Court justice), 53, 64–65
Blanchard, Olivier (economist), 31
Bloomberg survey, 158
Bopp, James, Jr., 91
Bork, Robert, 60
Bormann, Nils-Christian (political scientist), 182
bots, 205, 217, 222
Brady, Henry E., 40
Brandeis, Louis (Supreme Court justice), 27, 152
Breitbart News, 73, 205–207, 217
Brennan Center for Justice, 75, 99, 108, 111, 233
Brewer, David (Fuller Supreme Court justice), 79
Brexit, 169, 225
Breyer, Stephen (Supreme Court justice), 154
Brill, Steven (American lawyer), 104

Brisbane Times, 24
Britain. *See* United Kingdom.
Brown, Jeffrey (finance professor), 105
Brown, Jennifer (business professor),
    103–104
Brownback, Sam (Kansas governor), 72,
    108
Brusoe, Peter (political scientist), 165
Bryant, Chris (journalist), 125
Buckley v. Valeo, 6, 54, 230
    Buckley era, 6, 53–66, 81, 94, 113–124,
        149
Buffett, Warren, 53, 148
Burns, James MacGregor (historian),
    62, 149
Business Week, 128
BuzzFeed, 202, 203, 204

Calabresi, Guido (federal judge),
    153–154, 192
Caldwell, Christopher, 48
California
    Fair Political Practices Commission,
        168
    Proposition 30 attempt to influence
        voters, 168
    referendum on sugary drinks tax, 166
Cambridge Analytica, 169
campaign length, limits on, 148, 169
campaign donation limits (*see* Political
    donations)
Canada, 14, 18–19, 127, 140
    electoral system, 141, 143–145,
        161–166, 170
    Elections Canada, 144–145, 168
Capra, Frank (*Mr. Smith Goes to
    Washington*), 99
Carnegy, Hugh (journalist), 163
Cassino, Dan (political scientist), 194
Caterpillar (purchase of Electro-Motive
    Canada), 129
Cato Institute, 53
Center for American Progress, 109
Center for Rural Affairs, 43
Center for Strategic and International
    Studies, 212

Center for the Study of Democracy
    (Sofia, Bulgaria), 212
Chatterji, Aaron (business professor),
    167–168
Chavez, Hugo, 209
Citizens United, 76, 87, 91, 102, 109–115
    surveys in Colorado, Montana, 160
    referendums opposing ruling, 178
Cleveland, Grover (president), 52
Clinton, Hillary, 9, 10, 75, 122–123,
    196–198, 203–206, 212
CloudFlare, 224
Coca-Cola, foreigners distrust of,
    126–132
    Richlands, Australia, 126
codetermination, 8, 23–24, 29–31, 127
Colebatch, Tom (journalist), 236
Committee for Economic Development,
    114
Committee on Standards in Public Life
    (UK), 162
Conference Board, 115
Confessore, Nicholas (journalist), 55,
    114
Conkling, Roscoe, 61–65
Connecticut, public funding of
    campaigns, 173–177
Constitution, anti-bribery statues, 151
Cook Report, 73
Cook, Timothy (CEO, Apple), 168
Cooper, Betsy, 50
Corak, Miles (economist), 19
Corasaniti, Nick (journalist), 71
Corporate Reform Coalition, 90,
    115–116, 159, 172
Cox, Daniel, 50
CrossCheck, 184, 219
Crossland, David (journalist), 147
Cruz, Ted (senator), 75

Dahl, Robert (political scientist),
    Polyarchy, 7, 59
Daily News, 227
Daily Stormer, 224
Darwin, Charles, 237
Davenport, Carol (journalist), 78

DeLay, Tom (congressman), 33, 55
  "K Street Project," 68
DCLeaks, 213
Der Spiegel, 24, 215
DeSilver, Drew (economist), 43–46
Devins, Neal (law professor), 84
Dodd-Frank finance sector reregulation,
  100, 104–105
donations (*see* Political donations)
Döring, Tobias (journalist), 140
Douglas, Karen (psychology professor),
  123
Douglas, William O. (Supreme Court
  justice), 53, 64–65
Douthat, Ross (commentator), 74, 79
Dow Chemical Corporation, 91
Drake, Katharine (business professor),
  103–104
Driver, Justin (law professor), 88
Druckman, James (political scientist), 46
Drutman, Lee, 40
Duchin, Ran (finance professor), 104
Dutch law forbidding gifts to politicians
  (1651), 150

economic mobility, 16–20
Economic Policy Institute, 21–22
Economist, 161
Economist survey, 180
Edelman Public Relations *Trust
  Barometer*, 130–133
Edin, Kathryn, 196
Ehrenreich, Barbara, *Nickled and
  Dimed*, 196
Eichengreen, Barry (economist), 31
election-day registration, 142, 182–183,
  234
electioneering spending limits, 137–161
  effects on negative political
    advertising, 138, 162, 164
Election Integrity Project, 178–180
election runoff reforms, 182, 231, 234
Electoral College (Only in America), 96,
  148, 182, 233
Ellis, Emma Grey (journalist), 222
Ellis, Joseph J. (historian), 95

Eom, Kihong (political scientist), 155
Epstein, Lee (law professor), 89
Equal Justice Initiative, 63
Erdoğan, Recep, 108, 209
Europe work effort freater than US, 21
EY (Ernst & Young), 30

Facebook, 200–204, 213, 216, 219
  censorship inept, 222–226
  death of Lee Rigby, 215
  hate factory, 215
  streaming of violence, 215
  violation of community standards,
    216
Fairness Doctrine, 56, 191–194, 208, 219,
  223–224
fake news, 10–11, 71, 78, 123, 189–227,
  234
  conservatives gullible, 203
  Egan, John (Vancouver), 203
  Goldman, Ben, 204
  Harris, Cameron (Christian-
    TimesNewspaper.com), 205
  Horner, Paul, 204
  Latsabidze, Beqa (Tbilisi, Georgia),
    203
  Macedonian computer experts (Veles),
    203
  partisan gain, 202–205
  Vallorani, Brandon (Liberty Alliance),
    204, 206
  Wade, Paris, 204
Farhi, Paul (journalist), 196
Fauver, Larry (economist), 31
Federal Bureau of Investigation, 213
Federal Communications Commission,
  189, 191–195
Federal Election Campaign Act, 57
Federal Election Commission, 168
Federal Farmer, 4
Federal Reserve System, 47, 51
Ferling, John (historian), 93, 95–97
Financial Times, 15, 16, 21, 29, 71, 130,
  137, 139
Fleischhauer, Jan (journalist), 215
Fleming, Karl (journalist), 226

Florida, legislative weakening of
    gerrymandering reforms, 177
  Republicans reject referendum to end
    gerrymandering, 179
Foa, Roberto S. (journalist), 120
Folbre, Nancy (economist), 204
Forbes 400, 68
Fox News, 10, 56, 71–72, 193–197, 200,
    205–210
  gullible viewers, 195, 204
Fox, Richard (law professor), 115
founding fathers, 2, 56–58, 60–61, 81,
    84–85, 98, 149–161, 189, 230
Fourteenth Amendment, 53, 61–65, 85, 149
France, 17, 21, 31, 45, 97, 122, 127, 130,
    138, 141–146, 165, 169, 182, 212,
    219, 233, 236
Frank, Thomas, 76
Freedom House, 119–120, 140, 227
Freud, Sigmund, 190–191
Fried, Charles (Reagan administration
    solicitor general), 229
Friedman, Milton (economist), 208–209
Fritts, Edward O. (National Association
    of Broadcasters), 193
Frum, David, 206
Fuerst, Michael (economist), 31

Gab.ai, 224
Gallup survey, 7, 119, 122, 188, 208
Ganesh, Janan (journalist), 137
Garland, Merrick (federal judge), 52, 79,
    84–85
Gauck, Joachim (German president), 31
Gawker, 220
General Electric, foreign distrust of, 130
Gentzkow, Matthew (political scientist),
    202
Germany, 17–18, 21–22, 29–30, 42–46,
    48, 121–122, 126–133, 146, 162,
    218–226, 236
  Free Democratic Party (conservative),
    141
Gerry, Elbridge, 4, 190, 200
gerrymandering, 23, 76, 143, 176,
    181–185, 234

Gilens, Martin (economist), 34–40
Gini coefficient, 19, 43–46
Gladwell, Malcolm, 63
Glavin, Brendan (political scientist),
    165
GoDaddy, 218, 224
GoFundMe, 218
Goldberg, Marc, 215
Golder, Matt (political scientist), 182
Goldstone, Lawrence (historian), 59
Goldwater, Barry (senator), 58–60, 166,
    207
Google, 85, 200, 212, 219, 224
  YouTube, 85, 200, 212, 220, 224
Gore, Al, 87
Gorsuch, Neil (Supreme Court justice),
    6, 52, 84, 89, 146, 232
Graham, Howard Jay (historian), 62, 64
Graham, Lindsey (senator), 74
Grantham, Jeremy, 6
Greenberg, Stanley (pollster), 8, 83, 111
Greenstein, Robert (Center on Budget
    and Policy Priorities), 40
Griffin, Kenneth, 77
Groom, Brian (journalist), 125
Gross, Donald (political scientist), 155
Gross, Kenneth, 103
The Guardian, 203, 213

Hamilton, Alexander, 3, 4, 93, 96,
    215–216
  Federalist 68, 215
Hanna, Mark (senator), Grover
    Cleveland campaign, 151
Harari, Yuval (historian), 28
Harding, Luke (journalist), 213
Harlan, John Marshall (Supreme Court
    justice), 87
Harper v. Canada (Canadian Supreme
    Court), 145, 203
Harper, Stephen (Canadian Prime
    minister), 152
Hasen, Richard (law professor), 84, 152,
    157–158, 161, 226
Hatrone, 224
Heard, Andrew (political scientist), 168

Heydarian, Richard (political scientist), 200

Hitler, Adolf (*Mein Kampf*), 88

Hobbes, Thomas, 27

Hofstadter, Richard, 207

Hogan, Hulk (Terry Bollea), 220

Hopkins, Mick (journalist), 213

Horowitz, Paul (law professor), 226

Howard, Christopher (economist), 40, 42

Howard County, Maryland, 178

Howard, Philip (Oxford U Internet Institute), 201, 205

Huang, Jiekun (finance professor), 105

Huffington Post, 197
  Canada, 129

Hujer, Marc (*Der Spiegel* journalist), 24

Ignatius, David (commentator), 171

income bias, 5–6, 8, 31–41, 47, 52

independent political spending (*see* Political donations)

InfoWars, 205

International Monetary Fund, 17, 21, 46

International Social Survey, 42

Internet Research Agency (Russia), 213–214

Jacobs, Lawrence (political scientist), 46

Jefferson, Thomas, 23, 93, 148, 190

Jim Crow era, 63, 86–89, 148–149, 183, 226
  Nazi analogizing Jim Crow racism, 88

Johnson & Johnson, foreign distrust of, 130

Johnston, David Cay (journalist, economist), 81

Jones, Robert P., 50

Kagan, Robert, 210–211, 213, 237

Kaminski, Margot (law professor), 223

Kang, Michael (law professor), 109

Kansas, regressive tax structure, 108

Karmeier, Lloyd (Illinois Supreme Court justice), 108

Katz, Lawrence F. (economist), 25

Kennedy, Anthony (Supreme Court justice), 58, 60–61, 113, 155

opinion on independent political expenditures, 99–102, 114
  (*See also* Political donations)

Kennedy, Liz (journalist), 116, 159

Kerkmann, Christof (journalist), 140

Kerry, John (Secretary of State), Swift Boat ads, 170, 196

Kim, Jin-Hyuk (economist), 69

Kirchgaessner, Stephanie (journalist), 213

KKR (private equity fund), 23

Klarman, Michael (historian), 4

Klonick, Kate, 223

Klumpp, Tilman (political scientist), 76

Knox v. Service Employees International Union, Local 1000, 90

Koch brothers, 53, 69–74, 77–80, 85, 103, 108, 138, 146, 149, 168, 176, 194, 204, 207
  Charles, 140, 142
  David, 140, 142
  i360 enterprise, 169

Kostrzewa, Theresa, 103

Krueger, Alan B. (economist), 25

Krugman, Paul (economist), 67

Kushner, Jared, 195

Lahane, Chris, 74

Landes, William (law professor), 89

Lasser, Mitchel (law professor), 233

Lawless, Jennifer (law professor), 115

Le Figaro, 163

Lenfest, H.F. (Philadelphia's *The Inquirer*), 227

Le Pen, Marine (French rightist), 212

Lessig, Lawrence (law professor), 57, 97

Levendis, John (law professor), 110

Leventhal, George (Maryland politician), 175

Liebling, A.J., 193

Lienesch, Rachel, 50

Limbaugh, Rush, 195, 206, 209

limits on independent political spending including issue advocacy, 142, 161, 166–72

Lincoln, Abraham, 5, 51, 68, 89, 230
  Gettysburg Address, 97, 147
Linz, Juan (journalist), 125
Liptak, Adam, 89
Lipton, Eric (journalist), 78, 100
Locke, John, 27, 93
Long, Russell B. (senator), 102
Lynch, David J. (journalist), 213

Maas, Heiko (German justice minister),
  219, 222
Madison, James, 3–6, 11, 57, 59, 96–96,
  150, 214
  Federalist 10, 3
  Federalist 52, 4
  Federalist 63, 4, 190
Malbin, Michael (political scientist), 165
Maine, public funding of campaigns,
  165, 173–177
Mann, Thomas, 9, 50, 52, 78
Marcus, Ruth (journalist), 162
Marshall, John (Chief Justice, Supreme
  Court), 59
Marshall Project, 226
Martin, Jurek (journalist), 71
Masket, Seth (political scientist), 156
Mason, George, 57, 150
May, Theresa, 220
Mayer, Jane, 13, 70, 76, 194
Mayer, Kenneth R. (political scientist),
  155, 174
McAuliffe, Terry (Virginia governor), 88
McConnell, Mitch (senator), 49–52
McCutcheon v. FEC, 60, 154, 230
McCutcheon, Shaun, 60
McDonalds, foreign distrust of, 130
McGhee, Eric (political scientist), 156
McKenna, Joseph (Supreme Court
  justice), 87–88
Mediapart, 227
MediaQuant, 75
Mendleson, Rachel (journalist), 129
Mercer, Robert, 73, 75, 85, 169, 207
Merkel, Angela (German chancellor),
  138, 144, 146, 162, 170
Merkley, Jeff (senator), 79

Meyerson, Harold (economist), 50, 80,
  197
Mialon, Hugo (political scientist), 76
Milanovic, Branko, 35
Miliband, Ed (former UK Labour Party
  leader), 115
Mill, John Stuart, 180
Miller, Michael (political scientist),
  156–157, 174–174,
Mocetti, Sauro (historian), 77
Molex Corporation (Villemur-sur-Tarn,
  Haute-Garonne, France), 129
Montana, Corrupt Practices Act and
  "Copper Kings," 152
Montgomery County, Maryland, 173,
  175
moral turpitude, 88
Mounk, Yascha (political scientist),
  121–122
MSNBC, 194–195
Müller, Jan-Werner (political scientist),
  192
Murdoch, Rupert (publisher), 71, 143,
  194, 197, 224–225
Murkowski, Lisa (senator), 73
Murrow, Edward R. (journalist), 226

National Association of Homebuilders
  Political Action Committee
  (BUILD-PAC), 103
National Bureau of Economic Research,
  16, 105
National Center for State Courts, 172
National Enquirer, 205
National Institutes of Health, 51
National Popular Vote Interstate
  Compact (to neuter Electoral
  College), 233
Network Enforcement Law (German), 219
New Deal, 149
Newhouse, Neil (Mitt Romney aide), 207
Newton, Ted (Mitt Romney aide), 205
New York City election system, 164–165,
  174, 177
New York Times/CBS News survey, 43,
  114, 158–159

Nixon, Richard, 10, 33, 209
Norris, Pippa (political scientist), 180
Nuremburg racial discrimination laws,
    88

O'Connor, Sandra Day (Supreme Court
    justice), 84, 102–103, 107, 148, 151
O'Connor maxim, 162
Oesterle, William (CEO, Angie's List),
    168
Ohio state supreme court corruption,
    109, 112
O'Keefe, Eric, 113
Okun, Arthur (economist), 46
Olsen, Mancur (political economist),
    70
Omidyar, Pierre (eBay), 227
Organisation for Economic Cooperation
    and Development, 20, 25–26, 28,
    43–45, 51, 236
Organization of Petroleum Exporting
    Countries, 47
Ornstein, Norman, 9, 50, 52, 78, 188
Orwell, George, 81, 216
Oxford Internet Institute, 201

Page, Benjamin (economist), 34–40
Palast, Geri, 111–112, 173
Palmer, Vernon Valentine (law
    professor), 110–111
Pascaline, Mary (journalist), 122
Patreon, 218
Paul, Scott N. (economist), 31
PayPal, 218, 220, 222
Pew Research Center, 10, 25–27, 32,
    43–45, 69, 72, 113–114, 158, 164,
    194–196, 200, 208, 211
  DeSilver, Drew, 43–46
  Kochhar, Rakesh, 26
  Morin, Rich, 26
Phillips, Tim (Koch, Americans for
    Prosperity), 69
Pickett, Kate (public health), 46
Piketty, Thomas (economist), 31, 77, 135
  Endless Inegalitarian Spiral, 7, 34, 230
Pocock, J.G.A. (historian), 57

Polenz, Ruprecht (German politician),
    215, 222
political donations
  donation limits, 54, 58, 60, 68,
    138–140, 149, 153–69
    Missouri, 178
    Howard County, Maryland,
    178
    Berkeley, California, 178
  independent expenditures, 38, 57,
    101–107, 171
    Justice Anthony Kennedy
    embrace of, 99, 102, 114
Pope, Kyle (journalist), 223
Pope, James Arthur "Art" (North
    Carolina treasurer), 72
Porter, Eduardo (journalist), 41
Posner, Richard A. (judge, law
    professor), 83, 85–86, 89, 101,
    148
Post, Robert C. (law professor), 150,
    153–154, 164
Potter, Trevor, 33
primary elections, open nonpartisan,
    185, 234, 236
Priorities USA, 87
productivity levels higher than in the
    US, 17
proportional (legislative) representation,
    135, 143, 180–181, 231, 232, 234
ProPublica, 226
psychometrics, 169, 225
public campaign organization, 175
public funded elections,
    America, 58, 155–157, 164, 171-178
    "clean" elections, 173
    foreign, 140–146
    Tallahassee public funding of
    campaigns, 172
    use by Ronald Reagan, 171
    weakened by Roberts Supreme Court,
    176–177
    (see also Albuquerque, Arizona,
    Connecticut, Maine, Seattle,
    Tallahassee)
public funding of judicial elections, 172

Public Religion Research Institute, 17, 32, 50
Putin, Vladimir (support of Donald Trump), 122–123, 199, 209, 211–213
Putnam, Robert (sociologist), 21

Quinn, Paul (New Zealand lawmaker), 78

Ramsey, Ross (journalist), 117
Reagan, Ronald, economic era of, 6, 16–34, 56, 68, 126
    declining economic opportunity, 25
    middle class shrinkage, 24
Rasmussen survey, 113, 115, 117–118
Redick, Melvin, 213
Red Lion Broadcasting Co. v. the Federal Communications Commission, 189, 192–193
Republicans, slowing tax and spending to weaken the recovery, 50–52
Rich, Frank (journalist), 71, 74, 194
Ricketts, Joe, 52, 70, 194
Ringen, Stein, 28, 36
Roberts, John (Supreme Court Chief Justice), 1, 58–61, 83–89, 156
Robinson, James (economist), Why Nations Fail, 26–29, 33, 56
Rößner, Tabea (German Green Party official), 222
Romania, 121, 168, 213
Römmele, Andrea (political scientist), 1, 162
Romney, Mitt, 75, 142, 170, 205, 207
Roosevelt, Franklin, 15
Roosevelt, Teddy, 9, 56, 59, 171, 230
Rosen, Jeffrey (journalist), 84
Rousseau, Jean-Jacques (political philosopher), 93–94
Rowbottom, Jacob, 137, 166, 224–225
Rubin, Jennifer (commentator), 206
Rudd, Kevin (Australian politician), 224
Ruffing, Kathy (Center on Budget and Policy Priorities), 40
Russian interference in 2016 American elections

American documentation of interference, 199–200, 205, 210–213
    interference in Holland election, 212
    interference in France election, 212
    support of Donald Trump, 122–123, 191, 196
Rutenberg, Jim (journalist), 189

Saez, Emmanuel (economist), 47
San Mateo v. Southern Pacific Railroad, 61–63
Sanders, Bernie (senator), 9, 75
Santa Clara v. Southern Pacific Railroad, 59, 61, 63
Sarbanes, John (congressman), 166
Sarkozy, Nicolas (French prime minister), 163
Scalia, Antonin (Supreme Court justice), 60–61, 85, 91, 148–149, 155
Scheiber, Noam (journalist), 50, 80
Scholzman, Kay, 40
Schwab, Charles, 168
Scitovsky, Tibor, 6
Seattle, public funding of campaigns, 174
Sestak, Joe, 196
Shaefer, H. Luke, 196
Shapiro, Ilya, 53
Shays' Rebellion, 3, 94–95
Shelby County v. Holder (voting rights), 85, 88
Shepherd, Joanna (law professor), 109
Sherman, Arloc (Center on Budget and Policy Priorities), 40
Shkreli, Martin, 217
Sides, John (political scientist), 156
Simpson, Matthew C. (historian), 93, 96
Sinclair Broadcasting, 193–196
    Hyman, Mark, 196
Sitton, Claude (journalist), 226
skill levels higher in Europe than America, 17
Skocpol, Theda (political scientist), 67, 70–71, 74, 204
Smidt, Corwin (political scientist), 188

Smith, Adam, 229, 235
Snowe, Olympia (senator), 72
Snyder, Rick (Michigan governor), 141
social media,
    abuse of, 140, 142, 200–201, 205–212,
      215
    aid ISIS recruiting, 217
    censorship of, 220–226
    failure of self-regulation, 218–219
    fake news postings believed, 202
    "hate factories," 216
    source of fake news, 10
    platforms, 216
    (*see also* Facebook)
Solzhenitsyn, Alexander, 216
Soros, George, 69, 144, 227
Sosyura, Denis (finance professor), 104
South Dakota, legislative override of
    voter referendum on donations,
    176
Spalding, Matthew (Heritage
    Foundation historian), 94
stakeholder capitalism, 29–32, 127
Stanford Center on Poverty and
    Inequality, 19
Stanford Graduate School of Education,
    201
Starbucks, foreign distrust of, 130
Steen, Michael (journalist), 125
Stepan, Alfred (journalist), 125
Stephanopoulos, Nicholas A. (law
    professor), 102
Stevens, John Paul (Supreme Court
    justice), 56, 60, 91, 152, 161
Stevens, Stuart, 78
Stiglitz, Joseph (economist), 15, 28, 34,
    67
Stratmann, Thomas (economist),
    105–107
Suffolk University–*USA Today* survey,
    208
Sullivan, Margaret (journalist), 205
Sullivan, Martin A. (tax analysts), 30
Sumner, William Graham (nineteenth-
    century sociologist), 59, 75
"unfittest," 59, 60, 94

Sumner Darwinians, 83–91
Sunstein, Cass (law professor), 56, 152
Sussman, Dalia (journalist), 50, 80
Sutton, Willy, 6
Swan, Wayne (former Australian
    treasurer), 28
Sydney Morning Herald, 51, 236
Sykes, Charlie, 206, 209

Taft-Hartley, 57
Tax Analysts (think tank), 30
Tea Party, 69–72, 171–172, 176, 194,
    204
Teachout, Zephyr (law professor), 101,
    151–153
Telegram internet messaging, 217
Texas, University of, survey, 117, 172
Thee-Brenan, Megan (journalist), 114
Thiel, Peter, 75, 220
Thompson, Robert (state senator), 72
Tillman Act, 56–57, 151
tobacco industry, mendacious
    advertising, 208
Tocqueville, Alexis de, 180, 206
Toffel, Michael (business professor),
    167–168
Tor, 224
Transparency International, 7, 118–121
Tribe, Laurence (law professor), 56
Trump, Donald, 10, 51, 74–75, 77, 84, 87,
    103, 226
    demonizing mainstream media,
      207-211
    mimic Nixon, 10
    mimic tobacco industry, 208
    and Putin, 122–123, 211–214
    social media, 202–207
    Vietnam War draft deferments, 196
    white supremacists, 123
Twitter, 200–201, 205, 217
    bots, 20

unicameral legislature, 231
unions, central to prosperity, 17, 20–23
United Kingdom, electoral system, 137,
    141–143, 169

United Nations Development Program (Inequality-Human Development Index), 26–27

Vanderbilt, Cornelius, 54
Vanderbilt, William H., 63
Verga, Sidney, 40
Vogel, Kenneth (journalist), 73, 76
von Finck, August (Mövenpick), 141
vote buying (definition), 55
voter registration, automatic (Oregon), 184, 234
voter suppression, 63, 78–79, 182–184
    Iowa, Wisconsin, 86–89
    Voting Rights rollback, 85–89, 182–185, 232

wages,
    higher in Europe, 17–18
    stagnation, 5–9, 16, 19, 22–23, 55, 79, 187
Wagner, Ann (congresswoman), 101
Waite (Morrison) Supreme Court, 59, 62–64, 148
Wales, Jimmy (Wikipedia), 227
Wall Street Journal, 16, 30, 205
Walmart, 26, 128
    heirs, 48
    wage suppression, 128
Walton family, 104
Warren (Earl) Supreme Court, 149, 189, 192–193, 238
Warren, Elizabeth (senator), 9
Washington Post, 201, 226
wasted votes, 143, 180–181, 231
Watergate, 57–58, 171, 226
Watson, Glenn (Rugeley, Staffordshire, England), Amazon, 126
weapons of mass destruction deceit, 194
Weekly Standard, 48
Wellman, Laura (business professor), 103–104
Werner, Timothy (political scientist), 155, 174

WeSearchr, 224
Wesleyan Media Project, 170
Wessel, David (journalist), 30
Whelan, Ed (Ethics and Public Policy Center), 85
Whitman, James (law professor), 88
Wigglesworth, Robin (journalist), 230
Wilkinson, Richard (public health), 46
Will, George, 155
Williams, Amanda (political scientist), 155, 175
Williams, Evan (Twitter), 200, 220–221
Williams, Joan C. (law professor), 8
Williams, Michael (political scientist), 76
Williamson, Vanessa (political scientist), 67, 70–71, 74, 204
Wilson, E.O. (biologist), 237
Wilson, James (journalist), 125
Wilson, Woodrow, 54
Winkler, Adam (law professor), 62, 151
Wolf, Martin (journalist), 29
Woodward, Bob (journalist), 226
Woolley, Samuel (Oxford University Computational Propaganda Project), 217
work effort (see Europe work effort greater than US)
works councils, 23, 31, 127
World Bank, 35, 46
World Value Survey, 120–122
Wyden, Ron (senator), 73

Yale Law Review, 64
Yellen, Janet (Federal Reserve chairwoman), 51
Yiannopoulos, Milo, 217
YouGov survey, 122

Ziegler, John, 199, 210
Zingales, Luigi (economist), 226–227
Zucman, Gabriel (economist), 47
Zypries, Brigitte (German economic minister), 220

Want more from George R. Tyler?

What Went Wrong

How the 1% Hijacked the American Middle Class . . . and What Other Countries Got Right

"Tyler explodes numerous myths... Controversial but well-grounded in data and fact. Anyone with an interest in economic policy ought to have a look."
—**Kirkus Reviews**

"[Tyler] provokes outrage with his impassioned portrait of an America where job security is a relic of the past."
—**Publishers Weekly**

"Tyler's timely and convincing book confirms what Americans feel in their bones: the economy is rigged against them and something is definitely wrong."
—**Library Journal**

"Several books have examined the effects of the recent recession, but few have dug as deeply into the root causes of [our] country's current economic malaise as George R. Tyler's *What Went Wrong*... Though his conclusions are undoubtedly controversial, Tyler grounds his arguments in data and facts, providing a deep exploration of our current economic situation and the pre-Reagan policies that, if implemented again, may lead us out."
—**Shelf Awareness**

LEARN MORE AT GEORGERTYLER.COM